The
JAMESTOWN
EXPERIMENT

THE REMARKABLE STORY OF
THE ENTERPRISING COLONY AND THE UNEXPECTED RESULTS
THAT SHAPED AMERICA

TONY WILLIAMS

 sourcebooks

Published by Sourcebooks, Inc.
P.O. Box 4410, Naperville, Illinois 60567-4410
(630) 961-3900
Fax: (630) 961-2168

ISBN: 978-1-4022-4353-0

Printed and bound in the United States of America.

Book Club Edition

ALSO BY TONY WILLIAMS

Hurricane of Independence: The Untold Story of the Deadly Storm at the Deciding Moment of the American Revolution

The Pox and the Covenant: Mather, Franklin, and the Epidemic That Changed America's Destiny

To my dear mother who has always encouraged me.

CONTENTS

ACKNOWLEDGMENTS

I would like to thank the Sourcebooks team in our third book, especially my editor, Peter Lynch. Peter has once again proven himself an excellent editor and shared my enthusiasm, from our initial discussions about the idea to the final edits. The book assumed a very different character over time, and I thank Peter for helping me to shape and hone my thoughts. I have not met anyone in academia, teaching, or writing more sincerely committed to true collaboration. Many thanks go to my publicity team of Liz Kelsch and Heather Moore for organizing the book tours and events for our first two books together.

The Jamestown-Yorktown Foundation, Colonial Williamsburg, and the Swem Library at the College of William and Mary provided invaluable support and made this book possible. Two individuals went well beyond the call of duty, as they have done for me over the last several years. First of all, Jim Horn generously offered all assistance in using the materials of the Rockefeller Library at Colonial Williamsburg. Moreover, Mary Cottrill has invited me to speak often about my books and other historical topics to tourists, locals, and interpreters at Dewitt-Wallace Museum. One such pre-publication lecture on this book forced me to focus my thesis much more than just sitting in front of my laptop waiting for inspiration.

During the writing and editing of this book, I returned to teaching history at Peninsula Catholic High School in Newport News, Virginia. I want to thank Jenny Franklin and M.E. Rhodes for their daily support of all of my endeavors, even as I desperately attempted to juggle my responsibilities. I could not ask for a better group of colleagues than the faculty and staff at the school. The students at PC quickly reminded me of why I always loved teaching high school students and are an inspiration to me every day.

My wife, Lynne, has always loved and supported me unconditionally, while my children are still my biggest fans and excitedly await the publication of all of my books. Speaking about the Jamestown colony at their school was a great deal of fun. I would not be able to achieve anything without their love and support.

Finally, of all of my friends who have lent encouragement and been sources of joy, I want to single out Jeff and Jessica Lavoie and their daughter, Carlie. We have been friends since high school and have individually gone through many changes through the years. But our friendship has remained one of the rocks in my life. It is a priceless gift which I have long cherished.

I am dedicating this book to my dear mother, Fran Banta. She has faced many challenges, including the death of my brother, Craig, during the writing of this book, but has been a model of faith, courage, and perseverance. I thank her for all of the love and support she has given me throughout my life.

INTRODUCTION

The American Dream was built along the banks of the James River in Virginia. The settlers who established America's first permanent English colony at Jamestown were gentlemen adventurers and common tradesmen who bravely voyaged to North America despite its many dangers. They sought personal profit and the greater national glory of mother England. Their venture was part of a grand national struggle with Spain to satisfy their aspiring imperial ambitions.

Yet the hardy adventurers who settled at Jamestown were largely on their own with their venture. The Crown granted them a royal charter for a joint-stock company in which they shared the risk over several investors. But the Crown did not offer any direct financial support. Rather, these free and independent Englishmen were enterprising individuals who risked their lives and fortunes on the venture and stood to reap the rewards of their private initiative.

Whatever these grand visions of profit and glory, the history of the first several years of the colony was simply a struggle to survive and endure. The settlers died in droves, and the colony constantly hovered on the edge of collapse. The old military model of colonization established during the Elizabethan era persisted and threatened to doom Jamestown. The authoritarian model of absolute leadership and the communitarian methods of living were fundamentally at odds with the character of these free individuals. The colonists bristled at draconian systems of law and harsh rulers, while ambitious gentlemen jockeyed and conspired to seize the reins of government. A common storehouse destroyed individual initiative and dampened the work ethic. The result was that the colonists continued to perish in great numbers and disappointed investors in England lost their money.

Even when they utilized modern methods of promoting their colony, they successfully whipped up enthusiasm for settling in Virginia among a credulous English public but achieved little tangible success. After fits and starts for the better part of a decade, innovations were finally introduced that slowly turned things around and put the colony on the path to success. The answers were novel and surprising and yet very much in harmony with the longings of these free men and women.

The solutions to the troubles at Jamestown were rooted in the entrepreneurial spirit that would shape and define the American character. Private property, individual initiative, personal incentives to seek profit, and the freedom to pursue one's own happiness— these are the traits that helped the colony survive and built a nation. These were the qualities that defined the life and autobiography of Benjamin Franklin, drove Americans to move West and develop a continent, spurred on the Industrial Revolution and mobility of men like Andrew Carnegie, shaped the dreams of millions of immigrants who sought opportunity and a better life, created a global economic and technological powerhouse, and allowed thousands of ordinary men and women to start small businesses and pursue a dream.

These are the characteristics of the dream that are deeply rooted in the American character—and they began at Jamestown more than four hundred years ago. Yet, these results were by no means guaranteed in 1607 when the colonists landed in Virginia. The colony nearly duplicated the failures of other English settlements, most notably Roanoke. Any number of historical factors and decisions made by the settlers based upon the martial colonial model during the first decade could have led to very different results for the colony and America. History is full of contingencies, but the contours of the paths the adventurers took shaped the success of the first permanent English settlement in America and, in time, the creation of the American character. The first settlers themselves might have been surprised by the results of their venture—if they survived until 1624.

Chapter One

GENTLEMEN ADVENTURERS AND THE CALL TO EMPIRE

Long before Jamestown was settled, adventurous Englishmen were among the first Europeans to brave the dangers of crossing the Atlantic to stake a claim to the riches of distant lands. On May 20, 1497, the small ship *Matthew* embarked from Bristol on the west coast of England. The port city had a thriving trade with the Atlantic and Mediterranean in Icelandic codfish, Spanish wine, and local woolens. The captain had letters of patent from King Henry VII for a voyage to discover new lands "unknown to all Christians," though no financial backing from the Crown. The king would receive one-fifth of any riches that were discovered, but the captain had to fund the voyage himself. The captain was seeking a northern route across the Atlantic to Cathay (China) and the riches of the spice trade in the Indies. The man who captained the vessel was not even English; he was an Italian with the anglicized name John Cabot.

On June 24, the *Matthew* landed on the Feast of St. John in northern Newfoundland. He coasted for hundreds of miles along its eastern shore through dense fogbanks and floating icebergs.

His sailors went ashore once and saw signs of life but no natives. The men easily scooped up basketfuls of cod from the rich fishing grounds. Having made his discoveries, Cabot ordered his crew to set sail for England. The *Matthew* made landfall in Brittany in early August and returned to Bristol a few days later.

Cabot traveled to London, and four days later had an audience with the king at Westminster. The explorer did not have a baggage train of spices and gold to show the king, but he had valuable information of a great discovery—Cabot assumed that he had indeed discovered a northwest passage to Cathay and made landfall on an island off the Eurasian continent.

King Henry's imagination was stirred by news of this "new found land," and he offered Cabot a reward of £10 for his discovery. Henry also granted Cabot new letters of patent for a second voyage to establish a colony that would send shiploads of spices to London. This time the king provided and laded a ship, while British merchants invested in four ships filled with cloth to trade for spices. In May 1498, the five ships left Bristol with hopes of bringing home great riches. One of the ships returned shortly, but the other four, including Cabot's, were never heard from again.[1]

This was largely the extent of English overseas ambitions for more than half a century. After this faltering attempt at discovery, the English relinquished the initiative for daring voyages of discovery and the riches of the Far East and the New World to the Spanish and Portuguese.

The English were laggards in the race for overseas empire compared to their Iberian rivals, who had trade relations and imperial possessions in their far-flung empire stretching across the world in the Caribbean, the Americas, the Philippines, the Indies, Japan, and China. As would be later said of other empires, the sun never set on the Spanish Empire in the first half of the sixteenth century.

The Spanish Empire began when the admiral of the ocean sea, Christopher Columbus, sailed to the New World in 1492 and discovered gold on his first voyage, which prompted three more transatlantic crossings to the Caribbean and the South American mainland.[2]

Rival Portuguese and Spanish claims to the New World caused the intervention of Pope Alexander VI, who issued the papal bull *Inter caetera* (1493), which led to a claim dispute between the two imperial powers. The next year, the Spanish and Portuguese quickly negotiated the Treaty of Tordesillas, setting a line of demarcation at 370 leagues west of the Cape Verde Islands. Spain won the rights to the territory west of the line, and the Portuguese to the east.[3]

Over the next two decades, Spanish colonists exported an impressive fourteen tons of gold from the Caribbean to Seville. Still, some were dissatisfied with their personal gain and sought gold over agricultural pursuits, with Hernando Cortés famously quipping, "I came here to get rich, not to till the soil like a peasant." Settlers successively moved from Hispaniola to Puerto Rico, Jamaica, and Cuba in search of wealth. In 1519, Cortés led an expedition of settlers called *conquistadors* to the mainland and two years later conquered the Aztec Empire centered at Tenochtitlan in Mexico. In 1532, Francisco Pizzaro conquered the Incan Empire in Peru and seized tens of thousands of pounds of gold and silver.[4]

Bartolomé de Las Casas published an indictment of the Spanish cruelty toward the native peoples, wildly speculating that the colonists had killed twenty million. Although the natives did indeed perish by the millions and the Spanish settlers committed atrocities, the native populations were overwhelmingly wiped out more from smallpox, influenza, measles, and a plethora of other diseases than by the sword. Still, the rumor became fact in the mind of Spain's enemies, who used it for propaganda purposes to denounce Spanish imperialism.[5]

In September 1519, Ferdinand Magellan led the Armada de Molucca that set sail from Spain to the fabulous riches of the Spice Islands in the East Indies. He braved the tempestuous straits at the tip of South America and entered the vast Pacific Ocean. Although he was killed by natives in the Philippines, his men endured and reached their destination, trading for thousands of pounds of spices, including cinnamon, clove, and nutmeg. Scurvy and starvation claimed the lives of his men, while shipwrecks destroyed some of the vessels with their precious cargoes. Less than twenty of the sailors managed to circumnavigate the globe in one ship with a cargo that more than paid for the three-year voyage.[6]

The Mexican and Peruvian mines fed the Spanish treasure fleets that crossed the Atlantic to Seville every year laden with the precious metals. The wealth supported Spanish ambitions on the Continent, paying Spanish and mercenary armies in Italy and the Netherlands, when the Dutch revolted against Spanish rule. Initially, the fleets had to contend with deadly hurricanes and other dangers of the Atlantic, but then they proved too inviting a target for other Europeans.

For the English, some cod fishing boats joined hundreds of vessels from other European nations traveling back and forth to Newfoundland every summer, but that was the extent of the English overseas ventures. But by the middle of the sixteenth century, all that was about to change.

A new generation of men was on the make with the ascension of Queen Elizabeth. They were rising gentlemen, many of whom came to London from the West Country. Many attended the Middle Temple of the Inns of Court and received a legal education as they prepared to join the queen's court. They were thirsty for knowledge and intelligent, participating in the humanist circles of a thriving intellectual life at Oxford and Cambridge and London homes, where they exchanged ideas about navigation, cartography, mathematics, and science.

Yet the gentlemen were soldiers, adventurers, and men of action rather than monastic scholars. They were passionately patriotic and envisioned England becoming a great nation. They looked across the oceans and believed that England must build great highways of commerce in gold and spices and an empire of English settlements.

The gentlemen adventurers were fiercely Protestant and were deeply influenced by John Foxe's *The Book of Martyrs* (1563), which detailed the violent repression under Mary Tudor, wife of Spain's Philip II. They saw themselves fighting a worldwide, apocalyptic struggle against the Catholic antichrist. The war included battling the Catholic enemy in the British Isles, on the continent of Europe, and in the New World. It also carried the responsibility to evangelize the native peoples of the New World to Protestantism, not merely to civilize them and save their souls, but to prevent the spread of the falsehoods of Catholicism. The titanic political and religious struggle with Catholic Spain seamlessly wove together, shaping the course of the mid- to late sixteenth century.

But these Englishmen did not merely seek national greatness and glory. They were daring and adventurous and willing to risk their lives in search of their personal fortunes and glory. They wanted to test their resolve against great odds, strong enemies, and dangerous overseas voyages. They were pioneering and restless men who would persevere until they won personal and national honor. Many won great fortunes and fame, while others paid with their lives.[7]

Most of all, they were free Englishmen who enjoyed their liberty to pursue their destinies. The English lived under the protections of the Magna Carta, which limited the power of the monarch and helped create a Parliament. Law and liberty permitted individual initiative to thrive, and the gentlemen adventurers seized the opportunity with ardor. They usually acted without the direct, official financial support of the Crown and invested their own money in joint-stock companies, established trade stations and settlements in distant lands, and voyaged into unexplored regions of the wide oceans and newfound lands.

In the 1550s, English merchants invested their growing wealth in overseas trade ventures. Trade links were established with Morocco to exchange English textiles for African gold and sugar. Trade representatives, or factors, moved to northern Africa and were followed by diplomats dispatched by Elizabeth I to formalize relations and facilitate private trade.

In 1553, a collection of two hundred merchants, officials, and adventurers formed the Muscovy Company, the first joint-stock company. An enterprising group of London merchants funded a voyage to find a northeast route to the East Indies. Its first governor was the son of John Cabot, navigator Sebastian Cabot. The company sold shares to finance the first voyage of three ships, which were commanded by Sir Hugh Willoughby and Richard Chancellor and included several merchants to establish trade relations.

Willoughby and his scores of men froze to death that winter on land short of their destination. Meanwhile, Chancellor survived the brutal winter elements, disembarked in Russia, and made his way by sled to Moscow, where he and his men were welcomed at the court of Czar Ivan IV. They signed a treaty initiating commercial relations between the two nations.

The company was formally chartered in 1555 during the reign of Mary Tudor. Under the terms of the company charter, the consortium of merchants was granted a monopoly over the trade with the Russian port. The instructions directed the company to seek out trade routes by land and sea to the Levant, Cathay, and the Spice Islands, which future voyages followed. The trade links the Muscovy Company had with Russia were modestly successful and provided invaluable experience for the merchant and gentlemen adventurers in overseas voyages and trade.[8]

Sir John Hawkins launched three voyages to break into the highly lucrative African slave trade, which was dominated by the Iberian powers and delivered human cargo to the New World. In 1562 he won the backing of London investors and cruised the coast of Africa, where he purchased some slaves and stole a shipload of Africans from Portuguese slave ships. He sailed to the Caribbean, traded his cargo to Spanish planters in Hispaniola, and returned to England with boatloads of gold, silver, furs, and sugar.

Handsomely rewarded for their investment, the merchants funded Hawkins's return voyage to the western coast of Africa in 1564. Queen Elizabeth even privately lent her sixty-four-gun, seven-hundred-ton *Jesus of Lübeck* to the venture. Philip II was outraged by Spanish colonists, trading with the English, but his orders banning the trade were ignored, and Hawkins's second voyage returned an impressive 60 percent to his investors and won him fame as a national hero.

In 1567 the indomitable Hawkins sailed to Africa again with a fleet of six ships, two of which Elizabeth contributed. After a number of fruitless battles with Portuguese ships, deadly forays into the interior resulted in several wounded Englishmen. Disease claimed others. Meanwhile, the Africans could easily escape the clutches of the foreigners by running into the jungle. Only after a dreadfully murderous raid on a village, with the help of their local enemies, were four hundred Africans rounded up to sell, much fewer than the expected number.

The difficulties Hawkins's fleet encountered only multiplied when the Englishmen reached the West Indies. Although Hawkins managed to trade the slaves at several ports along the Caribbean coast of South America, it was only after he fired on and burned the towns and captured the uncooperative Spanish officials that he managed to force them to trade with him. Then, in late August, a hurricane battered the ships for three days and sank one of his treasure-laden vessels.

The storm forced the English ships to limp into the Gulf of Mexico, where they put in at San Juan de Ulúa on the Yucatán by hiding their identity until it was too late for the Spanish garrison. The English were making repairs to their ships when a Spanish treasure fleet appeared and trapped them in the harbor. The tense days that followed came to a boil when the Spanish finally attacked, boarding and firing on the enemy ships. The English fleet tried to break out, but the *Jesus* was mortally wounded, and Hawkins transferred his men and the wealth to another ship. The ships fired broadsides at each other while the cannon of the fort thundered away. When the smoke cleared, Hawkins and Sir Francis Drake managed to sail only two ships out of six away. Hawkins landed in Plymouth in early 1569 with fifteen gaunt survivors of an Atlantic crossing plagued by starvation and scurvy.

Hawkins did not break the lucrative Iberian monopoly over the trade in human beings, but he and Drake soon hatched another, more daring idea.[9]

During the sixteenth century, Spanish treasure fleets brought back tons of gold and silver to fund Philip II's profligate spending on his armies, which he marched across Europe and tried to quell the Protestants revolting in the Netherlands. Philip's needs were so great that not even the treasure fleets could adequately pay for his armies, and he was forced to borrow money abroad. Two fleets, one bound for Mexico and one for Peru, sailed from Spain to Hispaniola. The Mexican fleet then went to San Juan de Ulúa, the site of Hawkins's fiasco. The Peruvian fleet stopped at Cartagena and at Nombre de

Díos in Panama, where Peruvian silver was brought by mule trains. Both fleets rendezvoused at Havana before arriving at Seville in Spain. In 1571, Sir Francis Drake roved between Cartagena and Nombre de Díos, intercepted a dozen Spanish ships with the small, forty-ton *Swan*, and plundered their cargo, netting some £66,000 and exposing the weaknesses of the Spanish Empire.[10]

In May 1572, Drake sailed to take his revenge on the Spanish enemy for events at San Juan. His two ships were joined by a third English ship, the *William and John,* and they rowed three pinnaces (small vessels propelled by sails or oars) to Nombre de Díos. They successfully raided the town, but their leader was wounded, and they were forced to pull out. Drake recovered and plunged into the jungles of Panama to ambush the silver train. He became the first Englishman to look upon the waters of the Pacific and prayed that "almighty God of His goodness to give [me] life and live to sail once again in an English ship to that sea." Drake eventually hit the convoy of men and mules carrying several tons of gold and silver. The Spanish pursued him, and he was forced to bury most of his treasure off the trail.

Drake returned to England, and his cargo of precious metals made him and his investors very wealthy. More important, it was "evidence of God's love and blessing towards our gracious Queen and country," as the English believed Providence was on their side against Catholic Spain. Drake also proved that the flow of gold and silver to Spain was vulnerable.[11]

In late 1577, Drake sought to fulfill his promise to sail the Pacific when he took a fleet toward the Strait of Magellan to plunder the west coast of Spanish South America with the firm support of the queen and her court. Drake's fleet had not passed the Cape Verde Islands before it started raiding its competitors, taking a Portuguese prize and an experienced pilot named Nuño da Silva.

After making landfall in Brazil, there were troubles in the fleet centered on Thomas Doughty, a proud gentleman. He challenged Drake's authority on several occasions and was accused of fomenting a mutiny. Drake finally put in at Port San Julián in Argentina and tried and convicted Doughty. Doughty was executed, and Drake addressed his men, laying down the principle of unity of command and discipline in the person of the captain. He stated: "Let us show ourselves all to be of a company, and let us not give occasion to the enemy to rejoice at our decay and overthrow…If this voyage shall not have good success, we shall not only be a scorning unto our enemies, but also a great blot to our country forever; and what a triumph that would be for Spain and Portugal."[12]

After scuttling an unseaworthy ship and renaming the flagship the *Golden Hind,* the fleet of three ships and two pinnaces under the firm command of Sir Francis Drake entered the treacherous Strait of Magellan on August 21, 1578, during the Antarctic winter. Drake had just emerged from the strait a little over a month later, when a storm beat him back into the strait and caused one of his captains to sail the second-largest ship in the fleet back to England. Drake persevered and sailed north for the Spanish ports along the Chilean and Peruvian coasts, which were virtually undefended because no Englishmen had sailed the waters of the Pacific—until now.

Drake surprised the Spanish and looted one port after another as the unsuspecting Spanish believed his ships were their own. First he sacked Valparaiso and took chests of twenty-five thousand gold pesos. Next, the fleet captured two barks with forty large bars of silver. The Englishmen then snatched another thirteen silver bars on a beach from a sleeping guard and joked that they had "freed him of his charge." Drake's men seized another prize with another thirty-seven bars of silver, a chest full of coins, and wine. In mid-February 1579, rather than sack the port of Callao, Peru, he disabled the ships in the harbor and pursued the grand prize of a treasure ship: *Nuestra Señora de la Concepcíon* (or *Cácafuego*).

The *Golden Hind* and her companion ships captured prizes and gathered intelligence as they chased the *Nuestra Señora*. Drake offered a great prize to the man who spotted her first, which was claimed by his cousin a few weeks later. On March 1, Drake came alongside the Spanish ship and demanded her surrender, causing the master of the ship to reply, "What English demands I strike sail? Come do it yourself." Drake did so. His men opened fire, tearing down the mizzenmast and wounding the master in a hail of arrows. The treasure loaded on to the English ships for nearly a week was an incredible twenty-six tons of silver, fourteen chests of gold coins, jewels, and gilt items.[13]

Drake could hardly return back through the Strait of Magellan now that the Spanish were alerted to his presence and seeking him. He made for the North American coast, landing at Oregon and California for repairs, fresh food and water, and to look for the western entrance to the Northwest Passage. He named the land "New England" and erected a brass plate claiming North America for the queen of England.

From there, Drake knew he would have to circumnavigate the globe and plunged across the Pacific. In late 1579 he made landfall at Portuguese possessions in the Philippines and the famed Spice Islands of the Moluccas, where he traded for six tons of invaluable cloves, pepper, and other spices. Although the *Golden Hind* struck a reef, forcing Drake to lighten her load by dumping half his cloves, the ship miraculously got off and remained seaworthy as it rounded the Cape of Good Hope and reached England in September 1580. After nearly three years at sea, the patriotic Drake first inquired, "Is the queen alive and well?" She was, and she was very pleased with the 4,700 percent return for investors and knighted Drake for his accomplishments for the nation.[14] But the English still pursued trade and settlement in North America as well as plunder to the south. The gentlemen adventurers continued to strike out across the ocean to the new world in pursuit of these goals.

In June 1576, mariner Martin Frobisher initiated decades of serious English exploration and colonization of the New World when he embarked on the first of three voyages to North America looking for the Northwest Passage. He was convinced that the voyage to Cathay was "not only possible by the northwest, but also as he could prove, easy to be performed." He was trained in the navigational arts by court astrologer John Dee, who was skilled in astronomy, mathematics, and geography, and served as principal advisor to the Crown on navigation.

In mid-July, a pair of barks and a pinnace reached the eastern coast of Greenland, but icepacks frightened off one of the masters, who sailed back to England, and the pinnace sank. Frobisher endured and managed to sail around the southern tip of Baffin Island and up what is now Frobisher Bay, which he believed was a strait and the fabled passage to Cathay. He claimed the land for England and captured a native before sailing home.

When he returned to London, Frobisher was "joyfully received with the great admiration of the people, bringing with them their strange man and his boat, which was such a wonder onto the whole city and to the rest of the realm that heard of it." The native Eskimo helped spark a wild popular enthusiasm for the exotic in distant lands and was a spectacular flesh-and-blood example of the exotic rather than just a dramatic travel narrative. The pyrite that Frobisher had found turned out to be fool's gold, but it nevertheless set off a wave of gold fever in London and great enthusiasm for additional voyages.

Merchant Michael Lok formed the Cathay Company, and subscribers (including the queen) invested in Frobisher's second and third voyages to search for gold and the Northwest Passage. Frobisher sailed in May 1577 and again exactly one year later. During the former, he brought home 140 tons of ore and ten times as much as that during the latter. In July 1578, he sailed up the Hudson Strait, but fog and ice forced him to turn around. Nevertheless, he believed he had found the passage to China. Although his voyages had cost a whopping £20,000 and showed virtually no return, the English remained resolute in their pursuit of wealth and empire.[15]

Humphrey Gilbert, half brother to Sir Walter Ralegh and an acquaintance of colonial promoters Richard Hakluyt and John Dee, also sought the Northwest Passage and the English settlement of North America. Gilbert was a ruthless soldier who had fought for England and the cause of Protestantism in France, Ireland, and the Netherlands. He was knighted for his service in Ireland, during which he brutally repressed the Munster Rebellion through terror and slaughter. He was elected to Parliament and supported a practical education in the navigation arts.

In 1576, he published *A Discourse of a Discovery for a New Passage to Cathay,* arguing for the existence of the Northwest Passage. In June 1578, with the support of his influential men at court, Gilbert won a patent from Queen Elizabeth for all North American lands "not actually possessed of any Christian prince or people." He was given extensive rights to govern any settlements, although English colonists would retain their traditional rights. The Crown would take one-fifth of any gold and silver he discovered, but controlling the trade of the East was beyond the imagination of an ambitious Elizabethan gentleman adventurer.[16]

On November 18, 1578, the expedition departed from Plymouth. It was destined to fail. Storms dispersed the fleet and forced Gilbert to Ireland, the farthest point he sailed to on this voyage. Other ships went privateering off the coast of France and Spain, and Ralegh made it to the Cape Verde Islands until a leaky ship forced him to turn back. The abortive voyage was nothing short of a disaster.

Yet, in June 1583, Gilbert organized another fleet after selling millions of acres of land in North America to investors. The queen did not want her beloved pet Ralegh nor Gilbert to risk the dangers of the voyage, but she relented with Gilbert, who made a northern crossing and landed at St. John's Harbor in Newfoundland. The large island with its waters teeming with codfish was visited annually by dozens of ships from several different European countries, but that did not stop the haughty Englishman from formally claiming Newfoundland for Elizabeth. The dumbfounded fisherman looked on with barely concealed amusement at Gilbert's actions and let it pass without comment.

When disease wracked the English fleet, Gilbert made for England in late August. Terrible storms struck the fleet north of the Azores. One of the ships was wrecked, and eighty men killed. Then, on September 9, Gilbert was aboard the *Squirrel* when "suddenly her lights were out, whereof as it were in a moment, we lost sight, and withal our watch cried, the general was cast away, which was too true. For in that moment, the frigate was devoured and swallowed up of the sea." Gilbert paid with his life, but his dreams of settling North America did not die with him, for other adventurers who believed in colonization picked up his banner.[17]

In the 1580s the vision of overseas colonies and a global English Empire most clearly took shape in the writings of Richard Hakluyt, which were used to attract royal support and investor interest as promotional literature. The Oxford-educated young man was drawn to the study of geography and exploration when he visited "the chamber of Mr. Richard Hakluyt my cousin, a gentleman of the Middle Temple…at a time when I found open upon his board certain books of cosmography, with a universal map; he seeing me somewhat curious in the view thereof, began to instruct my ignorance."[18] The encounter set off a lifelong interest and study of every travel manuscript that he could lay his hands on and conversations with every mariner who would be willing to speak with him.

In 1582, Hakluyt the younger published a pamphlet called *Divers Voyages Touching the Discovery of America, and the Islands Adjacent* in which he advocated the colonization of America "to advance the honor of our country." He produced an inexpensive edition in order to reach as wide an audience as possible. Hakluyt stated that the English had a legitimate claim to North America because of the voyage of John Cabot and because the lands were "unpossessed by any Christians." Addressing the recent failures of Frobisher and Gilbert, Hakluyt argued that the English explorers were driven by "a preposterous desire of seeking rather gain than God's glory." Moreover, they must establish great centers of learning in navigational arts like their rivals. He gave what he believed was ironclad proof of a great river or northwest passage cutting through North America to China and the Spice Islands. North America also promised to yield great amounts of gold, silver, and pearls, just as the Spanish had found to the south. He also advanced the idea that the English could reap a number of commodities from the undeveloped, fertile lands to England, which could then challenge the Spanish monopoly over treasure and commerce as well as convert the natives to Protestant Christianity, thus saving them from heathenism or Roman Catholicism.[19]

In 1584, Hakluyt wrote *Discourse on Western Planting* to promote the schemes of Sir Walter Ralegh—who developed plans to colonize North America after his half brother perished at sea—to the queen. The blueprint for colonization repeated many of the ideas of *Divers Voyages,* but he also presented a concise economic and commercial blueprint for empire. All the accounts he read spoke of the potential wealth in precious metals and of a bountiful, fertile land that would provide many commodities to the industrious English. The chronically poor and unemployed would find opportunity in the North American colonies. The colonists would serve as producers of raw materials, but also they would be consumers who demanded products from England, which would stimulate the English economy. A prosperous economy would lead English parents to have more children and strengthen the nation. Experience in navigation and great wealth would also allow England to build a navy to defend the realm and its far-flung empire. The colonies could serve as a base for privateers to intercept and plunder the Spanish treasure fleets, but Hakluyt's scheme was dedicated primarily to building the English empire.[20]

Hakluyt was an intellectual who laid down a cohesive framework for the rationale behind the English empire, but he left it to the gentlemen adventurers with whom he conferred to execute his vision.

In 1584, Sir Walter Ralegh received Gilbert's exclusive patent to North America and planned to settle on the Outer Banks of North Carolina. Ralegh was educated at Oxford and the Middle Temple. He had made the acquaintance of Hakluyt and served Sir Francis Walsingham. In 1580, he fought in Ireland and participated in the slaughter of hundreds of foreign mercenaries at Smerwick Fort. He was a favorite courtier of Queen Elizabeth, by whom he was rewarded with generous estates and incomes. His Durham House became a center of discussion for navigation and colonization and included all of the leading figures involved in the schemes.[21]

On April 27, 1584, Ralegh dispatched an expedition of two ships to the Outer Banks for reconnaissance of the area to establish privateering bases from which to strike the Spanish treasure fleets. By July 13 they had discovered Roanoke Island as a suitable site and captured two Indians (Manteo, son of the Croatoan chief, and Wanchese) who served as a promotional vehicle for the venture among English investors to fund colonization. Written propaganda accounts claimed, "The soil is the most plentiful, sweet, fruitful, and wholesome of all the world." In fact, Ralegh was trying to secure London investors even before the expedition returned. The military nature of the colony Ralegh envisioned meant that the gentlemen adventurers were not yet prepared to establish Hakluyt's proposed trade colony.[22]

Soldier Ralph Lane was released from his service in Ireland and appointed governor of the colony, while Sir Richard Grenville served as admiral for the fleet. On April 9, 1585, seven ships and some six hundred men sailed for Roanoke. A storm scattered the fleet and sank one of the smaller pinnaces, causing Lane to put in at Puerto Rico to build a new one. They landed at Roanoke in late June, but a storm grounded the flagship, *Tiger,* and ruined most of its provisions. Lane ordered the Roanoke colonists to erect homes, a storehouse, and a diamond-shaped fort with a firing step. In August the fleet departed, leaving behind 107 colonists to live off the land until a relief expedition arrived. Grenville returned to England and encouraged Ralegh to send supplies, but not before Grenville seized a Spanish prize, the "richly laden" *Santa Maria de San Vincente,* before reaching home. The prize paid for the expedition and confirmed in the mind of many investors the value of focusing on taking Spanish treasure ships. In June, Ralegh had already acted without waiting to hear of the colony's fate and sent supplies, but the ships were diverted to Newfoundland at the request of the queen to warn them of an impending sea war with Spain. The priority of the Crown was battling Catholic Spain, even to the detriment of Roanoke.[23]

Roanoke was largely a sideshow for the audacious privateering voyage of Sir Francis Drake, who left England in September in command of the largest English fleet ever in American waters. After narrowly missing the main treasure fleet by hours and losing several hundred men to disease after plundering the Cape Verde Islands, he sailed for the Caribbean. On New Year's Day, 1586, Drake sacked Santo Domingo and seized sixteen thousand furs before ransoming the city. Cartagena fell to the sea dog, who liberated hundreds of African slaves and won another ransom. After losing several hundred men, Drake sailed for Roanoke but stopped on the coast of Florida and burned the Spanish settlement at St. Augustine to the ground.[24]

On June 8, Drake arrived at Roanoke and agreed to provide boats, men, supplies, and guns for Lane's colony. A mighty storm rolled in and destroyed several smaller ships and damaged the others. The situation was precarious for the hungry colonists, and they yielded to what they imagined to be inevitable and returned to England with Drake's fleet. Drake left the hundreds of slaves liberated from the Spanish to their fate. Only a few weeks later, Grenville arrived at the deserted colony with three supply ships, and when he did not find anyone, he sailed back to England. Had he not sought Spanish prizes on the voyage to Roanoke, he might have reached the colony in time to convince Lane to remain. Grenville left fifteen men with artillery and supplies to find the missing Roanoke colonists. The men were never heard from again.[25]

Despite the failure, Ralegh and his backers still believed that Roanoke could serve as a privateering base and that the colonists could find gold, the Northwest Passage, and marketable commodities to

keep investors interested. A third expedition to Roanoke was organized under the weak leadership of painter Governor John White.
The model of settlement seemed to change from a mostly privateering
base to land development, as a number of families were sent who
received land grants and were governed by a council. On May 8,
1587, three ships sailed from England and arrived by late July. They
moved into the existing houses built by Lane's colonists. By the end
of August, the settlers begged White to return home and lobby Ralegh
for additional provisions. Upon White's return, Ralegh attempted
to organize a supply fleet for the spring of 1588, but it was stopped
when every available ship was called into service against the Spanish
Armada.[26]

On April 22, amid the confusing preparations for war and the
impounding of all ships, Ralegh finally won permission to send a
few small supply ships with Governor White. The ships, however,
never made it to Roanoke, because they engaged in privateering
battles and were heavily damaged. They sailed back to England.
Ralegh could not persuade the Privy Council to send another relief
expedition and soon lost interest.[27]

The outrages the English perpetrated against Philip's overseas
possessions, as well as the execution of Mary Queen of Scots in
1587, led the Spanish king—with the assistance of papal funds—to
go to war against Protestant England. But while he was assembling
his massive war fleet, Drake secretly brought a large fleet of ships
to the Spanish coast to take the war to the enemy. On April 29,
1587, Drake appeared at the port of Cadiz and immediately
attacked. English firepower drove six Spanish galleons back into
the harbor. Drake's men proceeded to plunder and sink two dozen
vessels and depart nearly unscathed. The size of the monetary return
mattered much less than the devastating psychological impact on
the Spanish.[28]

By July 1588, after many delays and storms at sea, the Spanish fleet of about 130 ships reached the English coast. It sailed in a crescent formation past Plymouth and the other coastal towns into the English Channel, where it planned to embark the Duke of Parma's soldiers waiting at Dunkirk and invade England. The larger English fleet of some 180 ships pursued the Spanish and skirmished a bit. On July 21, the English sank the colossal 1,150-ton Spanish warship *Nuestra Señora del Rosario*. The two fleets otherwise largely exchanged ineffective broadsides, although the Armada was becoming desperately short of food, water, and gunpowder. When the Spanish put in to pick up Parma, he was not there. Subsequently, the English sent eight fireships toward the Spanish and dispersed the enemy fleet, which headed north. The Armada sailed north around the British Isles but was punished by storms off the coast of Ireland that drove many ships into the rocks, where the survivors were slaughtered by Irish Catholics (who were supposedly friendly) and English troops. The remnants of the Armada limped back to a dispirited Spain, where the defeat could be seen as nothing less than a national tragedy, whereas the victory set off great patriotic celebrations in England. The English believed God had blessed their victory over the Catholic king.[29] The epic battle between the two nations had direct implications for their imperial struggle and the English drive for empire in North America.

While the English defended their home against invasion, Governor White was determined to learn the fate of the Roanoke colonists and sought to rescue them. But he did not sail until 1590, when he boarded a privateering vessel in a small fleet without supplies for the colony. Rather than sailing directly for Roanoke, the ships hunted Spanish prizes in the Caribbean. In August, after several encounters, the ships finally reached the abandoned Roanoke colony. The settlers White had left behind years before were gone, but they had left two messages—CRO carved on a tree and CROATOAN carved on a palisade post—but they had not left the prearranged distress signal, meant to indicate that they had moved of their own accord rather than facing an Indian attack. White fruitlessly searched for them, but he had to return to England without learning their ultimate fate.[30]

The aging generation of explorers and sea dogs who had braved the oceans and unsettled lands, as well as given war to the Spanish enemy for decades, died out in the 1590s. At home, England suffered rising inflation, failed harvests, plague, and increasing poverty for the landless masses. Nevertheless, the English had quelled the Spanish threat, and voyaging overseas for trade and colonies persisted.

The most successful of the ventures was the East India Company, founded to participate in the lucrative spice trade. From 1591 to 1594, an English merchant adventurer, Sir James Lancaster, sailed to the East Indies to reconnoiter the area for opportunities. Dutch ships simultaneously conducted similar voyages. Although the trip was a financial failure, London merchants continued to meet and plan additional expeditions to break into the Portuguese trade and block Dutch challenges. On September 22, 1599, 101 London merchants (including members of the Levant Company and Drake's crew) pledged money for and petitioned the queen "to venture in the pretended voyage to the East Indies."[31]

Elizabeth hesitated because of peace negotiations with King Philip's successor, Philip III, but when they stalled interminably, she gave her consent. On December 31, 1600, the collection of what was now 218 members was granted a charter to "the East Indies, the countries and ports of Asia and Africa, and to and from all the islands' ports, towns, and places of Asia, African and America, or any of them beyond the Cape of Good Hope and the Straits of Magellan." Sir Thomas Smythe served as the first governor of the company. Lancaster sailed within only two months to Sumatra and Bantham, and he triumphantly returned to England three years later with five ships laden with five hundred tons of pepper.

Within a decade, trade "factories" were established in Africa, India, the Spice Islands, China, and Japan, where the English traded for ivory, silks, cloves, nutmeg, sugar, coffee, and tea, among other valuable commodities, all of which returned great profits to investors. By 1620 the company owned a fleet of more than thirty armed ships that accompanied convoys of more than a dozen trading ships at a time. Competition with the Dutch East India Company (VOC) was fierce, as England reaped growing profits from its global trade.[32]

The record of English expansion during the latter part of the sixteenth century produced mixed results, though it was largely a story of failures and disappointed hopes that fell far short of what most of its supporters had envisioned. England was still far from achieving the global imperial status of its chief rival Spain. Except for a few noteworthy successes, such as Drake's circumnavigation and the successful Dutch East India Company, English attempts at trade and settlement had resulted in few tangible gains. Virtually none of the trade companies generated large profits, explorers had perished, colonists had died, the coasts of North America still did not have any permanent English settlements, and the Northwest Passage remained elusive. Nevertheless, the promise of great wealth and glory continued to draw English gentlemen adventurers to voyage or invest in overseas ventures. They were still interested in the North American coast for several reasons. The lure of gold and silver, an undiscovered route to the East, and the endless bounty of a fertile land could not be contained.[33]

And as a new century dawned with a new king, a new generation of independent, enterprising men sought to realize the dream of a global English empire. Among these rising young gentleman was an adventurer named John Smith, who would help initiate the plan to colonize Virginia, shaping the course that settlement in Virginia would take in the opening years of the seventeenth century.

Chapter Two

JOHN SMITH
AND THE IDEA
OF VIRGINIA

When the twenty-four-year-old gentleman adventurer John Smith returned to England in 1604, he found the realm much changed from when he had left only a few years before. In 1603 the beloved Virgin Queen had died after nearly half a century on the throne. The Scottish king, James I, succeeded her as the first monarch of the Stuart family. The following year, he signed a peace treaty with England's mortal enemy, Spain, ending the decades-long sea war that had culminated in the destruction of the Spanish Armada.

Peace presented a new series of opportunities for a new generation of gentlemen adventurers and investors overseas. The old generation of Elizabethan sea dogs and promoters had largely passed away during the previous decade. One of the firmest supporters of overseas ventures at court, Sir Francis Walsingham, had died in 1590. The elder Richard Hakluyt, who had published so many tracts to promote investment and support for colonization, had passed away in 1591. Renowned privateers Sir Francis Drake and Sir John

Hawkins perished in an ill-fated 1595 expedition to Panama. Sir Thomas Cavendish was lost at sea, and Sir Richard Grenville was killed assaulting a Spanish fortress. Grenville's half brother, Sir Walter Ralegh, the guiding force behind the failed attempts to colonize Roanoke, lost favor at court, and James had him imprisoned in the Tower of London.

John Smith was a gentleman adventurer of the new generation who moved English schemes for colonizing North America forward. He was born of humble origins in 1580, the son of a middling yeoman farmer in Lincolnshire, far below the previous generation of well-heeled gentry with ties to court. He received an elementary education and apprenticed with a merchant in Kings Lynn. At sixteen years old, Smith discovered that he was not going to sea on trading voyages as he wished and then learned of his father's death. Since he thought his future prospects were dim, Smith traveled to the Low Countries to join an English regiment in aiding the Dutch in their revolt against the brutal rule of Catholic Spain.

After battling Spanish forces for a time, Smith returned to his home of Lincolnshire and received a martial education in the art of war. He read Machiavelli's *Art of War* and the Roman emperor Marcus Aurelius, among other works, and was tutored in the military arts by Theadora Polaloga, who had traveled to England from the Byzantine Empire, which was now controlled by the Ottoman Turks. Seignior Polaloga trained Smith in riding, languages, conversation, and oratory, as befit a young Renaissance gentleman.

In 1600 the restless twenty-year-old Smith left England to battle the Ottoman Turks, who were then threatening Christendom in Eastern Europe. He traveled across France, where four rogues pretending to be adventurers robbed the young man of his gold and baggage. A number of French women patronized his voyage through the country until he boarded a ship at Marseilles bound for Italy.

Smith encountered a great deal of animosity from his fellow passengers. The Roman Catholic passengers from different nations disliked the young English Protestant because of his religion and his nation's reputation for piracy. He similarly held the Catholics in disdain, particularly because they were on a pilgrimage to Rome. When severe storms threatened the ship, the superstitious among the passengers blamed the Protestant soldier of fortune for their woes and threw him overboard to improve their luck.

Smith was able to swim to a nearby island, where another ship was fatefully riding out the storm and offered to take him aboard. The hapless traveler encountered additional dangers when a Venetian ship fired on the vessel after it entered the Adriatic Sea. The two ships exchanged a ferocious barrage as they lined up broadside. Fifteen men were killed on Smith's ship, and twenty men lay dead on the opposing ship. As flames raged aboard his vessel, Smith and his new companions boarded the Venetian ship and engaged in hand-to-hand combat in an attempt to take the ship. The Venetians surrendered before the onslaught, and Smith joined in the plunder of the ship for his efforts. The ship carried valuable silks, velvets, gold, and other riches. He netted a princely sum, including £225 in coin and a gold box worth again as much.

Smith spent time in Italy, where he saw the pope, and then made his way over land to the combined armies of Christian Europe arrayed against the Turks. He made an immediate impression upon the leaders of the European forces. In order to help a relief army break the enemy siege of Limbach, Germany, he demonstrated a communication network with torches, which he recalled reading about in Machiavelli's *Art of War*. He also offered a means to deceive the enemy by hanging burning cords that emulated soldiers firing their muskets and made the army appear larger than it was. The Turkish army retired and the siege was lifted, and he came to the attention of his superiors, who gave him command of a cavalry unit.

Smith's unit was deployed in the siege of Szekesfehervar, which had been occupied by the Turks since 1543. He suggested making bombs from large pots filled with gunpowder, pitch, turpentine, and musket balls. The incendiary devices were ignited and launched over the walls of the city with dramatic effect. He later described the scene as "a fearful sight to see the short flaming course of their flight in the air, but presently after their fall, the lamentable noise of the miserable slaughtered Turks was most wonderful to hear." His innovative "fiery dragons" were partly responsible for helping to break the siege and storm the city.

In 1602, Smith was serving under Szigmond Báthory, a Transylvanian prince under Mózes Székely, who was in command of the siege of Alba Julia. Although it was not a military necessity, a Turkish commander issued a challenge to the Christian allies to send out a champion to meet him in single combat. The Turkish commander rode on to the field with armor adorned with gold, silver, gems, and eagle's feathers. Smith donned his modest armor and mounted his warhorse. At the sound of a trumpet, the two foes charged each other and lowered their lances. Smith impaled the Turk with a sickening crunch and drove him off his mount, killing him instantly. He then unsheathed his sword and beheaded the man, carrying his gruesome trophy across the field to the cheers of his army.

A friend of the dead Turk challenged Smith to a duel the following day. Smith took the field of honor armed with a lance, firearm, and sword. After their lances shattered on each other's shields, they withdrew their firearms. Smith drew a bead on his opponent and knocked him off his horse with one shot. He then drew his sword and took another head for his collection.

In the euphoria of these victories, Smith's arrogance was fueled and he threw down a gauntlet to anyone in the Turkish army. His next competitor gladly took the chance to humiliate the swaggering mercenary. After an exchange of pistol shots missed their marks, the adversaries unhooked their battle-axes and took aim at each other's skulls.

Smith explained that he "received such a blow that he lost his battle-axe," though luckily for him not his head. Nevertheless, he managed to dodge more blows, unsheathe his sword, and turn the tide of battle. "Beyond all men's expectation, by God's assistance, [he] not only avoided the Turks' violence but...pierced the Turk so...thorough back and body that although he alighted from his horse, he stood not long ere he lost his head as the rest had done."

Although the fights did not alter the outcome of the siege, the Europeans assaulted the city and the garrison surrendered. Most of defenders lost their heads, and the victors sacked the town and carried away a great deal of plunder.

An immediate legend in the army, John Smith was awarded a promotion, a warhorse, a sword, a gilded belt, an annual pension, and a coat of arms bearing the heads of the three Turks whom he defeated.

Only a few months after his victory, Smith's fortunes turned for the worse. The army encountered a force allied with the Turks, and he was gravely wounded on the battlefield and left for dead. He was discovered alive by some pillagers, and he was taken away to a slave market on the Danube, where he was clapped in chains and sold with others "like beasts in a market-place." He was chained to other slaves and then subjected to a five-hundred-mile death march through the Ottoman Empire. An iron ring was clasped around his neck, his head and beard were shaved, and he was fed a meager diet.

Smith's military training led him to spend every waking

moment probing for a way to escape. One day he found his chance. Smith was threshing grain in an isolated field, alone with his owner, who was taking sadistic pleasure in "beating, spurning, and reviling" him. Smith gripped his thresher until his knuckles turned white and swung a vicious blow that killed his master. He hid the body in some straw, put on his master's clothes, and ran away.

The fugitive desperately rode north into Russia for weeks, trying to avoid detection and find a way home. Smith came upon a camp where the commander took off his neck ring and issued him a safe-conduct pass. The Englishman journeyed back to Transylvania, where Prince Sigismundus gave him fifteen hundred gold ducats for his service and troubles. He traveled home through a circuitous route in Europe and Northern Africa. The final leg of his voyage was spent aboard a French man-of-war that was struck by storms and had a two-day running broadside battle with two Spanish warships. With cutlasses and blunderblusses in hand, Smith and the Frenchmen barely repulsed the Spaniards. In 1604, Smith finally arrived home in England and learned of the planning of another adventure to North America. Although Smith had spent his time battling enemies on the continent, he now joined others in winning glory by settling distant lands for England. The dangers would be just as great, but the rewards could be beyond imagination.

In 1604, London and other cities were abuzz with several different schemes for overseas voyages. Merchants, adventurers, politicians, and members of the court were discussing the potential risks and rewards of the different ideas that were proposed. They were generally guided by a desire for profit, but they were also fierce patriots who wished to support England's imperial ambitions, particularly against the hated Spanish, even if they were officially at peace. Many were committed Protestants who combated the spread of

Catholicism on the Continent and in the New World by joining the enemies of Spain, fighting closer to home, or colonizing Ireland. The promoters of colonial ventures were also generally involved in more than one scheme with an almost unlimited appetite for personal profit and imperial greatness. They were gentlemen, but they also were men of action, willing to risk their lives and fortunes on gold and the glory of mother England.

When John Smith returned from his adventures, one such promoter was Bartholomew Gosnold, who was actively lobbying merchants and politicians to support a venture to North America. Indeed, Smith called Gosnold "one of the first movers of the colony." For many years, Gosnold had "solicited many of his friends" but mustered little interest. He persisted, nevertheless, and slowly won people over to the idea of a Virginia colony. Smith himself became interested in the colony and had money to invest in the venture.[34]

Gosnold was born of a well-connected Suffolk family. He was a cousin of gentleman adventurer Edward Maria Wingfield. When he was a young man, Gosnold had gone to sea and fought as a privateer. He also joined other English adventurers in the Low Countries against the Spanish. In 1602 he led an expedition to the coasts of New England at Cape Cod and Martha's Vineyard to establish a trading station in furs and fish with the local Indians. He brought back an Indian canoe to England to stir enthusiasm for overseas ventures and promoted the great beauty and bounty of the land. He also carried some commodities—furs, sassafras roots, cedarwood—to show the potential goods to be found there.

Gosnold interested his cousin Wingfield in the Virginia colony. Wingfield had come from a similarly distinguished family, and his father was a member of Parliament. Wingfield had served in Ireland and the Netherlands, where he was held as a prisoner of war in 1588 before returning to Ireland. He had fought in the Low

Countries with Fernando Gorges, who was the governor of the fort at Plymouth and willing to support Gosnold.

Another critical supporter of the Virginia colony was the extraordinary merchant Sir Thomas Smythe, who had recently been knighted by the king. Smythe had participated in a number of groundbreaking overseas ventures, including the incorporation of the Turkey Company in 1584, the development and activities of the Muscovy Company in 1587, and an expedition to the East Indies in 1591 to explore the opportunities to participate in the lucrative spice trade. He was the first governor of the English East India Company. Smythe also held a number of government positions that helped him build up his connections for global voyages and trade. He was the sheriff of London, the master of customs, an ambassador to Russia, and a member of Parliament. There were few men whose support was so critical for winning the support of the Crown and private investors for a colony. Other powerful and influential men in the government also lent indispensable support for Gosnold's vision.

Any North American colony needed to have official royal sanction, although James would not provide any financial backing, just as Elizabeth had not. Sir John Popham, lord chief justice of the King's Bench, and the king's first minister, Robert Cecil, Earl of Salisbury, were prime movers in winning government permission to settle in American and in assembling the necessary wealthy investors among the merchants of London, Plymouth, and Bristol. Smith would later describe the relationships that were forged and proclaimed, "Nothing could be effected" without "certain of the nobility, gentry, and merchants." In the summer of 1605 the various interests came together and discussed their purposes and means of achieving them where many other Englishmen had failed.[35]

On April 10, 1606, Popham and Cecil persuaded the government to grant a patent, or royal charter, establishing two companies to colonize the territory called Virginia, "which are not now actually possessed by any Christian prince or people."[36] The king did not wish to see any conflict with a European power over contested lands. The Plymouth Colony would settle in the northern part of Virginia from thirty-eight degrees to forty-five degrees latitude. It generally comprised merchants from the West Country cities of Exeter, Bristol, and Plymouth.

The Virginia Company would consist of "certain knights, gentlemen, merchants, and other adventurers of our city of London and elsewhere."[37] They would be allowed to plant a colony between thirty-four and forty-one degrees latitude. Both companies were allowed to settle within a hundred miles of the coast.

A Virginia Council of thirteen important investors appointed by the king was to direct both companies from London. The colonies would have a local council to administer the government locally, but the Virginia Council would manage the general affairs of the companies and instruct them on the proper policies to implement in North America. The patent included protecting the rights of Englishmen "as if they had been abiding and born within this our realm of England," when they traveled to settle in distant lands.[38]

The Englishmen were charged with carrying the Protestant faith to the native peoples, who were said to be living "in darkness and miserable ignorance of the true knowledge and worship of God."[39] The council directed the settlers to set up their colonies inland and to erect fortifications to defend against competing nations, such as Spain. Most important, the economic grounds of the colonies were laid when the company was granted rights to all the "lands, woods, soil, grounds, havens, ports, rivers, mines, minerals, marshes, water, fishing, [and] commodities."[40] No other subjects would be granted a competing patent that would violate this monopoly. The king also authorized the colonists to "dig, mine, and search for all manner of mines of gold, silver and copper," with the only caveat that the Crown was to receive a fifth of the gold and silver and a fifteenth of the copper.[41] The king also prohibited the colonists from trading with any other country, thereby enforcing an early expression of the idea of mercantilism: colonies existed solely for the good of the mother country and were limited to providing raw materials and trading with it.

The gentlemen adventurers won the royal patent and organized the complicated venture rather quickly. First, ships and sailors were found to traverse the Atlantic with the colonists. Tons of supplies were bought and loaded for the lengthy four-month voyage and to support the colonists while they planted crops. Prospective hardy adventurers, including many who had seen military service, were persuaded to risk settling in unexplored areas of North America. A variety of tradesmen were hired in London and other cities.

Through the raw days of November, the last-minute preparations moved forward at a rapid pace. Three ships were moored at the docks along the Thames at Ratcliff Cross some four miles upriver from Blackwall and were taking on supplies. The merchant flagship *Susan Constant* was some 120 tons and measured 116 feet. She carried cannon to defend herself against any Spanish marauders on the high seas. The *Godspeed* was half the tonnage of her sister ship but would carry more than fifty men and tons of supplies. The third ship in the small fleet was the *Discovery*, a pinnace that was rightly named, for it was small enough, at 20 tons, to navigate Virginia's rivers on voyages of discovery.

During the night of November 23 an accident damaged the *Susan Constant* while it lay in its berth, fully loaded with supplies. The *Philip and Frances* was a mostly empty ship of 100 tons, and some of her young sailors had too much cable out. The more experienced sailors on the *Susan Constant* warned them to correct the problem, but the youths ignored them. The *Philip and Frances* was swept by the ebb tide and crashed into the *Susan Constant*. Four carpenters were hired and worked for three days to make the necessary repairs to the ship. By December 10 the Virginia Council reported that the ships "are now ready, victualed, rigged, and furnished for the said voyage."[42]

While the ships were busily readied in late November and early December, the Virginia Council issued a set of formal instructions to the leadership for governing the colony as well as some practical advice. They were prudent measures aimed at preserving law and order in the colony and instituted the English constitutional system of liberty. A colonial council was authorized to govern locally, according to the common law, and had to make laws that were consistent with the laws of England. The president was limited to a one-year term. An additional safeguard against any abuse of power was the empowering of the council "upon any just cause…to remove the president or any other of that council."[43]

The constitutional security against tyranny was an English trait and was a wise precaution for the distant settlement. But there was a potential problem with the directive. If there were disputes among the proud and competitive gentlemen adventurers, the power of removal could be used as a weapon to settle personal differences and grievances. The resulting misuse of the instruction and cancerous destruction of the leadership could theoretically cause more trouble for the enterprise than an overbearing president.

In an unwise move that caused much confusion in the highest ranks of the colony, the instructions were sealed with the names of those who were appointed to be leaders with the directive that the packet was not to be opened until "four and twenty hours next after the said ships shall arrive upon the said coast of Virginia." For the duration of the voyage, the admiral of the fleet, Christopher Newport, was quite reasonably to have "sole charge and command." But the members of the colonial council did not have the opportunity to offer their vision of leadership to the settlers or win over their allegiance. The restriction also prohibited any personality conflicts from being settled in the relative calm of the taverns and homes of London under the oversight of the Virginia Council, rather than amid the chaos of erecting the colony. The leadership of such a great undertaking across the Atlantic was startlingly secret to the people who were risking their lives in a largely unknown land.

The Virginia Council additionally laid down a general criminal code and jury system for the colony alternatively regulating behavior and protecting the rights of the settlers. "Tumults, rebellion, conspiracies, mutiny, and seditions…together with murder, manslaughter, incest, rapes, and adulteries" comprised the list of crimes that warranted the death penalty. The English settlers were entitled to having "twelve persons so returned and sworn [who] shall according to their evidence…be given unto them upon oath, and according to the truth in their consciences either convict or acquit ever of the said persons so to be accused and tried by them." Trial by jury was an ancient right of Englishmen, but whether it would always be applied fairly or merely receive lip service remained to be seen when the colonists were in America.[44]

The council also enumerated a list of lesser offenses that would receive a milder punishment. The range of penalties included "reasonable corporal punishment and imprisonment, or else by a convenient fine, awarding damages, or other satisfaction to ye party grieved." The misdemeanors incorporated a number of moral offenses in the attempt to regulate personal behavior for the common good. Drunkenness, idleness, loitering, and vagrancy were acts contrary to the survival of the colony and would be punished.[45]

The council also gave some practical instructions on what the settlers were to do once they landed. The commands were guided by the objectives of what the investors and planners were attempting to achieve. Although what they directed made general sense, it also denied the settlers some flexibility in adapting to events as they happened in Virginia.

The first piece of advice was to choose a site for the colony by sailing up a navigable river. The river should offer the most favorable opportunity to find the Northwest Passage to the "other sea" (the Pacific) to control the China trade through a shorter route to the west. It should also be the "most fertile and wholesome place." Another critically important consideration was that the location must be defensible against the Spanish enemy. The council mentioned the example of the destruction of the French colonies in Florida as proof against settling on the coast and offering an inviting target of plunder.

Once the colonists landed, they were to divide the men into teams to fulfill the mission of settlement. Forty of them were to build a common storehouse for their supplies. Thirty were to be employed in tilling the soil and sowing crops of corn to feed the settlers. There would thus be a communal character to the survival of the colony rather than individual initiative to spur on hard work. "First build your storehouse and those other rooms of public and necessary use before any house be set up for any private person and though the workman may belong to any private persons yet let them all work together first for the company and then for private men," the instructions noted. Captains Newport and Gosnold were to take another forty on a voyage of discovery armed with pickaxes to "find any mineral," whether gold, silver, or copper. Besides the search for great wealth, the hunt for a river stretching across the American continent to the "East India Sea" was part of the quest for unlimited riches, especially if they could find the legendary cities of gold and control the fabled passage.

The individuals of the council were acutely interested in protecting their investment and promoting Virginia among other prospective investors. They desired news of the commodities, soil, woods, and other sources of wealth to "advertise" the English colony in Virginia. But they were not terribly interested in any honest appraisal that might damage the perception of the venture in England, warning the leaders to "suffer no man to…write any letter of anything that may discourage others." Since their fortunes and the glory of England were invested in the colony, the council only wanted to publicize favorable news about the great successes in North America.

The council addressed the anticipated military and economic aspects of Indian relations. The primary consideration, before friendly relations were established and trust built, was to be wary of the Indians and carefully construct the defenses against possible aggressive actions. The colonists were to clear the trees on the land surrounding their town to deny the local peoples cover to launch an attack. Moreover, the colonists were not to expose their numbers of sick or dead, lest they give the Indians encouragement to attack. Only the best marksmen should handle weapons, "for if they see your learners miss what they aim at they will think the weapons not so terrible and thereby will be bold."

Once the security of the colony was guaranteed, the settlers were ordered to trade with the Indians, who could also be a great source of local knowledge about the search for gold and the Northwest Passage. The colonists must take "great care not to offend the naturals if you can eschew it," treating them justly and charitably. The

English believed in their own propaganda about the Spanish lie—the supposed mistreatment and slaughter of millions of Indians by the Spanish—and wished to avoid repeating the crime. Thus, the Indians would be receptive to the Protestant missions to "draw the savages and heathen people…to the true service and knowledge of God."

Although there were flaws in the planning, the members of the Virginia Council did the best they could to anticipate the conditions the settlers would face and instruct them in the vision of the investors. Now it was up to 107 brave souls to journey across three thousand miles of ocean into a virtually unknown land. Not every problem could be foreseen, nor would the wealthy investors have much to offer to fight the daily struggles to survive. The adventurers would have to adapt to circumstances and find innovative solutions to difficulties. They would also have to cooperate in pursuing their goals if they were to successfully plant a permanent English colony in North America.

When they stepped aboard their three vessels, no one could predict what the outcome would be for their purses, their very lives, or the glory of England. The council had generally planned well for the governance, profit, and survival of the colony. The instructions were closely related to fulfilling the goals of the investors. But the character of the instructions made it plain that the colony would resemble previous English attempts to settle in America. At this point, no one questioned the communal and centralized qualities of the colony for those more consistent with free Englishmen.

Chapter Three

VOYAGING TO VIRGINIA

It was very early on a chilly December morning when Capt. Christopher Newport dressed and went to oversee his fleet bobbing in the Thames. The forest of ship masts crowded the wharf of this busy port. A few friends and relatives came early to see off the small fleet, but London was the center of shipping for global trade networks, privateering, and exploratory voyages, so the fleet's departure did not garner much popular attention. Newport was satisfied that all was ready to sail.

Newport captained the *Susan Constant* and had sole command of the fleet. He was a one-armed military man who had sailed throughout the Atlantic as a privateer and raided Spanish treasure fleets. A bit of a mercenary acting in the interests of the Crown, he captured or sank dozens of Spanish ships. In 1592 he won renown by plundering the *Madre de Dios* of hundreds of tons of valuable spices, silks, and gems. Newport even took part in Drake's bold raid on the Spanish port of Cadiz, sinking part of the assembled armada months before it set out and was destroyed by storms at sea. He also knew American waters as well as anyone and was a good choice to lead the fleet.

The primary organizer of the voyage, Bartholomew Gosnold, was at the helm of the *Godspeed* and had similarly impressive credentials for piloting a ship in the waters of the New World. The captain of the *Discovery* was a mysterious gentleman turned captain, John Ratcliffe, formerly known as John Sicklemore.

Newport's three dozen mariners were busy with the final preparations for what was expected to be a ten- to fourteen-week voyage, although any number of problems could lengthen that journey by weeks—any such delay, however, would be deadly, as passengers and crews suffered the effects of scurvy. Orders were barked out as the crew speedily carried out their tasks. Some carried the final casks of food and water below, while others checked and rechecked their equipment as they had done over the last several weeks. Finally, the crew was ready to sail.

Passengers filtered toward the three ships. Some were escorted by wives, children, or parents making tearful good-byes; others simply came alone. Most were hardy young men in their twenties or thirties, although a few boys also could be seen. Almost half were gentlemen and expected the proper deference from the crew and the artisans aboard ship. The craftsmen included four carpenters, two bricklayers, a blacksmith, a tailor, a mason, and a sailmaker. No women boarded the vessels. There were no families. All the passengers were young men in search of adventure and glory—but most of all great amounts of gold (although other forms of wealth would do nicely too). Indeed, self-interest drove these men to take the great risks in braving the voyage and settlement overseas. They were risking the possibility of winning great wealth against the expense of their lives.

Newport kept the sealed box with the settlers' instructions from the Virginia Council in his cabin. For now, the settlers and mariners were simply to follow Newport's direction—period. Wisely, the Virginia Council placed a copy of the instructions on each ship. Many dangers—hurricanes, Spanish ships, epidemics—lurked during the long voyage, threatening to strike at any time. If the council sent only one copy of the instructions and it went down with its ship, the colony would be leaderless and prone to chaos and failure. This seemingly obvious prudential measure was not a routine that was always followed during later voyages.

On December 20, 1606, 144 sailors and adventurers set sail for Virginia as their three ships quietly slipped their moorings. They rode the ebb tide, sailing down the Thames and catching a last sight of the English countryside. The river pilots navigated them past the busy wharves, where ships from Britain's burgeoning global trade docked. The adventurers aboard the three ships were filled with both excitement and trepidation.

The Gulf Stream, little understood until Benjamin Franklin made his measurements while sailing across the Atlantic, brought warm water currents across the Atlantic, moderating the climate of England. However, westerly winds shot across the wave tops of the treacherous North Atlantic. They brought storms and daunting winds to sailors trying to ride the winds and tides southward.

The *Susan Constant, Godspeed,* and *Discovery* soon were caught in a maelstrom of winds. The gales blew hard against the sails for weeks on end, with no reprieve. A few days after setting off, Newport and the other captains dropped anchor to avoid being dashed against the rocks off the north coast of Kent, in the Downs, within sight of land.

One person in the fleet noted that on the "fifth of January we anchored in the Downs, but the winds continued contrary so long that we were forced to stay there some time, where we suffered great storms. But by the skillfulness of the captain we suffered no great loss or danger." In fact, church steeples could still be seen in the distance, though the winds muted their tolling bells. That, however, was of little consolation to many passengers.[46]

The boats rocked violently in the white-capped waves that the tempests kicked up. The horizon never seemed to settle in one position, and the landlubbers became violently ill. The fleet's only minister, the Reverend Robert Hunt, became terribly seasick. As the days became weeks, Hunt could not eat anything and lost weight and his strength. John Smith witnessed the unfortunate scene and stated that Hunt "was so weak and sick that few expected his recovery."[47]

The smell aboard the ships was almost unbearable. Besides the offensive smells resulting from the seasickness, dozens of unwashed bodies closely packed together on the ships made the vessels reek. Added to that was the smell of spilled chamber pots, livestock, and rotting food, all of which was bound to get worse as they crossed the Atlantic.

The three vessels stayed there for six long weeks. Many of the passengers, especially the gentlemen, wanted to know why they were not moving. They were consuming precious supplies of food and water while waiting for the storm to pass, but the ships could easily spring deadly leaks in such tempestuous weather. The decision to proceed without enough supplies or on a leaky vessel could be deadly.

The men grated on each other's nerves in the close confines of the ship. Fierce divisions and discord raged. Many wanted to abandon the voyage and return to England, which was still in sight. So they turned their anger against Reverend Hunt and blamed him for their difficulties. A faction of men, dubbed "atheists" and "godless foes" by John Smith, proposed putting the reverend ashore. The seasick minister "with the water of patience and his godly exhortations, but chiefly by his true devoted examples, quenched those flames of envy and dissension." However, others soon flared up.[48]

Finally, the adventurers caught a break in the weather and raised anchor—trying again to sail for the New World. They took a southerly course, and the weather gradually became warmer, giving the crew better working conditions and allowing the passengers to venture on the top deck for fresh air or a nighttime view of the stars. Many had time to reflect on their purposes for settling in Virginia.

The fleet stayed within sight of one another as they sailed toward the Canary Islands, west of the coast of Africa, where they stopped to refill their barrels of fresh water and purchase supplies. The passengers and crew went ashore briefly to enjoy a few moments of their last landfall until they reached the Caribbean, and then the refreshed fleet continued on its journey, sailing along the equator, riding the easterly trade winds and equatorial current toward the New World.

During the late hours of February 12, the sailors caused quite a stir on deck when they "saw a blazing star" in the nighttime sky. The superstitious mariners interpreted the comet as a bad omen. Sure enough, the signs from the heavens read true, as "presently a storm" rolled in and blew the ships.[49]

Besides the storm, the comet also portended another evil—more disputes aboard the flagship, this time centered on the proud and pugnacious John Smith. The next day, Smith was arrested as a mutineer and "restrained as a prisoner." He was clapped in chains and locked up for the duration of the voyage to Virginia. Smith was accused of conspiring to "usurp the government, murder the council, and make himself king." He was jailed under Newport's absolute authority and could be hanged or marooned on an island to die for mutiny.[50]

Smith may have openly challenged the directions of the captain or gentlemen on the *Susan Constant* one too many times. He could not help criticizing their decisions when he believed he had a better answer. Either way, Newport would not allow Smith to flout his authority. Additionally, the gentry on the ship did not respect Smith's status as a gentleman, regarding him as an upstart and a vulgar commoner. For Smith's part, his meteoric rise in the army through his intelligence, experience, and grit meant that he did not suffer fools lightly. All the same, his combativeness placed him in chains.

With Smith safely restrained, a semblance of peace was restored in the fleet. So far, the voyagers were remarkably lucky; they had not lost a single person to disease. Malnutrition endangered every transatlantic voyage. It was caused by increasingly foul water and a monotonous diet of fetid salt pork and moldy hardtack with every passing day. To counter this danger, ships stopped often for provisions at various islands throughout the Caribbean. The growing signs of scurvy—rank breath, bleeding gums, and wiggly teeth—were mitigated by the consumption of fresh fruit. These stops also presented opportunities for the crew and passengers to clean their filthy bodies, although many did not take advantage of the chance to bathe.

Finally, on March 23, a sailor sighted the island of Martinique to the relief of the passengers and crew. The fleet dropped anchor the following day at Dominica. One adventurer described the island paradise as "a very fair island, the trees full of sweet and good smells." They spotted several canoes being rowed toward their ships. The native Caribs were hesitant to get too close to the English ships because of previous hostile encounters with the Spanish. Once the peaceful intentions of the visitors were ascertained, however, the "savage Indians" provided different fruits and even some French cloth. In return, the English offered knives, hatchets, beads, and copper jewels.[51]

The natives, George Percy noted, put their jewelry "through their nostrils, ears, and lips, very strange to behold." He also recorded that "their bodies are all painted red." They went around "naked without covering." More frightening than their strange dress and paint was the fear that the natives "will eat their enemies when they kill them, or any stranger if they take them." Besides the Caribs' suspected cannibalism, the Englishman added, "They worship the Devil for their god and have no other belief." Newport and his men completed their trades, watched a thresher and a swordfish kill a whale for a few hours, and then departed.[52]

The three ships continued sailing with slack winds through the maze of islands for another day, until they halted at Guadalupe. They found a spring that was so hot that no one could stand it for very long. Newport even boiled a piece of pork in it. They sailed past the island of Montserrat and then anchored at Nevis and landed for a week of rest and exercise. They disembarked (except for Smith and whatever crewmembers were on watch) and enjoyed a respite from their long journey.

The men marched onto the island "well fitted with muskets… fearing the treachery of the Indians." They finally had the opportunity to clean themselves and their filthy clothes. The stinking, sweating men "bathed ourselves and found it to be of the nature of the baths in England, some places hot and some colder—men may refresh themselves as they please." They were able to live off the land rather than dipping into the ship's rotting supplies, which was perfectly acceptable to all. During their stay, "Some went a hunting, some a fouling, and some a fishing, where we got great store of conies, sundry kinds of fowls, and great plenty of fish." They built campfires and enjoyed the warmth and a freshly roasted meal. The reverie was unbroken by any Indian attacks, although the English maintained a guard. The natives were sighted but did not interact with the visitors.[53]

Meanwhile, the contentious character of the voyage once again surfaced. Either John Smith stirred up more trouble because he could not keep his mouth shut while jailed, or Newport decided that, now that they had made landfall, it was time to execute the insurrectionary. A few of the crew hastily constructed a gallows by which to hang Smith; however, Gosnold and Reverend Hunt intervened and discussed the matter with Newport. They convinced him not to hang Smith for the time being. Smith barely avoided death, but he was still confined.

As part of their island-hopping voyage through the Caribbean for supplies before they resumed their journey of riding the Gulf Stream to Virginia, the fleet anchored at the Virgin Islands, where the men once again stretched their legs and enjoyed some much-needed elbow room. Their Easter dinner consisted of tortoises, fish, and fowl. "On this island we caught great store of fresh fish and abundance of sea tortoises, which served all our fleet three days, which were in number eight score persons. We also killed great store of wild fowl."[54]

A few days later they put in at an island between Puerto Rico and Haiti, where they were amazed at the sight of a six-foot iguana that some described as "a loathsome beast like a crocodile" and "in fashion of a serpent and speckled like a toad."[55] The others feasted daily on "iguana, tortoises, pelicans, parrots, and fishes," John Smith recorded.[56] The only fatality of the voyage occurred as a result of heatstroke and lack of water during a six-mile hike in the stifling, humid weather. On another island the adventurers spent a couple of hours lading two boats with waterfowl and eggs "to our great refreshing."[57] The sailors and settlers enjoyed exploring the exotic islands, but they were just brief stops on their way to Virginia.

On April 10 they sailed with eager anticipation from the Caribbean northward toward their final destination. Eleven days went by as they cruised with happy, refreshed spirits. However, tensions were whipped into a frenzy again by a terrible thunderstorm that struck the fleet off of North Carolina. The storm kept them from landing at their intended destination.

As evening approached, thunderclouds rolled in across the horizon, and the sailors automatically furled their sails and sent everyone below decks. The ships rode out the storm at the mercy of the choppy seas. Blue streaks of lightning flashed across the dark sky, and rain rattled heavily on the upper deck. Passengers jumped with every clap of thunder. After a harrowing night, the next day dawned clearer, but the sailors had lost their bearings. For a few days they wondered why no land was in sight. "We were forced to lie at hull that night because we thought we had been nearer land than we were. The next morning, being the twenty-second we sounded; and the twenty-third and twenty-fourth day, but we could find no ground. The twenty-fifth day we sounded, and had no ground at an hundred fathom."[58]

The ill will among some of the leaders again reached a boiling point, although John Smith was not involved. This time, Ratcliffe, who commanded the pinnace *Discovery,* decided to capitulate and "rather desired to bear up the helm to return for England than make further search." Although they were so close to Virginia, he threatened to terminate the voyage and sail for home when the seemingly fruitless several months at sea had frayed his nerves. The mariners and settlers needed their leaders to demonstrate perseverance and fortitude in accomplishing their mission. Newport persuaded Ratcliffe to complete the voyage.[59]

John Smith, not a particularly pious man, attributed the storm to "God the guider of all good actions, forcing them by an extreme storm to howl all night, did drive them by his providence to their desired port, beyond all their expectations, for never any of them had seen that coast." Although this view of the storm reflected a common view of hurricanes—that God providentially sent storms to punish sin and stilled the winds as a sign of divine mercy—Smith's words were more a snide comment about the skill of the ships' captains.[60]

With the rising sun painting the clouds first a faint pink and then a brilliant orange in the wee hours of the morning of April 26, watchmen atop the masts shouted, "Land, ho!" Ratcliffe and the faint of heart were thus prevented from departing for England. All had arrived at their destination after a four-month winter voyage. They had braved the winter elements to land in Virginia during the spring, a propitious time for planting crops.

The fleet sailed into the Chesapeake Bay. They were lucky and thankful to be alive. The men spoke in rhapsodic terms of their first sighting of Virginia. George Percy wrote: "We landed and discovered...fair meadows and goodly tall trees, with such fresh-waters running through the woods, as I was almost ravished at the first sight thereof."[61]

The men were not yet out of danger. In fact, in many ways, although the ocean crossing had been completed, the dangers of the New World were just beginning. At Cape Henry, a landing party was organized to begin the first of many exploratory expeditions. They armed themselves and marched out to search the territory. Although they saw no natives, they were being watched. A hunting party saw the Englishmen and tracked them back to the shore. These Indians were skilled archers and deadly accurate, and they could loose several arrows per minute. Suddenly the sky was filled with flying missiles—several of which hit their mark. The discoverers experienced their first attack during their first steps in the New World and suffered two casualties.

At night, when we were going abroad, there came the savages creeping upon all four from the hills like bears, with their bows in their mouths. They charged us very desperately in the faces. They hurt Captain Gabriel Archer in both his hands, and a sailor in two places of the body very dangerous. After they had spent their arrows, and felt the sharpness of our shot, they retired into the woods with a great noise and so left us.[62]

John Smith was still confined aboard the *Susan Constant*. He offered a different reason for the attackers' withdrawal: they had not been frightened off by the powerful English guns, but rather their supply of arrows was spent. The attack itself was a foreboding welcome to Virginia. But if Smith were correct in his assumption that English technology did not simply overawe the Indians, the settlers might be entering a very dangerous situation.

After tending to their wounded and keeping a vigilant eye for further attacks under the cover of darkness, the adventurers' first order of business was to open their instructions and learn the membership of the first council now that they had landed and Christopher Newport had relinquished his authority. Newport retrieved the box and read the names of those appointed to the council: Bartholomew Gosnold, John Ratcliffe, Edward Wingfield, and himself. John Martin, son of a goldsmith and politician, and George Kendall, a privateer with ties to Sir Edwin Sandys and Lord Salisbury, also joined the council. Most surprising, under the circumstances, was the company's appointment of the prisoner suspected of mutiny: John Smith. He was, however, not seated, because of the opposition of the other councilors.

The leadership crisis of the venture continued. By failing to seat Smith, the councilors directly disobeyed the orders determined by the Virginia Council in London. If they broke this basic instruction, others might follow. Moreover, as everyone already saw from the troubles aboard ship, Smith was a self-assured man who would fight for his appointed position on the council and cause trouble until he was seated. Seating Smith, however, presented a danger in that he might seek retribution against his foes on the council, especially after factions formed and divided the leadership of the colony. Few alternatives boded well for the cohesive rule over the colonists in the strange land.

For now, though, there was harmony among the colonists as they explored the area in search of a place to settle that was in accord with the instructions of the Virginia Council. They also assessed the bounty of the land while they sailed around Chesapeake Bay and its rivers. During their exploring, they came into contact with different Indian tribes that were friendlier than the initial confrontation had indicated.

The day after the attack, the English launched a shallop, a small open boat, to explore the river system. The shallop crew entered a smaller river and came across a recently deserted plot of land where they found a canoe and some burning brush. In addition, they discovered a "good store of mussels and oysters, which lay on the ground as thick as stones. We opened some, and found in many of them pearls." While on this march, they saw an "excellent ground full of flowers of diverse kinds and colors, and as goodly trees as I have seen, as cedar, cypress, and other kinds." They also discovered strawberries "four times bigger and better than ours in England." Pleased by the bounty of the land, they rowed over to a place they quixotically named Cape Comfort.[63]

The following day the English settlers assembled for a ceremony led by the council members. Reverend Hunt offered prayers for their endeavor. They "set up a cross at Chesapeake Bay" in honor of their Christian majesty, James I, thereby claiming Virginia for mother England. It was a symbol of their Christian mission to the

Indians as well as their religious and patriotic mission to settle the land before their enemy, Catholic Spain, could. They named the place Cape Henry in honor of the royal prince.[64]

The explorers went back to Cape Comfort, sailed up the James River the next day, and encountered the Paspahegh Indians, who invited the strangers to their village. The Englishmen were entertained with singing and dancing, along with an oration by the werowance, or king, which of course was incomprehensible to them. The Englishmen took their leave and were then greeted by the Quiyoughcohannocks, whose werowance wore an impressive headdress. The Englishmen were primarily interested in the signs of wealth that he wore. He had a "great plate of copper" on his head, and his face was painted blue and "sprinkled with silver ore." His ears hung with pearls and a bird's claw set "with fine copper or gold." The decorations belied possible sources of great wealth and greatly excited the settlers. They did not hold the Indians in great esteem, condescendingly noting that they gave one of them "trifles which pleased him." Nevertheless, the tribes would be an invaluable source of knowledge about the mineral wealth of Virginia.[65]

By May 8 they rowed up the James River as far as Appomattox, where they again encountered the Appomattoc. This time, there were "many stout and able savages to resist us with their bows and arrows, in a most warlike manner, with the swords at their backs beset with sharp stones, and pieces of iron able to cleave a man in sunder." Having been warned off, the explorers departed peacefully. The mixed reactions of the natives to the English affected their decision of where to settle during their journey along the James. They sought a defensible position against further hostility. [66]

Meanwhile, the discord among the colonists did not end: they clashed over the best place to erect their settlement. John Smith recounted that when they searched for "a very fit place for the erecting of a great city, about which some contention passed betwixt Captain Wingfield and Captain Gosnold." There were too many important tasks to be accomplished once they landed for the friction to persist. The root of their problem was the secretive nature of the council membership. But the pride of the gentlemen adventurers and their individualistic English heritage added to the mix.[67]

The first month of exploration yielded important clues about the opportunities for riches that Virginia might yield. Mineral wealth, pearls, abundant food, and a plentiful land beckoned them to land and exploit the wealth they claimed. The interactions with the different Indian peoples varied and led the settlers to maintain their vigilance. Disputes among the colonists were perhaps even more unsettling than any external threat. After navigating farther downriver, they finally decided on a marshy peninsula they called Jamestown Island in honor of their king. They landed with great hopes of striking it rich and establishing the first permanent English settlement in America.

~ *Chapter Four* ~

SETTLING VIRGINIA

T he peninsula on the James River seemed the perfect place for the 108 colonists to settle. It seemed to be a bountiful garden that provided all of their needs. Along the banks of the James, they saw "the goodliest woods as beech, oak, cedar, cypress, walnuts, sassafras, and vines in great abundance." Besides timber to build their grand city and export home, there was a profusion of "many fruits as strawberries, mulberries, raspberries, and fruits unknown." The variety of game for food and valuable furs included a "great store of deer, both red and fallow. There are bears, foxes, otters, beavers, muskrats, and wild beasts unknown." The romantic vision of the settlers saw fair meadows on which to raise domesticated cattle as well.[68]

Besides apparently having everything the colonists needed to survive, the James River also had the essential quality of being a deep enough channel where "ships of great burden may harbor in safety." As instructed, it was roughly fifty miles upriver to hide its location from prowling Spanish warships. Likewise, the peninsula offered a defensible position against hostile natives, and the guns of the English ships could easily be brought to bear to thwart an attack. The river also provided a means of launching voyages of discovery for gold and a passage to the Pacific. The river and its branches provided a "great plenty of fish of all kinds, as for sturgeon all the world cannot be compared to it."[69]

On May 14, since the spot was as good as any—despite the opposing opinions of some—the men disembarked and unloaded their ships as they set about starting the colony. On that day the leaders of the colony were sworn into their offices. According to their instructions, they elected Edward Maria Wingfield their first president.[70] He delivered a speech explaining why John Smith was still not seated with the rest of the council. Smith nevertheless gained his freedom from captivity and escaped execution.[71]

After the ceremony, all of the men were put to work on building the settlement and fortifications. The members of the council directed the work and determined the shape of the defenses. Several of the men hefted axes and cut down trees, which they "cast together in the form of a half-moon" as ordered by Capt. George Kendall. The fort was not palisaded and not very strong. As work on the defenses progressed, other men cut down trees and cleared brush in order to make an area in which to pitch their tents. Some cut up the trees to "provide clapboard to relade the ships." Land was cleared to prepare gardens, and the soil was tilled for fields of corn. Meanwhile, sailors mended nets to fish in the river for food. The demanding work continued for weeks.[72]

During the coming days they had several encounters with some Indians. Both sides proceeded warily with each other because they were still evaluating the other's intentions. Incredibly, the English left most of their arms packed in crates aboard the *Susan Constant, Godspeed,* and *Discovery.* On the first night, the settlers frightened off a couple of Indians who were skulking about at midnight near the encampment.

A few days later a werowance came to Jamestown accompanied by a group of one hundred warriors armed with bows and arrows. The warriors guarded their leader "in a very warlike manner." The leader demanded that the English lay down what small arms they had, but this order was refused. Tensions reached a fever pitch when one of the visitors stole a hatchet and subsequently had it violently snatched in turn from his hands. "Another savage seeing that came fiercely at our man with a wooden sword, thinking to beat out his brains." Angry, the Indians departed quickly.[73]

In a few days a smaller party of Indians came to the settlement. Although they brought a deer to share, another incident occurred between the two peoples. The Indians invited themselves to stay the night, but they were kindly refused since the English "would not suffer them for fear of their treachery." One of the gentlemen sought to test the Indian weapons and set up a target, thinking that it would resist an arrow. A willing warrior withdrew an arrow, nocked it, and let it fly. Surprisingly, it sank into "the target a foot through or better, which was strange, being that a pistol could not pierce it." The miffed Englishman then had a bit of fun with the warrior and set up a steel target for the Indian to shoot. When he loosed the arrow, it "burst all to pieces." The enraged warriors departed in frustration while the settlers howled with laughter. The English did not notice the Indians subtly sizing up their defenses.[74]

On May 21, Christopher Newport led John Smith, Gabriel Archer, George Percy, and several sailors on an investigation of the James River, seeking any sign or news of mineral wealth or the Northwest Passage waterway to the Orient. They wondered if the James itself were the actual river that connected the Atlantic and Pacific oceans,

England with the wealth of the East. Newport was determined that the party would not return to Jamestown until it found the "head of this river, the lake mentioned by others heretofore, the sea again, the Appalachian mountains, or some issue." The voyage of discovery was prompted by the Virginia Council as well as the desire of the gentlemen adventurers for great wealth.[75]

During their journey upriver, they traded and exchanged gifts with various Indian peoples several times. Archer noted, "We went ashore and bartered with them for most of their victuals." While the party dined with several Indians, they learned of a great king, Wahunsonacock (also known as Powhatan), who was the "chief of all the kingdoms." They discovered that Wahunsonacock had conquered dozens of local tribes and exacted large tributes from them. His enemies, the Monacans, lived to the west in the mountains. The English inquired "where they got their copper, and their iron," but they received few answers.[76]

The English explorers dined with an Indian chief they believed was Wahunsonacock, but it was actually his son Parahunt. They exchanged gifts of friendship, including "knives, sheers, bells, beads, and glass toys." Parahunt denied any involvement with the attack on the English at Cape Henry and falsely blamed it on the Chesapeakes. He then offered the English a "league of friendship" with ceremonial gestures of goodwill. Little did the explorers know as they took leave of him and proceeded up the river that it was all a ruse.[77]

Despite their instructions not to fire their weapons too often, lest the natives become accustomed to the shock value of the explosive sound or understand their limitations, Newport yielded to some requests to see the weapons discharged during the voyage. When he fired a musket, the Indians were very frightened. "At the noise [a chief] started, stopped his ears, and expressed much fear…some of his people being in our boat leapt overboard at the wonder hereof."

The leader was pleased to hear that the English promised to "terrify and kill his adversaries" with the strange weapons, thereby altering the balance of power among the tribes. These were dangerous precedents for Newport to set.[78]

The small party visited the Pamunkeys and were entertained by King Opechancanough. The colonists were excited to see that the king had a "chain of pearl about his neck thrice double," which they estimated was worth £300 or £400. Many of his people wore copper jewelry: "They wear it in their ears, about their necks in long links, and in broad plates on their heads." They also had many "rich furs." The evidence of such valuable metals and furs was a very welcome sight to the English.[79]

The explorers were grieved to discover that their dreams of wealth up the James River came to naught. At present-day Richmond, the falls, rocks, and shallow water intervened, making it impassable by any large vessels and "ended...our discovery." A disappointed Newport consoled their dashed hopes by setting up "a cross with this inscription—Jacobus Rex. 1607. and his own name below." After they erected the monument, "we prayed for our king and our own prosperous success in this his action, and proclaimed him king, with a great shout." One of the Indians who was with the English was displeased with the ceremony, so Newport told him, "The two arms of the cross signified King Powatah [Wahunsonacock] and himself, the fastening of it in the middle was their united league, and the shout the reverence he did to Pawatah." The Indian was apparently satisfied with the explanation.[80]

The voyage of discovery was frustrating in not living up to the grand expectations of the settlers, but it was not without promise. They might not have discovered the Northwest Passage or lost cities of gold, but there was proof that the land held valuable minerals and commodities that could be exploited for a return to the investors in England.

Despite whatever hopes were dashed or encouraged by the journey, they noticed that their Indian guide had begun acting strangely. They began to suspect some artifice, and Newport "made all haste home, determining not to stay in any place as fearing some disastrous happening at our fort." He made this decision on May 27: a day too late.[81]

On May 27, between two hundred and four hundred Indian warriors crept stealthily from tree to tree and crawled through the long grass surrounding the small Jamestown settlement. The undermanned English were clearing underbrush and hoeing the ground to plant gardens and crops, until arrows suddenly flew from every direction. It was a frightening surprise attack, and several settlers were wounded from the barrage of arrows. The unarmed and panicked English dropped their tools and broke into a run. They dove for cover in their tents and behind trees.

The colonists were hit randomly during the onslaught or targeted individually. The Indians pressed the attack, coming up "almost into the fort." They shot their arrows into the tents. The English had few weapons with which to defend themselves; most were still aboard the ships in boxes. Those who had weapons nervously tried to load the powder and balls and then aim with trembling hands. The skirmish "endured hot about an hour" while the men screamed in fright or from their wounds. More than a dozen settlers were struck during the "furious assault." A boy was killed outright, and one of the wounded men later died. The colony's leaders were experienced soldiers and did not shy from battle; four members of the council were in front of their men and wounded in the process. President Wingfield, who "showed himself a valiant gentleman, had one shot clean through his beard, yet escaped hurt."[82]

The sailors managed to mount a devastating bombardment from the ships' cannons in the harbor as the main counterattack. During their most desperate moments, when the raid seemed almost to "endanger their overthrow," the thunderous cannon fire frightened the Indians, who were driven back into the woods. Adding to the effect, a salvo shattered a large tree branch, raining deadly darts into any warriors in the immediate vicinity. John Smith wrote, "Had it not chanced a cross bar shot from the ships struck down a bough from a tree among them, that caused them to retire." The Indians gave up the attack and beat a hasty retreat. The English killed a handful of Indians and wounded several.[83]

Newport, Smith, and the company of explorers were shocked when they returned to Jamestown the following day and saw the effects of the Indian attack. The injured were being tended for their wounds, and the rest were at a high state of alert. Wingfield ordered the men to construct a real fort, with a palisade of wood surrounding it. They sweated while felling trees and cut them into clapboards. The colonists also loaded their weapons and prepared them for firing. Men shouldered muskets and drilled, while others mounted ordnance in the fort.

A colonist described the stronghold as a triangular fortification with "three bulwarks at every corner like a half moon." Two corners faced the James River because of the greater threat posed by raiding Spanish warships. In each corner, four or five cannons were mounted and pointed outward. The men worked hard, but it took them almost three weeks to erect the much-needed defenses.[84]

On May 29, the settlers were in the initial stages of building the fort when their enemy again began probing them for weaknesses and hampering the work. The Indians now feared the destructive firepower of the English cannons, and so they did not approach within range of the cannons and musket. Still, about forty arrows landed around the fort, but none of the colonists were hurt.

After a day's respite, the Indians harassed the English again. They silently approached the fort, "lurking in the thickets and long grass," looking for an opportunity to pick off the settlers in a war of attrition rather than by frontal assault. Eustace Clovell imprudently straggled unarmed outside the fort and was hit by six arrows. Bleeding profusely, he ran back into the fort, crying "Arms! Arms!" before collapsing. Everyone grabbed their muskets, scanned the woods from the relative safety of the half-finished fort, and awaited the expected attack that never came. Eight days later Clovell died of his wounds, although he had saved other lives with his warning. Certainly, few settlers wished to leave the confines of the fort.[85]

The attacks persisted as the colonists grew weary from their constant vigilance and worry that they would be overrun. On June 1, the day after Clovell was gravely wounded, twenty Indians appeared (there were more in the woods) and "shot many arrows at random which fell short of our fort." After the ineffective attack, the Indians melted back into the safety of the woods.[86]

Over the next two weeks several others were hit by arrows when they foolishly wandered away from the fort and were ambushed by the Indians. The nimble Indian warriors easily escaped and were never hit by English muskets. In one incident, on June 4, the Indians were hiding in the long grass when "a man of ours going out to do natural necessity [relieve himself], shot him in the head and through the clothes in two places but missed the skin." A few days later, "Savages lay close among the weeds and long grass…shot Matthew Fitch in the breast somewhat dangerously."[87]

Despite their instructions and a small bit of common sense, no one thought to cut down the grass surrounding the fort. Instead, they stationed a few men in the woods to surprise the skulking enemy, and the guards managed to frighten off a few Indians. Yet the warriors still came to kill the settlers one by one.

Finally, after two weeks of almost continuous attacks and constant fear, an unarmed pair of Indians approached the fort. President Wingfield and Captain Newport went out to parley with them. They turned out to be friendly, having met the ships' crews during their voyage up the James. They promised that the Indians were negotiating among themselves and that a greater peace would ensue. One of the Indians counseled the English with the sound, albeit rather obvious, advice to "cut down the long weeds round about the fort, and to proceed in our sawing."[88]

With the Indian willingness to call off the attacks, and by acting on the sage advice of the visitors, the English lived peacefully over the next week. Nevertheless, they kept a vigilant watch, posting guards and setting a watch each night. But divisions amongst English leaders had begun to weaken the harmony of the colony— and its ability to repel the attacks.

In the midst of these terrifying episodes, the internal leadership problems of the colony reignited the flames of dissension. The leaders were again divided, after less than a month ashore. On June 6, the colonists began murmuring and complaining about "certain preposterous proceedings, and inconvenient courses." They wrote out a petition and submitted it to the council for its consideration. The council read the petition on June 10, and Christopher Newport won over the fidelity and goodwill of the men with soothing words. Gabriel Archer wrote, "We confirmed a faithful love one to another, and in our hearts subscribed an obedience to our superiors this day."[89]

Perhaps feeling magnanimous in the restoration of respect and amity, the council finally swore in John Smith as a member that day. Smith had just won a judgment against Edward Wingfield for £200 because "many untruths were alleged against him, but being so apparently disproved begat a general hatred in the hearts of the company against such unjust commanders." Smith put the money back into the common treasury. He credited Reverend Hunt with successfully exhorting the leaders and colonists to reconcile with one another.[90]

Meanwhile, the settlers spent the time busily preparing the ground for planting as well as reloading the ships for Newport's return trip to England. They cut down trees and made clapboard to send to England as a viable indigenous local commodity to persuade investors to support the colony. Christopher Newport had been hired only to carry the colonists to Virginia and then return with word of how the colony fared and with proof of its riches. On Sunday, June 21, the men attended a Sabbath service. Later that afternoon, Newport dined ashore with the council and "invited many of us to supper as a farewell." The dinner might have generated some levity among the leaders, perhaps allowing them to reflect on their accomplishments: they had sailed to the New World, conducted some exploration, found clues to great sources of wealth, established relations with the native peoples, planted food, built fortifications, and started building their colony. And they had accomplished this with relatively minimal loss of life. Despite the respite, tensions still simmered among them.[91]

President Wingfield later reported that he had a private conversation with Newport a few days before the dinner. Obviously concerned about the discord, Newport asked Wingfield how well the government was settled on the eve of Newport's departure. Wingfield was confident that he could govern the colony, but he suspected Bartholomew Gosnold and Gabriel Archer might foment trouble. The president believed Gosnold had a dangerous following of loyal men; he viewed Archer as an ambitious character. Newport again addressed the men and believed he had "moved them with many entreaties to be mindful of their duties to his Majesty and the colony." Newport believed he was leaving the colony in harmony when he departed.[92]

During the dinner, the members of the council also presumably conferred on the contents of a letter they were composing to the Virginia Council in London. After reflecting on the state of the colony and their accomplishments to date, and hoping that God would bless their future proceedings, they promoted the colony to the investors.

They reported that the easiest and richest commodity to find was sassafras roots, and they sent a shipment of more than two tons. The deep and navigable James River had great "sturgeon and other sweet fish as no man's fortune hath ever possessed the like." They sent home a "taste of clapboard" that the investors would have some idea of the bounty of trees in Virginia. Most tantalizingly, the council in Virginia warned that Spaniards must be prevented from laying their "ravenous hands upon these gold showing mountains." Indeed, the Jamestown council sent a barrel of earth back, because they were told that it contained gold. They also asked for Newport's speedy return with a relief expedition of supplies. The incessant Indian attacks and the friction within the council were not mentioned, because such news would discourage investment.[93]

On the morning of June 22, Christopher Newport promised the colonists that he would return within twenty weeks with supplies. He then sailed down the James River with a few dozen sailors aboard the *Susan Constant* and the *Godspeed*. The sight of the colony was quickly lost as the ships headed for the ocean. Newport had left the colony with provisions (although they were generally worm-ridden) in a land of bounty where they could fish, hunt, farm, pick berries, and trade with the natives. He felt confident in the welfare and survival of the colony. He could not have foreseen just how disastrous the summer would be for the one hundred settlers left behind.

When Newport arrived in Plymouth at the end of July, he wrote Lord Salisbury praising Virginia for being "very rich in gold and copper." The returning mariner promised to show the gold to Salisbury, the other lords, and the king "shortly."[94] One leading member of the company, Sir Walter Cope, also wrote to his friend Salisbury a few weeks later, after hearing of the colony's supposed wealth. With biblical imagery, Cope wrote that many in Virginia were claiming, "Instead of milk we find pearl, and gold instead of honey." The "barrel full of earth" that Newport had brought with him appeared to be solid gold, "a treasure endless proportioned by God." But as soon as the next day, Cope wrote another letter bearing the bad news that the ore was worthless. It had seemed so much like gold that the "best experienced about [London]" tested it four times. In the end, "all turned to vapor."[95]

The leaders and investors of the company were disappointed but undaunted. By August 17, Sir Thomas Smythe wrote to Salisbury that Newport intended to sail back to Virginia, resolved "never to see you[r] lordship before he bring with him [that] which he confidently believed he had brought before." Smythe was already preparing two ships for Newport's return voyage and hoped he would arrive in Jamestown by January with more than one hundred men and supplies for the colony.[96]

The Englishmen were not the only ones interested in the initial success of the colony. Their Spanish rivals watched events closely, especially the Spanish ambassador in London, Pedro de Zúñiga. At first, he calmly reported to King Philip III that, "Of the ships which went to Virginia, one has arrived at Plymouth, and…they do not come too contented." They had a few commodities, his spies informed him, but little of any real value.[97] Within a month, as the preparations for Newport's second voyage advanced, Zúñiga's diplomatic posts became more urgent.

On September 22, Zúñiga pressed for an audience with King James and wrote his own king, predicting that James would claim that he had no direct responsibility for the actions of the merchants and members of the company. The ambassador directly advised his king to "root out this noxious plant while it is so easy." So many were arranging to sail for Virginia that it was imperative "not to regard it lightly, because very soon they will have many people and it will be more difficult to get them out."[98] His pleas to his sovereign became more desperate because it was evident—to him—that the English were starting a base for piracy, since they took no women to plant a lasting colony and had found no great sources of wealth. "It will be a service to God and Your Majesty to expel those rogues from there, hanging them while so little [effort] is needed to make it possible."[99]

Zúñiga must have been incredulous when he finally received Philip III's reply. Rather than pledging to destroy the Protestant enemy, the Catholic king simply thanked the ambassador and told him to "report to me what you learn." Philip ignored the frenetic advice of his hot-headed diplomat and instead waited to see how the English would fare.[100] If he could have known the deadly conditions of the Jamestown colony that summer, the Spanish king would have been even less concerned than he appeared in his correspondence with his ambassador.

Chapter Five

DEATH IN JAMESTOWN

If the settlers' hopes were a bit dashed because they had not yet found mountains of gold, they were even more surprised that the land of milk and honey did not supply their basic necessities. The summer months did not provide the expected bounty of provisions. In fact, the summer proved a deadly killer that almost wiped out the colony and stressed the tensions among the leaders to the breaking point.

Since the men were no longer drinking from the casks of water and beer on the ships—even if stale—they drank directly from the James River. "Our drink cold water taken out of the river, which was at a flood very salt, at a low tide full of slime and filth, which was the destruction of many of our men," noted one of the colonists.[101]

Beginning in late July, salt poisoning, dysentery, and typhoid fever raged among the colonists. "Scarce ten amongst us could either go or well stand, such extreme weakness and sickness oppressed us," John Smith wrote.[102] By early August, the first men started dying. On August 6, John Asbie died of the "bloody flux" when dysentery drained his bodily fluids. A few days later George Flowre perished from "the swelling," or salt poisoning.[103] Men started dropping everywhere during the following two weeks, with nearly a dozen more succumbing to fatal illnesses.

The feeble men were languishing from waterborne diseases. They groaned weakly and wept in despair in every corner of the fort—the cries were "most pitiful to hear." The hardest heart was pricked to "hear the pitiful murmurings and out-cries of our sick men without relief every night and day for the space of six weeks, some departing out of the world, many times three or four in a night." In the morning, those who had the strength to stand and do any labor (which were very few) would drag the bodies "like dogs to be buried."[104]

Even one of the council members—Bartholomew Gosnold—died from disease. He was buried with honors, "having all the ordnance in the fort shot off with many volleys of small shot." But his death contributed to the tension and confusion among the colony leaders. In the week after his death, another seven men perished, including gentlemen. The diseases did not respect social class, and no amount of family wealth or prestige could save the gentlemen adventurers in a distant land. As the dreadful heat of August gave way to a more temperate September, men continued to die.[105]

Disease was not the only cause of death; malnutrition killed the colonists too. Prior to their return voyage to England, the sailors had provided the settlers with biscuits and other foodstuffs. Now, the colonists were subsisting on only "a small can of barley sod in water to five men a day."[106] John Smith confirmed that the daily ration for each man was a half-pint each of wheat and barley, but the allotment "contained as many worms as grains, so that we might truly call it rather so much bran than corn."[107] The massive sturgeon and sea crabs in the river supplemented their diet and provided some relief from their hunger, but it was not enough to keep them alive. Half of the colonists were dead by September 10, but within a few months they would be facing the arrival of winter with very few provisions, until Newport returned with the promised relief fleet. The tottering colony faced very dim prospects in its race against death.

The survival of the colony depended almost entirely upon the Wahunsonacocks' goodwill and willingness to bring supplies of food to the settlement. The Indians did not launch any attacks, though they could easily have seized the fort and killed everyone inside. No longer could the colonists bring the guns of the *Susan Constant* and the *Godspeed* to bear in the defense of the settlement. Moreover, the Englishmen lacked the strength to man the fort and fire either muskets or cannons to impede any attack. Most of the men lay in their beds or on the ground, and the fort was left almost completely unguarded. "Thus we lived for the space of five months in this miserable distress, not having five able men to man our bulwarks upon any occasion," George Percy wrote.[108]

In September, in fact, the Indians shared with the colonists the bounty they had harvested from the land. "It pleased God, after a while, to send those people which were our mortal enemies, to relieve us with victuals, as bread, corn, fish, and flesh in great plenty." Many different Indian chiefs brought the English a "store of provision to our great comfort." The feeble men sat up and thankfully ate the food and soon recovered their strength. Moreover, although the sturgeon in the river had retreated, a great abundance of waterfowl appeared on the river and were shot for food. It did not escape the notice of the settlers that they were vulnerable to an attack that never occurred and that "we [would have] all perished" if the Indians did not bring the food. [109]

All of the stresses within the leadership stretched to the breaking point as a result of the suffering and deaths, and they finally exploded in an eruption of blame and mutual recrimination. In late August, the council accused fellow councilman George Kendall of fomenting discord between the council and the president. Kendall was arrested and taken aboard the pinnace, where he was kept under guard. He was subsequently released from his incarceration after a fortnight, but he was prohibited from bearing arms. The leadership also removed him from the council.[110]

On September 10, council members John Ratcliffe, John Smith, and John Martin—all of whom were recovering from being "very sick and weak" and very nearly dying—summoned President Wingfield from his tent. They were accompanied by a few armed guards. Since only four or five dozen settlers were still alive, all of them stopped whatever they were doing and silently watched what ensued. Wingfield's alleged despicable actions roused their "dead spirits" to confront the president and arrest him.[111]

The three councilors presented Wingfield with a "warrant signed by them to depose him of the presidency." He was relieved of his duties as the president as well as on the council. He publicly and vehemently denied all the charges in a heated exchange with the three men. He then said that "they had eased him of a great deal of care and trouble." The guards marched him to the pinnace, where he was imprisoned.

Smith explained that the charges against President Wingfield stemmed from the fact that he had hoarded food and did not open up the store of general provisions for the colonists throughout the summer, when they were dying in great numbers. "The sack [wine], aquavitae, and other preservatives for our health, being kept only in the president's hands, for his own diet, and his few associates," caused numerous deaths in the eyes of his enemies. Even Martin, Ratcliffe, and Smith claimed to be sickened by Wingfield's policies. Smith charged that the colonists were adversely affected through the president's "audacious command."[112]

Wingfield defended his actions, claiming that leadership some-times required difficult decisions for the common good of the men under his command. He argued that the supplies of oil, vinegar, sack, and aquavitae were down to two gallons each, and he was saving the wine for the Communion table. The men had emptied all of their own private supplies, and now they wanted to "sup upon that little remnant" and any that they could "smell out."[113]

The council members had pestered the president for a "better allowance for themselves and some of the sick." Wingfield refused, protesting that he could not be partial toward the gentlemen and that everyone should have "his portion according to their places." If he had caved in to the demands, Wingfield asserted that he would have in a very short time "starved the whole company."[114]

Wingfield had felt pressure from several angles that tested his leadership abilities. His men were dying of disease, supplies of food were getting dangerously low, and a relief fleet would not arrive for months. The Indians were bringing food, but their grace might end at any time. Because of the deadly early-summer attacks, Wingfield would not let the Indians come into Jamestown and see how weak the colony was, and thereby invite an attack. Meanwhile, his main advisors and their allies were growing desperate and angry about the state of supplies, which they increasingly blamed on him. The struggles the colony faced under Wingfield's administration came to a head when the president was formally accused of crimes and tried.

On September 11, the council summoned the prisoner before them, and Wingfield was put on trial. Gabriel Archer was made the official recorder for the colony. The council laid articles of impeachment against the president, and he was "thus displace out of the presidency and also of the council." Ratcliffe delivered a speech to explain why Wingfield should be deposed from the presidency.

He testified that the president denied him "a chicken, a spoonful of beer, and served him with foul corn," and he pulled some of the rotten grain out of a bag to present as evidence.[115]

John Martin testified next, stating that Wingfield "slacked in the service of the colony." The president, according to Martin, spent most of his time tending the roasting meat on his spit and the food in his oven while the company literally starved to death.[116]

The prisoner was allowed to speak in his own defense and demanded a written copy of the articles against him, but his request was summarily refused. Wingfield denied the charges of hoarding food and drink. "I did always give every man his allowance faithfully," he swore. He averred that he was ready to answer any man's complaint against him. In his account of the trial, Wingfield noted that no one stood up to contest with him. He commented that Ratcliffe's speech "savored well of a mutiny" and was "easily swallowed" by the council. As a result, the president was thrown back into his prison on the pinnace.[117] With Wingfield deposed, the council selected Ratcliffe as the new president.

Wingfield labeled his opponents a "triumvirate." In his view, they sought to overthrow His Majesty's government in Virginia and violate the lawful instructions of the Virginia Council. He named Gabriel Archer as one of the ringleaders who helped organize the intrigues that led to his overthrow.[118]

On September 17, the justices of the court convened again and summoned Wingfield to answer more charges. Jehu Robinson testified that the former president told him that he was conspiring to take flight in the pinnace to Newfoundland "to escape these miseries." Wingfield therefore stood accused of plotting to desert the settlement to a probable death for his own well-being.[119]

Wingfield entreated Ratcliffe, Archer, and the council to take him to England. He wanted justice in the mother country, because the government of Jamestown and its laws were so unjust that he had no desire "to live under them any longer." Their triumvirate was not governed by the rule of law, but rather ignored the instructions of the Virginia Council in London. He was also determined to go to England to "acquaint the council there with our weakness." The leaders of the colony ignored his pleas and kept him locked up on the pinnace. With the miscarriages of justice, the removal of rivals on the council, and growing factionalism, the leadership was at war with one another. The entrepreneurial mission of the colonists was lost temporarily in the chaos.[120]

A more fundamental problem in governing the colony was that the settlers had no voice in the selection of their governors. The Virginia Council appointed the leaders of the colony based upon their presumed abilities as gentlemen. Wingfield proved that social status was not an indicator of ability to lead in the nascent colony. Indeed, the gentlemen remained locked in a struggle for power, and the commoners could do little but witness the spectacle and suffer the consequences.

During the fall, the situation in Jamestown remained dire. Ratcliffe and Martin, Smith related, "being little beloved, of weak judgment in dangers and less industry in peace," were poor leaders with little vision for the colony beyond their own political ambitions. The settlers were completely dependent upon the Indians for food, and the pair did nothing to remedy the fact that the colony was down to only eighteen days of rations. The weak and discontented men lived in misery and spent their time grumbling and muttering about their condition rather than acting to save themselves. They had no houses to cover them, their tents were rotted, and their cabins were unfinished.[121]

John Smith took over the daily management of the company,

imploring the men to work and setting an example of industry. The men, he complained, "would rather starve and rot with idleness." He directed them in building houses and thatching them against the elements. But the colony was still very low on food supplies, especially since the Indians had stopped bringing provisions. Smith and the other leaders could force the colonists to work under threat of great punishment, but they could not offer any better incentive to work hard. When individual workers did take initiative, they were not rewarded for it. Under the circumstances, the men did enough labor to avoid punishment and continued to consume the food in the common storehouse.

Smith went out to trade with the Indians for corn to survive.[122] Smith and a handful of workmen (who were not sailors) sailed downriver in the pinnace to the Kecoughtans at the mouth of the James; this tribe had attacked them when the colonists had first arrived in Virginia. The Indians were shrewd traders. At first they "scorned him as a famished man." Seeing how desperate the settlers were, the Indians derisively offered Smith and his companions a "handful of corn" or "a piece of bread" for the Englishmen's muskets and swords. Smith was greatly angered by the contemptuous terms and decided that bold actions on strong terms were required rather than courtesy. He fired his musket into the air to frighten them and ran his boat aground, causing them to flee.[123]

Smith stormed into the nearby village and saw great heaps of corn. Sixty or seventy armed warriors suddenly appeared, wielding clubs, bows, and arrows. Smith and his company fired their muskets, felling several Kecoughtans and smashing an idol. The rest of the warriors fled into the woods, but they returned shortly to make peace with the Englishmen.

The two sides were now ready to trade fairly with each other.

The Indians brought "venison, turkey, wildfowl, and bread" in return for beads, copper, and hatchets. This combination of using firm tactics to press for fair trading terms would be the basis of the soldier's future trade expeditions among the Indians. Smith returned to the colony and then set out on three or four more trade voyages. He discovered the Chickahominy tribe, who came by the hundreds with baskets to trade when they learned of the impending arrival of Smith's ship.[124]

During one of Smith's returns to Jamestown in November, President Ratcliffe physically beat a smith named James Read, who returned the blow against the leader of the colony and his social better. Read was condemned to be hanged. He was standing on the gallows with a noose around his neck, and just before the ladder was kicked away, he bellowed for clemency and warned that a conspiracy was afoot. Read nervously stated that he wished to speak with Ratcliffe privately. The two conferred for several minutes while the rest of the colonists wondered what was being said. The president soon announced that Read had accused George Kendall "of a mutiny."[125]

Read gained a last-minute reprieve with his accusation and thereby escaped the death penalty himself, but Kendall was sentenced to die. A short time later, Kendall "was executed being shot to death." The shots of the firing squad rang out a lesson to all who witnessed the event.[126]

On December 10, as the winter cold descended upon the Chesapeake, John Smith led some men back up the Chickahominy River to discover its source. Only this time, the colonists at the fort had sufficient supplies of corn and harvested crops. They had also acquired an abundance of waterfowl from the James and animals from the woods. So this time, Smith's group took the barge upriver until they could proceed no farther in the shallow waters. They stumbled across a couple of Indians in canoes who were willing to guide the Englishmen. Smith gave strict orders to the remaining men "not to go ashore until my return" because of the potential danger. Thomas Emry and Jehu Robinson climbed into the canoe with Smith, and the small party set out.[127]

Smith and his companions paddled some twenty miles upriver, observing the depth and breadth of the river. Stopping for a meal and to stretch their legs, Smith decided to explore a bit with one of his Indian guides. Fearful of an attack, he ordered Emry and Robinson to "discharge a piece" to signal to Smith "for my retreat at the first sight of any Indian." He was gone for no longer than fifteen minutes when he "heard a loud cry, and a hollering of Indians." No warning shots had been fired, but the scream was enough of an alarm for Smith.[128]

Immediately suspecting a trap, Smith believed he had been betrayed by his guide. He immediately "seized him and bound his arm fast to my hand in a garter, with my pistol ready bent to be revenged on him." The Indian claimed ignorance about the attack and told the Englishman to fly into the woods to escape the raiding party. Smith's mind was racing as he decided what to do. But it was too late to take a different course of action—the camouflaged Indians already surrounded him.[129]

Suddenly, an arrow pierced Smith's right thigh. He quickly scanned the woods, confirming that he had been deceived. Several Indians came into view and tightened the circle around him. He was afraid but maintained his discipline, drawing a bead on two warriors who were pulling back the strings of their bows to shoot again, "which I prevented in discharging a French pistol." The noise frightened them off, giving him a moment to reload his weapon. The warriors moved closer and drew their bows back.

Again, they were momentarily frightened by the firing of Smith's weapon. He shot at his enemy a few more times; they answered with twenty or thirty arrows. Fortunately for Smith, the arrows could not penetrate his thick winter clothing.[130]

Two Indians lay bleeding on the ground, but Smith was surrounded by as many as two hundred warriors. Escape was impossible. Smith's terrified captive called out to the others that Smith was a leader among his people, hoping to stop the flights of arrows intended for Smith and protecting himself as well. Smith tried to parley and asked to "retire to the boat," but the Indians "demanded my arms." They tried to discourage him by claiming that his companions were dead. During the tense standoff, Smith used his prisoner as a shield and began moving slowly toward the river. Hundreds of arrows were trained on him.

While Smith was watching his enemy and holding his prisoner fast, he lost his footing and fell into some water. "In retiring being in the midst of a low quagmire, and minding them more than my steps," Smith related, "I stepped fast into the quagmire and also the Indian." Giving into the inevitable, Smith surrendered and "resolved to try their mercy." The warriors grabbed him out of the muck, stripped him of his weapons, and dragged him before Opechancanough, Chief Wahunsonacock's brother.

Smith had a history of quick thinking to get out of tight situations. He thought of a way to forestall his execution. Trying to prove himself a man of importance while simultaneously impressing the Indians with his "magic," Smith pulled out his compass. They "marveled at the playing of the fly and needle, which they could see so plainly and yet not touch it because of the glass that covered them." He followed up the physical examination of the object with a wondrous explanation of the "roundness of the earth and skies, the sphere of the sun, moon, and stars." He told them of the "greatness of the land and sea, the qualities of our ships, shot, and power, the diversity," and many other things that held their attention rapt.[131]

Nevertheless, the ploy seemed to fail when they tied Smith to a tree and crowded around to shoot him with their arrows. Then Opechancanough intervened and stopped his warriors from executing the prisoner. Smith was led to the spot where he had disembarked from the canoe. Robinson's corpse lay nearby with "twenty or thirty arrows in him," and Emry was presumed dead. Smith was then marched off to a dance and feast, though he was held "by three great savages holding him fast by each arm" and under an armed guard "on each side six...with their arrows nocked." He was treated rather well and feasted on platters of bread and venison.[132]

Meanwhile, the seven men Smith left behind ignored his injunction against going ashore. They were lured ashore by several attractive Indian women trying to capture their attention. While approaching the women, they were ambushed by several warriors. The Englishmen ran back to the barge in terror. George Casson tripped while glancing over his shoulder and was unable to get up before he was knocked down again from behind. While he screamed for his departing companions to come back, the Chickahominies seized him and then "stripped [him] naked and bound [him] to two stakes."[133]

The Indians started a fire behind Casson and began to torture him slowly. His captors cut off his fingers at the knuckles with shells and threw them into the fire. The Englishman shrieked in agony at the torment, but worse was yet to come. The bloody shells were used to skin him alive, starting with his face. Casson was barely conscious when the warriors slit his abdomen and pulled out his intestines, which they also tossed into the flames. Casson finally died and was burned at the stake.[134]

In an Indian village of thirty or forty mat-covered homes, the line of warriors marched in file, guarding Smith and honoring Opechancanough with an escort. The Indians formed into a ring and danced, "singing and yelling out such hellish notes and screeches, being strangely painted." They danced with quivers of arrows and clubs, celebrating their victory over the Englishmen. Three dances took place before they departed, and Smith was brought to a well-guarded longhouse.[135]

Smith was kept in captivity for several days but treated well, getting back his compass and cloak. He and Opechancanough discoursed in a civil manner and exchanged information about each other's cultures. Their mutual admiration and affection grew during the course of their conversations. Smith told the Indian king more about astronomy, about Europe's oceangoing ships and sailing across the expansive seas, and about the Christian God. In return, Opechancanough told the Englishman about the dominions of Virginia. He explained that the course of the James River was the Northwest Passage because "within four or five days journey of the falls, was a great turning of salt water," or the Pacific Ocean. Smith also learned that there was a place where "certain men clothed at a place called Ocanahonan, clothed like me" might just be the lost colonists of Roanoke. Both individuals were intrigued by what the other related, with Smith receiving some valuable information about the route to the China trade.[136]

Opechancanough plied Smith for information about the Englishmen at Jamestown and their military capabilities. The Indians continually "threatened to assault our fort," which alarmed Smith. He reasoned through a way to alert the settlers at the fort. He asked to write a letter to Jamestown to inform the colonists that he was alive and being treated well. He let it slip to Opechancanough in a barely concealed threat, "I would write...that I was well, least they should revenge my death." Since Smith felt that "their cruel minds" were bent on attacking the fort, he exaggerated its strength. He told them about its many cannon and a fictitious minefield.

Smith's request to send a letter was eventually granted, and three warriors were dispatched to deliver the written message. In the letter, which the Indians could not read and which Smith believed they thought was a magical form of speaking, he gave instructions for the settlers to give the Indian messengers a sample of Jamestown firepower to bring back to the village: they should fire a deafening salvo from the pinnace.[137]

Smith was marched through several Indian villages and still treated well. At one, he was brought before another brother of Wahunsonacock, Kekatuagh, who asked him to "discharge my pistol" while guarded by forty bowmen. The Indian was attempting to ascertain the strength of Smith's weapon, and he set up a target more than one hundred feet away to test it. Fearing that the Indians would learn that the English weapons were not accurate at such a distance (while Indian arrows were), Smith decided "to spoil the practice I broke the cock." The Indians were greatly disappointed not to receive their demonstration.[138]

After two weeks, Smith was finally escorted to the large home of Chief Wahunsonacock at Werowocomoco on the northern side of the York River. It was the first time that a European was permitted to have an audience with the great werowance.

Wahunsonacock had a "grave and majestic countenance" and welcomed Smith. The chief was covered in a great robe made of raccoon fur and sat before a fire, while "more than two hundred of those grim courtiers" stared at Smith as if he "had been a monster."

Wahunsonacock was angry that the Englishmen had settled on his lands and demanded to know why they were there. Smith lied and said that they stumbled upon the Chesapeake after a battle with the Spanish and a tempest blew them off course, with one of their boats taking on water. He also related to Wahunsonacock the same message he had delivered to the chief's brother: the English were a vengeful people. Smith told his host of King James and "the innumerable multitude of his ships…and terrible manner of fighting under Captain Newport, my father."[139]

Smith received a great deal of information from Wahunsonacock, which must have pleased the Englishman. Wahunsonacock confirmed the existence of the South Sea that was perhaps five days' journey away. The chief regaled his visitor with a tale of "people with short coats, and sleeves to the elbows, that passed that way in ships like ours." It was additional proof of the survival of the Roanoke colonists. Finally, Wahunsonacock divulged that there was a place called "Anone" where "they have an abundance of brass."[140]

Wahunsonacock deliberated with his advisors while numerous armed guards looked on. After several agonizing minutes for Smith: "Two great stones were brought before Powhatan. Then as many as could, laid hands on him, dragged him to them, and thereon laid his head, and being ready with their clubs to beat out his brains." At that moment, Pocahontas, Wahunsonacock's daughter, intervened and saved John Smith from death. Or so he believed, since it may have only been a ceremony.[141]

Two days after the spirited young girl saved Smith from death, Wahunsonacock "disguised himself in the most fearful manner he could…made the most doleful noise Smith ever heard. Then Powhatan more like a devil than a man, with some two hundred more as black as himself, came unto him and told him now they were friends."[142]

Wahunsonacock invited Smith and the few dozen English

settlers to forsake their people and live among his people in harmony and bounty. The werowance asked in return that they provide him with copper and hatchets. He astutely wanted to control the trade for useful raw materials that could strengthen his control of the area. He also sought the powerful cannons of the English so that he could maintain the dominance of his empire and expand it.

As a captive, Smith was in no position to refuse the conditions that his adversary offered, but he discerned an opportunity to arrive at Jamestown and reject the offer simultaneously. Wahunsonacock promised to make Smith a chief and grant his release in exchange for "two great guns and a grindstone" that twelve warriors would carry back to Werowocomoco. Smith readily agreed, chuckling inward at his own joke. Back at Jamestown, Smith offered the party a one-thousand-pound cannon, although as he wryly put it, "They found them somewhat too heavy."

He scared them off yet again with a blast of the guns, which were filled with stones. The shot splintered some great trees covered in icicles. The "ice and branches came so tumbling down that the poor savages ran away half dead with fear," and without the werowance's prized weapons. After a great laugh, Smith called the Indians back and gave them a few trifles for their women and children.[143] The powerful leader of the Powhatans had seized up one of the most formidable Englishmen in Virginia and released him. Perhaps he found Smith a man worthy of mutual admiration or of possible use in maintaining control over the extensive Powhatan empire, especially since the settlers' numbers were dwindling and soon might be easily taken over and integrated into the Powhatans. Whatever the reason, Smith was free and faced numerous troubles among his own people.

When Smith returned to Jamestown on January 2, 1608, he discovered that escaping captivity and death at the hands of the Indians was the least of his problems. Only forty colonists were still alive. Moreover, President Ratcliffe and newly elected councilman Gabriel Archer were leading a plot of several gentlemen to commandeer the pinnace *Discovery* and return to England to escape the suffering, but they would be leaving behind the rest of the colonists to face "the fury of the savages, famine, and all manner of mischiefs and inconveniences." Smith explained, "Now in Jamestown they were all in combustion, the strongest preparing once more to run away with the pinnace for England." In a daring move, Smith ordered the cannon and muskets pointed at the ship to keep it in Virginia. Smith forced them to "stay or sink."[144]

The first seven months of the colony were an abject failure. Diseases had ravaged the settlement. The land was not nearly as bountiful as they described in their promotional letters to investors in England. The native peoples recognized the difficulties of the colony and used it to their advantage, threatening Jamestown and dominating trade or helping it survive for their own benefit. Moreover, the settlers fought as much with one another as they did with the Indians. Ambitions and intrigues drove the Englishmen apart. The reality of the colony hardly matched the grand expectations of the investors little more than a year before. Their salvation seemed imminent when Christopher Newport's ship put in at Jamestown during the frightful cold of the winter. Newport landed the same day that Smith returned to Jamestown. It was fortuitous timing for John Smith, for his life hung literally in the balance.

Chapter Six

GOLDEN DREAMS

Christopher Newport was shocked by the condition of the colony when he returned, as he had left the settlement in good shape in late June. He now witnessed the hunger that had plagued the colony. The few surviving colonists were also at each other's necks. Former president Wingfield was suffering from months of confinement. The colony had sunk into anarchy.

Newport's ship, the *John and Francis,* carried five dozen colonists and copious provisions for the settlement. In early December they had sailed up from Puerto Rico and sighted America on December 24. A dense fog rolled in, causing them to lose visual contact with a sister ship, the *Phoenix.* After a voyage of thousands of miles together, the pair became separated only ten to twelve leagues from the wide mouth of the James River. The sailors on the *John and Francis* had "no further news of it" and its forty settlers. Newport decided to sail up the James when the fog lifted, fully expecting the *Phoenix* to join him shortly at Jamestown.[145]

When Newport and the settlers disembarked from the *John and Francis,* the captain immediately conferred with the president and the council. That same morning, January 2, Smith had returned from captivity. Rather than being relieved that a member of the council was alive after weeks of going missing with the other men, the council accused Smith of the deaths of Thomas Emry and Jehu Robinson. In a matter of hours, he was tried, convicted, and sentenced to hang. "Great blame and imputation was laid upon me by them, for the loss of our two men which the Indians slew," Smith reported. The council convicted him in accordance with the scriptural "eye for an eye" principle of Leviticus 24, which says that a man who slays another must be put to death. Although Smith did not kill the men, he was held responsible for their deaths. For the second time in less than a year, he was awaiting execution. Newport's ship arrived that evening, and Newport ordered Smith released, barely saving his life. Smith was even restored to the council.[146]

Newport brought sixty more settlers and months' worth of provisions to keep the colonists alive through the winter. Intent on finding gold to satisfy investors in England and to pay for the steep cost of the provisioning expedition, the new settlers included two refiners and two goldsmiths among many artisans who were to do various tasks around the colony. Yet the arrival of so many colonists further strained the housing shortage, so Newport ordered the new men to build a storehouse, a stove, and a church. They worked quickly, finishing "cheerfully and in short time."[147]

Unfortunately, on January 7 one of the houses erupted in flame and smoke. Sparks leaped to the thatched roofs of nearby dwellings. The heat of the conflagration rapidly grew more intense. Panicked men yelled a warning to the others and quickly ran to safety. They desperately attempted to quench the flames with water, but it was an impossible task. The blaze even claimed the wooden palisade that surrounded the settlement as their main protection. From a distance, the settlers watched in silence as the fire consumed the storehouse, their homes, and all their earthly possessions, including their food and clothing.

One of the new settlers had accidentally set fire to "their quarters and so the town, which being but thatched with reeds, the fire was so fierce that it burnt their palisades, though eight or ten yards distant, with their arms, bedding, apparel, and much private provisions…Our preacher lost all his library and all he had but the clothes on his back, yet none never heard him repine at his loss." They looked over the pile of ashes and the three surviving houses that was their colony. When the fire waned and the last embers burned out, they shivered in the frigid cold.[148]

The fire was particularly disastrous for the colony to experience in the middle of the brutally cold winter that had settled in Virginia. Although Wahunsonacock kindly sent supplies of "deer, bread, and raccoons" to help feed the colony, several settlers died from exposure in the wake of the fire.[149] At the time, the world was experiencing a little ice age in which global temperatures dropped by a few degrees for a few centuries, which affected crop yields and led to dramatically cold and snowy winters. "It got so very cold and the frost was so sharp that I and many others suffered frozen feet," a colonist reported. There was a great deal of frost and snow on the ground. The cold became so intense that "the river at our fort froze almost all the way across, although at that point it is as wide again as the one at London."[150]

The situation had been desperate before Newport arrived; now it was dire. They had virtually no food and no means of acquiring enough to feed everyone in the colony. They slept in the freezing cold, exposed to the elements. It was a battle for survival in which they were completely at the mercy of the Powhatans, just as Wahunsonacock had hoped.

When he sent provisions to Jamestown, Wahunsonacock also invited Christopher Newport to come to Werowocomoco, as Wahunsonacock wanted to meet the "father" he considered the leader of the English. Continually importuned by messengers and presents of food, Newport finally agreed to travel to Werowocomoco. A few weeks later, Newport set out from Jamestown in the pinnace with John Smith, Matthew Scrivener, and thirty to forty armed guards. Smith urged Newport and his men to go heavily armed.

The group traveled along the James, around Point Comfort, and up the Pamunkey River toward Werowocomoco. Because of his mistrust of Wahunsonacock, Smith went ashore first with twenty men to discover the leader's intentions. Smith and his men were kindly received and marched to the town with a large escort of more than two hundred warriors. Smith suspiciously watched for any sign of danger, either a sudden ambush by his host or booby-trapped bridges that would collapse and catch the English in a treacherous predicament. He sent the Indians first over the bridges as a precaution and to test the strength of the spans. Keeping a wary eye open at all times, Smith was led to the werowance without incident and grandly welcomed by the werowance.

Wahunsonacock and his people greeted the former captive and his men with shouts of joy and great orations. In stark contrast to the dire food shortages at Jamestown, he offered a feast of almost endless platters of meat and bread. The werowance sat down on a large pillow of pearl-embroidered leather and was himself adorned with a fair robe of furs. His female attendants and hundreds of warriors stood at his side.

Finally, Wahunsonacock spoke to Smith. "Your kind visitation doth much content me," the werowance began, "but where is your father whom I much desire to see? Is he not with you?" Smith replied that he would be arriving the following day. After Wahunsonacock considered this, he remarked on the joke that Smith had played on him about the guns he promised from their last encounter. Since the guns Smith had offered his Indian escort at Jamestown were much too large to transport, Wahunsonacock asked for "some of less burden." He also requested that the Englishmen lay their arms down at his feet "as did his subjects" as a sign of submission and trust. Smith refused, saying, "That was a ceremony our enemies desired, but never our friends," showing that he was no fool.[151]

Smith raised the question of trade and asked "for the corn... he promised me." Wahunsonacock did not enter into negotiations quite yet, offering to fill the Englishmen's baskets with as much bread as they could carry to their vessel as a present to Newport and a gesture of good faith.[152]

Smith and Wahunsonacock conversed for hours, and the dancing, singing, and feasting continued into the night, until everyone finally retired. It was a lavish entertainment for the settlers who were starving and freezing to death, as well as a sign of Wahunsonacock's power and wealth vis-à-vis his visitors. Smith stated that he witnessed "such a majesty as I cannot express, nor yet have often seen, either in pagan or Christian."[153]

Christopher Newport came ashore the following morning, and Wahunsonacock entertained him with celebratory feasts and entertainments lasting three or four days. During that time, Newport offered a teenage boy, Thomas Savage, to Wahunsonacock to learn their language and their ways. In exchange, the Indian leader offered Namontack, "his trusty servant and one of a shrewd, subtle capacity," to go among the English and learn about the strangers. The cultural exchange might help each learn the ways of the other to facilitate trade and foster a relationship between the two peoples while also gaining for each side valuable intelligence that might be used to their advantage.[154]

Knowing that he held all of the power in the trade relationship with the English and that they survived at Jamestown at his whim, Wahunsonacock finally allowed the subject to be broached. He addressed his counterpart with respect and an apparent willingness to get down to business: "Captain Newport, it is not agreeable to my greatness in this peddling manner to trade for trifles, and I esteem you also a great werowance." Wahunsonacock shrewdly invited Newport to "lay down all your commodities together. What I like I will take, and in recompense give you what I think fitting their value."[155]

Smith immediately saw through Wahunsonacock's strategy and turned to confer with Newport, whispering that "his intent was but only to cheat us." Smith was hardly about to reveal his hand and lay down "all our hatchets and copper together" for his trade partner to see. Wahunsonacock's strategy was "that ancient trick the Chickahominies had oft acquainted me," although Europeans were not ignorant of this common method of gaining an upper hand in trade. Newport, though, was a proud man who foolishly believed he could outwit those he considered savages. He haughtily "thinking to outbrave this savage in ostentation of greatness, and so to bewitch him with his bounty," rashly acceded to Wahunsonacock's wishes. Smith was beside himself with frustration at how poorly Newport understood trade with the native peoples.[156]

Because of Newport's careless trading, Wahunsonacock predictably offered Newport a trivial amount of corn for the settlers' goods. "We had not four bushels," Smith complained, "for that we expected to have twenty hogsheads." He rescued what would have been a disastrous move that might allow his Indian adversary to dominate their trade relationship for a long time to come. Smith helped win better terms when he introduced blue beads into the negotiations, which Wahunsonacock highly prized as great jewels. Smith thought he tricked the Indian with "many trifles," although the Englishmen were similarly mesmerized by the sight of pearls and what they considered to be precious metals. Regardless, Smith apparently steered the negotiations back to an equal footing, and the English left with a few hundred bushels of corn for the settlement.[157]

The leaders discussed the possibly of an alliance to fight the Powhatans' enemy, the Monacans. Newport, wishing to learn more about the possible location of gold and "to discover the South Sea" (which Smith deprecated as a "fairy tale"), almost agreed to such a joint venture. They took their leave of Wahunsonacock and went to Opechancanough to trade for more corn. Smith went off to "dig a rock, which we supposed a mine," and brought the ore and what he thought was twelve weeks' worth of provisions back to Jamestown in March.[158]

Despite the relative success Smith and Newport achieved in trading with the Indians, the colonists continued to suffer wretched conditions in the razed settlement. By staying for fourteen weeks, the sailors on the *John and Francis* consumed much of the provisions—the "beef, pork, oil, aqua vitae, fish, butter and cheese, [and] beer"—intended for the colonists. In exchange, the sailors charged exorbitant prices, gouging the survivors of the calamity and forcing them to trade their "money, spare clothes…gold rings, furs, or any such commodities" for a decent meal. The supplies, which they had to "buy…at fifteen times the value," John Smith reported, "could not be had for a pound of copper which before was sold us for an ounce."[159]

For many weeks the colonists were reduced to a miserable existence by the avarice of their fellow countrymen. They tried to subsist on a daily ration of some "meal and water," placing them in a condition no worse than before the relief expedition arrived, and their numbers were ravaged by the "extremity of the bitter cold frost." Half of the colonists died, including some of the first settlers and the more recent arrivals.[160]

As the men perished of malnutrition and exposure, Smith reported that instead of rebuilding the fort in the wake of the fire, most of the settlers were more interested in finding gold. He wrote: "The worst mischief was our gilded refiners with their golden promises made all men their slaves in hope of recompense. There was no talk, no hope, no work but *dig* gold, *wash* gold, *refine* gold, *load* gold." The men neglected all the necessary work on spring planting or erecting a new fort to "fraught such a drunken ship with so much gilded dirt."[161]

On April 10, the sailors were busily preparing the *John and Francis* for its return trip to England. Having gathered up enough of what they thought to be gold ore and believing the colony adequately provisioned, Newport stepped aboard the ship accompanied by former president Wingfield and councilman Archer. The Indian Namontack also joined the ship's passengers; he would excite Londoners and investors about the exotic peoples of Virginia. Londoners might be taken in by the spectacle of native American peoples, but no amount of promotion could hide the fact that the dreams of investors were not being realized. The gold was found to be fool's gold, and their dreams to be a fool's hope.

With Newport returned home, the gold fever that captivated the settlers' attention did not abate, especially since John Martin encouraged the search for gold and President John Ratcliffe was laid low by an illness for months. But Smith and Scrivener tried to restore some semblance of order and discipline among those who had survived the winter. The two men divided up the remaining colonists and put them to work rebuilding Jamestown. The men repeated the scene of the previous spring, sweating under the temperate spring sun, "repairing our palisades, cutting down trees, preparing our fields, planting our corn, rebuilding our church, and recovering our storehouse." The discipline recovered some order and led to the completion of some necessary tasks for their survival, but its martial character was not proving to be a viable long-term solution to their problems.

On April 10, while their hard work was going forward, an alarm went up through the settlement. The men dropped their axes and saws and grabbed their muskets and manned the cannons. At first they anticipated a "new assault of the savages." When no threat materialized from the woods, they learned that there was a "boat under sail" approaching Jamestown. They expected Spanish warships to appear at any moment, with cannons roaring against the fort. If Newport had not sailed the *John and Francis* back to England so recently, they might have had a better chance against their greatest enemy. Still, it could be a friendly vessel—perhaps Newport had encountered storms and was forced to return. Tense minutes passed slowly.[162]

The settlers relaxed their guard when they saw St. George's flag and were pleasantly surprised when the *Phoenix,* commanded by Francis Nelson and presumed lost and the men dead, sailed gently to the berth at Jamestown. Nelson came ashore with his sailors and some additional settlers and related their tale to the eager colonists. Nelson explained to Ratcliffe and the council that he had sailed alongside Newport until they encountered the fog off the Virginia coast. After becoming lost, Nelson's ship was pounded by "many perils of extreme storms and tempests" that ripped his sails and destroyed his masts. The captain decided to make for the West Indies to winter there while undergoing repairs and replenishing his supplies of water. He now had finally reached his destination.[163]

The colonists were relieved that Nelson brought dozens of settlers and plenty of provisions, because he had fed his company with local food in the West Indies. The supplies Nelson carried to the colony would last for months and supplement whatever crops they raised that year. "His victual [added] to that we had gotten," noted Smith, "was near after our allowance sufficient for half a year." Moreover, the Virginia Council in London would send another relief expedition after Newport returned home. Unlike the price-gouging sailors on the *John and Francis* who shared few provisions with the starving colonists, Nelson's mariners willingly unloaded their provisions and sold a few items at fair prices. Nelson "had not anything but he freely imparted it, which honest dealing (being a mariner) caused us to admire him. We would not have wished more than he did for us."[164]

President Ratcliffe wanted to send Smith and Nelson on a voyage to the falls and the Monacans to discover "his fantastical gold" and the suspected passage to the South Sea. Nelson, however, intervened and refused to let his sailors be employed in such a venture. A relieved Smith preferred to load the *Phoenix* with cedar to promote the wealth of commodities available in Virginia to English investors. The impasse would continue until Nelson returned to England, and Smith went separately to explore the region.[165]

In early June, having delivered his shipload of provisions and the remaining settlers to Jamestown and reloaded his ship with commodities for the company, Nelson sailed for England. John Martin, who was "always very sickly and unserviceable," was allowed to go home aboard the *Phoenix*. The colony was back on a proper footing, but how long this would remain true was anyone's guess.[166]

On June 2, 1608, with the crops sown and the settlement rebuilt, John Smith went out on a voyage of discovery accompanied by six gentlemen, seven soldiers, and a physician. He set out alongside the *Phoenix,* which continued into the expansive ocean, while Smith's barge made for Chesapeake Bay. Smith journeyed to continue the search for gold and the Northwest Passage, either of which would bring great wealth and renown to him in England. At the very least, he would certainly find valuable commodities to send to England or find new native peoples with whom the English could trade. The adventurers landed at the Eastern Shore and talked with the natives, who spoke the Powhatan language and related their knowledge of the river system to Smith.

A storm suddenly rolled up. The tempest stirred up "mighty waves" that crashed over the small barge and threatened to sink her. The "foremast and sail blew overboard" as the Englishmen struggled to keep the vessel seaworthy. They had to bail out the vessel and barely made it to an island, where they waited out the "gusts, thunder, rain, storms, and ill weather" and appropriately labeled the place Limbo. The crew found innovative solutions to their problems, erecting a new mast and sewing together some of their shirts to repair the torn sails so they could continue their endeavor.[167]

Many of their encounters with Indians were initially hostile and then smoothed into friendly relations, but not before a hail of arrows hit their barge or they fired their muskets into groups of natives on shore. Establishing relations was often accomplished through the mixture of force and diplomacy that Smith had practiced with the Powhatans and other peoples near Jamestown. In one incident after the storm, the Englishmen were angrily assaulted with arrows.

The next day, the Indians appeared unarmed and carrying baskets, but Smith suspected a trap. The Englishmen "discharged a volley of muskets charged with pistol shot," dispersing the Indians into a cluster of reeds where their companions "lay in ambush." The settlers landed and fired into the reeds and hit their unseen enemies, soon finding "much blood" but no Indians. Smith and his men left "pieces of copper, beads, bells, and looking glasses" near some homes and departed. The next day, first a few and eventually hundreds of Indians approached the strangers to trade and share information. Smith called these peoples "the best merchants of all other savages."[168]

The voyagers headed for the western shore and continued up toward the head of Chesapeake Bay. They sailed for thirty leagues but did not encounter any more Indians—only miles of wooded shoreline and some wild animals. At this point, the Englishmen began grumbling about being fatigued from rowing. The provisions of bread they brought with them were growing moldy after being waterlogged. Moreover, the unbroken monotony of the landscape with few human encounters and few discoveries made them wonder if they were wasting their time. They angrily complained to Smith that they wanted to return to the settlement.

Smith, fearing a mutiny and possibly for his life, appealed to his men to endure on their journey. He asked them to "abandon these childish fears" and behave like men. Then, arguing as many commanders have throughout history, he told his men that he had shared and would continue to share in their privations. "You cannot say but I have shared with you in the worst, which is past. And for what is to come—of lodging, diet, or whatsoever—I am contented you allot the worst part to myself." Although he quelled any incipient rebellion, more storms two days later "added such discouragement to our discontents that three or four fell extreme sick, whose pitiful complaints caused us to return." Smith sailed back down the Chesapeake to appease his irate men, but the voyage of discovery continued.[169]

Between sailing and rowing up the Potomac River, they encountered several peoples. Then some sparkling rocks caught their eyes toward the end of their journey. In many places, "where the waters had fallen from the high mountains, they had left a tinctured, spangled [layer] that made many bare places seem as gilded." They went ashore and dug into the ground finding "a clay sand so mingled with yellow spangles as if it had been half pin-dust" or proof of some precious metal for manufacturing.[170]

Smith's party was thrilled with the discovery and took some samples. They showed their discovery to the Patawomecks, whose werowance informed the visitors that there was a mine nearby. They enthusiastically set out for the mine, marching seven or eight miles to the spot. The Indians had excavated the mine near a brook, where they washed the dirt to separate out the precious material. They used the silver-colored mineral to paint their bodies or special objects. They gladly offered the Englishmen as much of it as they could carry back to their barge. It would "prove of no value," but they determined copious sources of valuable furs (bears, beavers, minks, otters, and sables) and fish. Moreover, Smith learned from the Indians that there was good reason to hope "our bay had stretched into the South Sea or somewhat near it."[171]

Smith's band of explorers returned to Jamestown on July 21 after discovering many native peoples and potential sources of wealth for the colony. They had good news to share. But when they went ashore, they were greeted with terrible news that the colony was again being ravaged in the deadly summer months.

The colonists, particularly the "last supply" who had recently migrated, suffered from the same maladies—typhus, dysentery, and salt poisoning—that had afflicted the settlers the previous summer. Just as in 1607, the men fell "sick...some lame" and were "unable to do anything but complain." Smith noted that the new settlers "were sick almost to death until they were seasoned to the country."

The suffering once again bred resentments and disputes that tore apart the leadership.[172] Many in Jamestown criticized President Ratcliffe for his "unreasonable, needless cruelty." As with Wingfield, the men were nearly mutinous and charged that Ratcliffe had "riotously consumed' the provisions of the common storehouse as the food supply began to dwindle. Although they had willingly contributed to the building of houses in the spring, they criticized the arrogant president because he compelled them to erect "an unnecessary building for his pleasure in the woods." (Smith had disparagingly called the building "Ratcliffe's palace," representing the popular anger against the would-be lord.) The colonists were bent on revenge.[173]

The circumstances of the colony were pregnant with danger, but Smith smoothed over relations by relating to everyone the opportunities in the Chesapeake for precious metals, commodities, and the Northwest Passage. Smith may have "appeased their fury," but they remained adamant that "Ratcliffe should be deposed." In his stead, they turned to Smith to seize the reins of government.[174]

Smith's conceit was satisfied by their wishes, but he demurred on actually taking over as president. The lure of discovering great riches in the Chesapeake drew him to return and continue his explorations. Smith nevertheless exploited the divisions to place his friend, Matthew Scrivener, in the presidency while he was away. He also succeeded in getting "more honest officers to assist Master Scrivener," especially because the new president was then suffering from one of the summer fevers that plagued the colony. Rather than remaining for the good of the colony while one president was deposed and his replacement was deathly ill, on July 24, Smith sailed off after spending only three days in Jamestown.[175]

Smith headed up the Chesapeake with twelve men on the barge. He had replaced nearly half his men—presumably the troublemakers who had almost diverted the last trip. Unfortunately, seven of the men had acquired lethal diseases in Jamestown and were laid low during the voyage as they sailed around Point Comfort. Fearing an Indian attack during their distress, Smith put the men's hats on sticks to make it appear that they were all hale, and the men who were able to stand held two muskets each to thwart any offensive.

They continued sailing into the upper bay and went up the Tockwough River in the northern end of the Chesapeake. Smith was very interested to see that the men had "many hatchets, knives, pieces of iron, and brass," which they explained they had gotten from the Sasquehannocks. Before the English departed to visit this other people, Smith learned that several native peoples "inhabit upon a great water beyond the mountains." A somewhat disappointed Smith guessed from the description that it was not the Pacific, but "a great lake or the River of Canada, and from the French to have their hatchets and commodities by trade." Still, they did relate that at least one of the peoples lived "on the ocean sea." A frustrated Smith was left with nothing but vague clues of the proximity to the Pacific and the passage leading there.[176]

The barge sailed as far as Smith's Falls at the Sasquehannock River, where he was forced to turn back. While they were sailing down the bay, they gave the places English names and left crosses either carved into trees or erected "crosses of brass to signify to any [that] Englishmen had been there." The company explored the Pawtuxunt and Rappahannock rivers, but they never saw the Pacific as hoped. Smith's party completed their relatively comprehensive expedition of the Chesapeake Bay. A gentleman, Richard Fetherstone, perished during the journey and was honored with a volley of shot.[177]

Chapter Seven

THE RISE OF JOHN SMITH

O n September 7, John Smith sailed back to Jamestown and learned what had transpired in the seven weeks of his absence—the news was mixed. He was greeted by Matthew Scrivener, who had recovered from his illness and fever, and the members of the council. Many of the colonists, however, were dead from the summer diseases and others were still suffering. Former president Ratcliffe was locked up on charges he had fomented a mutiny. Scrivener had been a fine leader and had organized the gathering of the harvest. Unfortunately, most of that year's crop was spoiled in the common storehouse from rain. Even worse, there would be food shortages again that winter unless Christopher Newport returned with another relief expedition. Smith was prepared to take the reins of government and provide leadership that would permanently establish the law and order he thought necessary for the colony to thrive. He had a sense of destiny (and hubris) that Jamestown would rise or fall depending upon his leadership and did not consider the possibility that it might succeed because of the energies of the individual colonists.

A few days later, on September 10, the council followed the will of those who liked and respected John Smith's leadership style, and elected him president. The ambitious Smith later enumerated his many accomplishments to contrast himself with his predecessors. He was a gentleman adventurer who wanted to emerge victorious in the contest for glory in the New World, and he was finally about to receive his due.

The church and storehouse were rebuilt and additional buildings prepared "for the supplies we expected." He strengthened and expanded the fort and renewed the watch duty by the men. The colonists restored military discipline. They trained by squadrons and with the "whole company every Saturday exercised in the plain by the west bulwark." Curious Indians watched the spectacle and beheld a display of the men firing their weapons. Finally, the boats were trimmed and ready for trade missions. In short, Smith organized all aspects of the fledgling colony for it to survive and thrive. He was aided by the change of the summer tides and the restored health of the settlers. Moreover, Christopher Newport returned to Virginia with provisions on the *Mary and Margaret*.

The supercilious new president seethed when Newport disembarked in Jamestown. Smith did not wish to share his newly acquired power with anyone. The mariner represented the company's interests in Jamestown and would report what he found there. Smith coveted power and could not restrain his jealousy of Newport, complaining, "How or why Captain Newport obtained such a private commission as not to return without a lump of gold, a certainty of the South Sea, or one of the lost company sent out by Sir Walter Ralegh I know not." Smith thereby questioned the company's instructions and the company's vision for the economic foundation of the colony.

By this time, Smith had doubts that gold or a Northwest Passage existed around Chesapeake Bay because of his own voyages and investigations with the Indians. He envisioned a lasting colony founded upon an ordered and disciplined community of settlers who would plant crops and find commodities to ship back to England. When Newport informed Smith of his intended voyage to seek gold and a passage through America, Smith objected and wondered "how pitch and tar, wainscot, clapboard, glass, and soap-ashes could be provided to relade the ship." He was pleased that the company had sent skilled Polish and German artisans to manufacture those goods to ship to England, but he was confounded by the fact that it sent "them and seventy more without victuals."[178]

Smith fumed that Newport was foolishly wasting "that time to make provision whilst it was to be had." Winter would approach soon, but they were not devoting their precious time to stocking up their food supplies. The council, however, disagreed with Smith. Two gentlemen adventurers—Richard Waldo and Peter Winne—were seated on the council, according to the directions of the Virginia Company. Newport, in an ironic reversal that worked against Smith, freed John Ratcliffe, who was "permitted to have his voice" in council decisions. Even Smith's ally, Matthew Scrivener, supported Newport's exploratory voyage.[179]

Rifts opened when Newport informed the council that he was going to invite Wahunsonacock to a "coronation" ceremony in which he would crown the werowance as a local lord in the service of James I with the intent of winning his peaceful allegiance. Newport angrily asserted that Smith's propositions about provisions and commodities were only "devices to hinder his journey [and] to effect it himself." Smith, Newport charged, was attempting to cover up the "cruelty he had used to the savages in his absence" during Smith's previous journeys. Smith denied the allegations and offered to take four men to Werowocomoco to entreat Wahunsonacock to come to Jamestown.

Traveling overland and crossing the Pamunkey River by canoe this time, Smith, with four companions and Namontack, arrived at the capital. Pocahontas informed them that her father was gone but offered them hospitality. As they were sitting on mats in front of a fire, they were suddenly frightened by "a hideous noise and shrieking" from the surrounding woods that made the Englishmen scramble for their weapons. The Indian girl assuaged their fears that they were under attack, and they were soon entertained by a dance of thirty painted young women holding swords, clubs, and arrows. A feast with more singing and dancing finished their evening.[180]

The following day, Wahunsonacock appeared and granted an audience to Smith. After exchanging pleasantries, Smith bid the werowance to Jamestown "to come to his father Newport to accept those presents and conclude their revenge against the Monacans."[181]

Wahunsonacock was a proud and intelligent ruler, and he quickly surmised the Englishmen's purpose. He turned the tables on Smith, asserting his dominance in the relationship with as much grandeur as Smith ever witnessed. Wahunsonacock retorted, "I also am a king and this is my land." He dictated the terms of meeting with Newport, even adding a deadline for him to arrive: "Eight days I will stay to receive them. Your father is to come to me, not I to him nor yet to your fort, neither will I bite at such a bait."[182]

The Powhatan leader continued, renouncing any implication that he needed the strength of English arms to assert his imperial might over other native peoples. "As for the Monacans, I can revenge my own injuries," he averred. With each statement, the confident Indian chief stared into Smith's eyes and knocked him and his people several notches down.

For good measure, Wahunsonacock then deflated the shred of hope that Smith maintained that the Pacific was nearby and that a Northwest Passage might be discovered. He thereby undermined

Newport's voyage of discovery, as well as one of the main objectives of the colony, in a single blow. Wahunsonacock stated simply, "[As] for any salt water beyond the mountains, the relations you have had from my people are false."[183]

Smith was severely beaten in this verbal jousting and contest of authority. He and Newport had no choice but to submit to the chief's wishes and come before him. He noted simply, "So I returned with this answer." Whatever Newport thought of Wahunsonacock's response and Smith's diplomatic fiasco, he acceded to the reality of the balance of power and set out for Werowocomoco the next day rather than receive the Indian he considered a subordinate.[184]

Many fine presents were given to Wahunsonacock, including a basin and pitcher, bed, and furniture, although what he thought of them was not recorded. Next a "scarlet cloak and apparel with much ado [were] put on him." But the werowance adamantly refused to bow down to the English "to receive his crown, he neither knowing the majesty nor meaning of a crown nor bending of the knee." Wahunsonacock would never submit to the English, particularly in front of his people. He would instantaneously lose his authority with them, as well as his control over his subject peoples.

Wahunsonacock quickly tired of the ceremony and finally bent slightly at the waist and allowed Newport to place the crown on his head. He gave the visitors a trifling gift of a few bushels of corn to thank them, and Newport received his old shoes and his mantle. He had inverted the coronation and enhanced his own prestige. It boded poorly for future relations as the Indian leader gained the upper hand in trade with the colonists and possibly in driving the invaders off his lands. The Englishmen "returned to the fort," with Smith knowing they had just been bested to their great detriment.

If Smith had further evidence that Newport was a miserable failure at Indian relations, Newport commandeered 120 settlers on yet another search for gold. The large party sailed up to the falls, where the men disembarked and marched west some fifty miles toward the Blue Ridge Mountains. They established contact with the Monacans, who greeted the English in a neutral manner. Refiner William Callicut used his equipment to dig at some mines and wrongly believed that he "extracted some small quantity of silver." The fruitless "poor trial" was wasted effort, and their "gilded hopes" were dashed again.[185]

Meanwhile, President Smith followed what he believed was a more practical desire to find valuable commodities for export. He dispatched teams of men for tar and pitch, and clapboard. He organized work teams, including one to experiment with manufacturing glass. Consistent with his worry about having enough corn for the winter, he ventured out to trade with the Indians for provisions. He first visited the Chickahominies, relating that they refused "to trade, with as much scorn and insolence as they should express." Smith imagined that Powhatan might be trying to starve out the English by directing others not to trade corn to the settlers. Smith did not cajole them with a coronation ceremony, nor did he lay out his goods for them to inspect. He directly confronted their antagonism and responded with threats of his own in order to force them to trade. He informed them "he came not so much for their corn as to revenge his imprisonment and the death of his men murdered by them." They complained of "their own wants" because of the low-yielding harvest that year. Smith expressed little empathy for their plight as he loaded the hundred bushels of corn on to his barge.

When Smith returned to Jamestown, he encountered similar resentments and hostility as when he escaped from captivity the previous year, even though he was now the president of the colony. Newport and Ratcliffe, he inferred, were responsible for many of the intrigues against him. The faction may even have attempted to persuade some of the council members to depose Smith, but they were unsuccessful. His enemies even wanted to use his trade mission as evidence that he had left the colony without the consent of the council. He threatened to charge them with mutiny if they continued their grumbling about his leadership.

Smith had other significant problems to contend with in the colony. The sailors aboard the *Mary and Margaret* repeated the previous year's scandalous episode by pilfering the ship's provisions and selling them to the colonists at inflated prices. Colonists and Indians used their "money or wares" to purchase foodstuffs at the waterborne "tavern." Most infuriating of all, after six weeks at Jamestown, only twenty "axes, hatchets, chisels, mattocks, hoes, and pickaxes" from the original stock of more than three hundred remained. These were intended to produce food to keep the colonists alive, but almost all of them had been sold or bartered away. Alarmingly, the settlers had traded the "pike-heads, knives, shot, [and] powder" to the Indians for pelts, baskets, and young animals to trade for butter, cheese, pork, biscuit, and oil from the ship. "Ten times more care to maintain their damnable and private trade," Smith railed, "than to provide for the colony things that were necessary."[186]

Smith was thoroughly disgusted with Newport, his allies, the sailors, and the company when he sat down to compose a letter to London answering the complaints it had sent him. The company had expressed a great deal of dissatisfaction about the "faction and idle conceits" that were dividing the colony. Meanwhile, it charged, the company was footing the bill for relief voyages to the tune of £2,000 and rarely received any commodities defraying more than a small portion of the cost. The company also protested that the colonists only offered ifs, ands, and buts to the entreaties to find gold and a passage to the Pacific.[187]

Smith denied sowing dissension among the colonists and told the company that finding great riches was highly unlikely. He carped that in comparison to other English companies, such as the one in Russia, the Jamestown colony faced the unique circumstances of struggling to feed themselves and suffering Indian attacks. They were subsisting on a daily diet of "a little meal and water" and did not have the strength to hunt or fish because they were sick and famished.[188]

The land had abundant natural resources, Smith maintained, but the colony needed "carpenters, husbandmen, gardeners, fishermen, blacksmiths, masons, and diggers-up of trees' roots" rather than a thousand such men as were then at Jamestown. Rather than paying the "unnecessary wages" to Christopher Newport to drop off "lame and sick" settlers while remaining to consume all the provisions, Smith suggested sending skilled workers and plenty of provisions. He also counseled them on having realistic expectations about the potential profits flowing from the colony. First, the colony would need to get on a firm footing rather than living from "one supply to another."[189]

Finally, after all the difficulties engendered by his voyage to Virginia, Smith happily watched Newport and his sailors depart with some samples of commodities for the company. Newport had brought additional settlers to the colony but few provisions. He left behind two hundred colonists, "the one half sick, the other little better," who had to fend for themselves in the coming winter months. They were under the command of President John Smith, who would do everything in his power to keep them alive.

In 1608 the harsh winter weather that plagued the colonists came early again across the Virginia landscape. Many colonists were sure to die, since their malnourished bodies were weakened and could not fight off disease in the extreme cold. The ground was "covered with snow and hard frozen," and the settlers were miserable. Traveling was extremely difficult as the settlers dug out the snow and tried to build fires. "Thus many a cold winter night have we lain in this miserable manner." Smith knew that their only hope to survive rested with the beneficence of the Indians. But Powhatan commanded the local tribes not to trade with the English, and the Indians suffered their own dwindling supplies.[190]

When Smith went to the Nansemonds, they denied him the four hundred bushels of corn they had promised and refused to conduct any trade at all. The rough Englishman had had enough and ordered his men to fire their muskets. Moreover, they "set on fire" the first house they saw to make an example of what would happen should the Indians continue their obstinate refusal to trade. Cowed by the show of force, the frightened and yet desperately hungry Indians offered to give Smith half of what they had. He returned to Jamestown with one hundred bushels of corn.[191]

Wahunsonacock completely dominated relations with the English and sent a messenger to the settlement with a taunting offer. He called for Smith to "come unto him" with workmen to build him a house. He also demanded "a grindstone, fifty swords, some pieces, [and a purse with] much copper and beads." In return, Powhatan would fill Smith's boat with corn. Smith recognized that his life would be in danger, but he decided to confront the mighty werowance and settle the issue once and for all.[192]

On December 29, Smith and forty-six volunteers sailed the pinnace and two barges to Werowocomoco with several artisans, since they were idle anyway. They landed first among the Warraskoyack on the south side of the James. Smith asked for two guides and directions for a soldier, Michael Sicklemore, to "seek for the lost company of Sir Walter Ralegh and silk grass." The Indian chief warned Smith gravely, "You shall find Powhatan to use you kindly, but trust him not…He hath sent for you only to cut your throats." Smith had guessed as much but sailed on to face Wahunsonacock and his destiny nonetheless.[193]

The normally short journey was further delayed for a week by "extreme wind, rain, frost, and snow" that drove the Englishmen to lodge with the Kecoughtan. Thus they spent part of their twelve days of Christmas feasting with the Indians and enjoying the welcome warmth of their dry and smoky homes. Continuing up the York River, the company was again forced ashore by the winter storms, although they spent three or four nights hunting fowl and trying to stay warm by their fires. Just as soon as they were able to sail again, "frost and contrary winds" caused them to put ashore again, this time among the Kiskiacks, who were less than hospitable. After a few tense days, the Englishmen had only a short, difficult voyage to reach Werowocomoco.[194]

On January 12, 1609, the traders navigated the river, which was "frozen near a half a mile from the shore." Furthermore, the ebb flow of the river left the barges in the "oozy shoals" as they struggled to break the ice. Rather than lie there impotently, Smith climbed into the frigid water and muck that reached up to his waist and waded the few hundred yards to the shore. A few dozen men followed their audacious president's example, and at least one nearly died of exposure. They dried off and warmed up inside some homes while they were provided with bread, turkey, and venison.

Wahunsonacock granted Smith an audience the following day and gave him a predictably icy reception. The chief disclaimed any knowledge of having sent for Smith and "began to ask us when we would be gone." He denied that he had any spare corn to trade, but he offered to procure forty baskets for forty swords. Smith asked his adversary how he had become so forgetful. Wahunsonacock simply laughed at Smith and asked to look over the commodities he would offer to trade. The Indian disdainfully assessed the lot and said he wanted nothing but weapons, "valuing a basket of corn more precious than a basket of copper." Smith smiled inwardly at the challenge and was prepared to fight a verbal duel that might very well have determined the fate of the Jamestown colony. Backing down could have sealed the settlement's doom.

Smith retorted that he had abided by Wahunsonacock's terms for trade when he sent the workers for his service. To counter the werowance's claim that he had no extra corn, Smith replied that he also had none to spare. He subtly warned Wahunsonacock, "…you must know those I have can keep me from want." He finished by reiterating the friendship of the English toward the Powhatans, although he added a caveat, "except you constrain me by our bad usage."[195]

Wahunsonacock listened to Smith's discourse and then accused him of duplicitous intentions in coming to Werowocomoco. "Many do inform me you coming hither is not for trade," he related, "but to invade my people and possess my country." Proof of this was that Smith and his men were armed. Wahunsonacock averred that Smith could relieve these fears if the Englishmen were to "leave aboard your weapons, for here they are needless, we being all friends."[196]

The pair continued their verbal sparring late into the night and the following day. Wahunsonacock demanded, "What will it avail you to take that by force you may quickly have by love? Or to destroy them that provide you food? What can you get by war when we can hide our provisions and fly to the woods?" He and his people could do these things, but they preferred to live in peace and harmony rather than a constant state of war. He was prepared to furnish the settlers with corn, asking only that they "come in [a] friendly manner to see us and not thus with your guns and swords as to invade your foes."[197]

Smith responded that the Powhatan warriors regularly came to Jamestown armed with their bows and arrows. The Englishmen were similarly wearing "our arms as our apparel." He also reminded Wahunsonacock with a thinly veiled threat of "the cruelty we use to our enemies as our true love and courtesy to our friends." The English embraced the dangers of war as "our chiefest pleasure."[198]

With a bit of disingenuousness contradicted by the fact that the settlers were just then seeking trade at Werowocomoco, Smith tried to discount the importance of the Powhatans to Jamestown's survival. "As for the hiding [of] your provision or by your flying to the woods, we shall not so unadvisedly starve as you conclude. Your friendly care in that behalf is needless." Smith was playing a very weak hand.[199]

Nevertheless, the two giants battled each other, both trying to gain the upper hand. An exasperated Wahunsonacock expressed disappointment that Smith did not rightfully bow down to his authority. "Captain Smith, I never use any werowance so kindly as yourself, yet from you I receive the least kindness of any. Captain Newport gave me swords, copper, clothes, a bed, tools, or what I desired; and would send away his guns when I entreated him." He did not realize how much Smith despised Newport for that and how Smith blamed Newport's weakness for his current predicament. Wahunsonacock continued, demanding due submission from one he considered his subject: "None doth deny to lie at my feet or refuse to do what I desire, but only you." He asked Smith one more time to lay down his arms.[200]

Smith asked the Indians to break the river ice so that his boat might come closer for the corn and his landing party. He also ordered his men to bring more soldiers ashore as a show of strength that would surprise and intimidate his host. Stalling for time, he kept up his repartee with Wahunsonacock, denying any submission to the Indian chief. "You must know as I have but one God I honor but one king; and I live not here as your subject but as your friend." He promised to lay down his arms the following day. But Wahunsonacock got wind of the fact that the Englishmen on the boats were planning to join forces with Smith, and he fled.[201]

An elderly Indian tried to delay Smith's departure, for the werowance had ordered his warriors to kill the Englishmen that night. Tensions ran high as the Indians offered to guard the muskets and pistols while the Englishmen carried the baskets of corn back to their boats. Smith saw through their ruse, and his men cocked their muskets into firing position, forcing the Indians to carry the corn on their own backs. Since the river was again at low tide and the boats were mired in mud, the settlers had to wait for a high tide that would speed them away. They spent that time in the village, being entertained as if nothing untoward had happened.

Pocahontas covertly warned Smith of the impending attack at dinner. Smith and his company sat down to eat, but they suspected they might be poisoned and forced the Indians to taste every dish first. They stayed until around midnight in good cheer, until the boats were ready to sail. Wahunsonacock returned shortly after the Englishmen departed.

Smith looked over the provisions that the Powhatans had given in trade and was grimly dissatisfied. It was not enough to last the colony through the winter. Before sailing for Jamestown, he went upriver and traded with the Pamunkeys for more corn. Chief Opechancanough was as combative and unwilling to part with his provisions as his brother Wahunsonacock. Smith knew that his life was in danger again, but he risked it for the survival of the colony.

Smith and fifteen others went to Opechancanough's home in Cinquoteck, a town only a quarter of a mile from the river. The Englishmen were entertained for a few days in the largely abandoned village when the chief allowed them an audience. As expected, Opechancanough surrounded himself with armed warriors and offered only a few baskets of corn at an outrageously steep price.

Smith had had enough. He wasted no time and admitted that he was the weaker partner in the negotiations: "Opechancanough, the great love you profess with your tongue seems mere deceit by your actions…You know my want, and I your plenty, of which by some means I must have part." Smith then lectured the Indian leader, "Remember it is fit for kings to keep their promise." He was forced to lay out his items and offer the chief generous terms, since both well knew just how desperate Smith was. Honesty lent strength to the negotiations, because only a fool would try to claim equality under the circumstances. "Here are my commodities, whereof take your choice. The rest I will proportion fit bargains for your people."[202]

Opechancanough feigned friendship and agreed to barter some corn, promising more the following day. One of Smith's party soon discovered that more than six hundred well-armed warriors surrounded the house. Smith held a spontaneous council of war to decide on how they should react. If they discharged their pieces, they might frighten their enemies off, but they would not get any provisions. Conversely, they might easily be slaughtered because of the overwhelming odds against them. "Let us fight like men and not die like sheep," Smith told them gravely. But he would attempt first to "draw them to it by conditions," getting what they wanted through the tested strategy of trade through diplomacy and force. His men were behind him and would follow his lead.[203]

Smith turned to Opechancanough and challenged his adversary to a duel. "I see, Opechancanough, your plot to murder me, but I fear it not," Smith asserted. "Take therefore your arms. You see mine. My body shall be as naked as yours. The isle in your river is a fit place, if you be contented, and the conqueror of us two shall be lord and master over all our men. Otherwise, draw all your men into the field. If you have not enough, take time to fetch more and bring what number you will, so everyone bring a basket of corn against all which I will stake the value in copper (you see I have but fifteen men) and our game shall be the conqueror take all."[204]

Opechancanough considered his options in the face of the Englishman's challenge. With so many warriors stationed outside his house, he did not need to risk his life needlessly in single combat. He offered the Englishmen a "great present" outside the door in order to draw them outside to face more than two hundred warriors, "each his arrow nocked ready to shoot."[205]

In a rage, Smith grabbed Opechancanough by his long hair and held him fast. Pointing his pistol squarely against the Indian's chest, Smith wrestled Opechancanough outside, where the warriors could see his predicament. The warriors lowered their bows and looked at each other. Smith shouted a warning for all to hear:

> I see, you Pamunkeys, the great desire you have to kill me; and my long suffering your injuries has emboldened you to this presumption. The cause I have forborne your insolence is the promise I made you before the God I serve to be your friend till you give me just cause to be your enemy. If I keep this vow, my God will keep me: you cannot hurt me. If I break it, He will destroy me. But if you shoot but one arrow to shed one drop of blood of any of my men, or steal the least of these beads or copper I spurn here before you with my foot, you shall see I will not cease revenge.[206]

Smith reiterated his intention only to trade fairly, assuring them that he would free their king and leave them in peace if they would abide by their former promises to load his ship with provisions.

Intimidated by the Englishman's threats of violence, the warriors put away their bows and went for corn. The men, women, and children of the village brought hundreds of baskets of corn to the Englishmen.[207]

Smith sailed back to Jamestown, but not before he fended off a few more attempts on his life. He considered the effects of his actions on the future of the colony. He had nearly three hundred bushels of corn to feed the colony for a short time because of his strong-arm diplomacy. It was only a short-term fix that would not alleviate the hunger problem for the long term. He had soured relations with the native peoples that surrounded the fledgling colony, and the colonists could not expect a relief expedition any time soon. The prospects for Jamestown were bleak when Smith stepped ashore, and the news kept getting worse.

In his absence, Smith discovered that two of the Germans sent to work on Wahunsonacock's house had betrayed the colony. After Smith departed from Werowocomoco, Wahunsonacock kindly offered the two settlers to free them from "those miseries that would happen [to] the colony" and provide all their necessities if they would go to Jamestown and trick the colonists into giving them a large supply of weapons.[208]

The two Germans did not have any allegiance to the national mission of the English settlers and looked out for themselves. Betting their survival on the Indians rather than the starving colonists, the pair agreed to the deal. Richard Salvage, the young interpreter in Powhatan's village, and another settler tried to warn the settlement of the betrayal, but they were discovered and held captive while the treachery was carried out.

The Germans, known only as Adam and Franz, set out for Jamestown and met with councilman Peter Winne. They convinced him that Smith had sent them to the settlement to retrieve the fort's weapons, tools, and a change of clothing. They even persuaded "six or seven more to their confederacy." Their subterfuge was so credible that they persuaded Winne to furnish them with "a great many swords, pike-heads, pieces, shot, powder, and suchlike." Winne even allowed some Indians to carry the arms away without question. Consequently, Wahunsonacock now possessed some three hundred hatchets, fifty swords, eight pieces (with powder and shot), and eight pikes. The balance of power was turning against the English settlers; the werowance and his people were strengthened in their ability to resist John Smith's demands in the future.[209]

Smith also learned that while he was gone, Matthew Scrivener had become ambitious and sought to contend with the president—his former ally—for authority. But then Scrivener and Richard Waldo, both members of the council, sailed to Hog Island with nine other men, and their boat capsized in the ice-laden river during an "extreme tempest." All of them either quickly drowned or died from hypothermia. The deaths were a severe blow to the leadership of the colony.[210]

As if the problem with the missing weapons were not enough, Smith assessed the woeful state of the provisions. The provisions Newport had left with the colony were nearly a year old by that point and almost completely rotten, moldy, and worm-ridden. They were so spoiled that the hogs apparently refused to eat them. The small harvest was similarly ruined. Still, Smith judged it "sufficient till the next harvest."[211]

Upon his return, Smith instituted martial discipline and forced the colonists into a work regimen of at least six hours a day. They were divided into small work teams for a variety of tasks. Smith declared, "He that will not work shall not eat," but he failed to give them any real incentive to work except to escape "his due punishment" for idleness. He was doing what was fair and just—after all, it was inequitable for "the labors of thirty or forty honest and industrious men…to maintain an hundred and fifty idle loiterers." But none of those two hundred colonists would reap any individual rewards for their hard work.[212]

While Smith was organizing the colony, the troubles with the rogue Germans and Wahunsonacock continued. Smith learned that one of the Germans was near Jamestown, hiding in the woods, and went out with a party of twenty men to apprehend him. While the settlers were conducting their search for the traitor, Smith was surprised by the chief of the Paspaheghs, Wowinchopunck. Neither man could fire his weapon, and the two grappled with each other. The "strong, stout" Indian maneuvered Smith into the river in order to drown him. Some of Smith's men heard the noises and ran to the shore, where they saw the pair wrestling for their lives. There was no escape for the Indian even if he killed the Englishman. Suddenly Smith grabbed the chief's hair "and got such a hold on his throat he had near strangled" his foe. Panting heavily, Smith finally released his adversary and took him back to Jamestown as a prisoner. Smith learned that Wahunsonacock was behind the attempted murder.[213]

Wowinchopunck escaped from the settlement, which fired Smith's bent for revenge, since he feared that appearing weak by not answering the violence would "but encourage the savages." He led a retaliatory raid against the Paspaheghs, slaying seven or eight Indians in the attack, and torched several homes. Smith and his men stole the Indian fishing weirs and canoes and brought them back to Jamestown. Wowinchopunck sent a messenger to Smith to parley. The chief promised to share some of the harvest, but he warned Smith that if he proceeded on his violent course, "we will abandon the country…[and] you will have the worse by our absence."[214] Smith fully understood the precariousness of the settlers' position and the Indians' knowledge of that fact. He continued to seek alternatives to keep the colonists alive.

Spring brought limited hope to the colonists, who were industrious thanks to the rules the president had laid down. The men had dug a well in the fort for a ready supply of water. Twenty houses were erected for shelter, and the church was rebuilt. The fishing weirs and nets were placed in the James River for sturgeon and other fish. A blockhouse held items for trade, and to prevent thievery, an armed guard allowed no one to pass—Indian or Englishman—unless they first secured the president's approval. The work rules resulted in the production of some commodities, including dozens of barrels of tar, pitch, and soap ashes for export.

Even then, the colony still struggled with its provisions because the Indian corn was found "half-rotten and the rest so consumed with so many thousands of rats that increased so fast...as we knew not how to keep that little we had." Once again, the English were completely at the mercy of the goodwill of the Indians, who brought game to the settlement as Wowinchopunck had promised.[215]

The lack of food became so serious that Smith was forced to divide the settlement and send several groups away from Jamestown, even though it left them vulnerable to Indian attacks. More than sixty settlers went downriver "to live upon oysters" while George Percy led another two dozen at Point Comfort to live off of whatever fish they could catch. Percy, however, was sick and afflicted with a nasty gunpowder burn, and his men did very little fishing, even though they were starving. Francis West took twenty men up to the falls, but they found nothing to eat "but a few berries and acorns."[216]

The settlers were desperate, especially when so little food was found even after they dispersed. The leaders forced them to scavenge for every bit of food before they starved to death or resorted to cannibalism. They were not too weak to make "exclamations, suggestions, and devices" to overthrow Smith and "abandon the country." Smith punished one man severely as an example, and he warned if any attempted to steal the ships and leave Virginia, the perpetrators would be caught and sent to the gallows. He appealed to them as he had done during their difficult time exploring the Chesapeake Bay: "I never had more from the store than the worst of you." This did not relieve their hunger, and the grumbling continued, but they could not accuse Smith of hoarding food the way they had with Edward Wingfield and John Ratcliffe.[217] So far, none of Smith's decisions had really set the colony on a solid foundation. His harsh regimens might have stopped some of the more egregious problems such as not working or pilfering food and weapons from the common storehouse, but he had not found a lasting model for the colony's prosperity.

So far the Jamestown colony was a nearly complete failure. The death rate from hunger and disease was atrocious. The colonists were dependent upon those they considered inferior for food, and they continually provoked them to increasingly hostile relations. Costly relief expeditions had been sent, but these stores were rapidly consumed and left the colonists as hungry as before. Nothing of great value had been found to reward the company's investors, and the colonists had not yet developed the natural resources the land possessed. The colonists, whose lives were invested in the survival of the colony, displayed a shocking unconcern about either their lives or the colony.

In England, the Virginia Council attempted to find a formula that would put the colonial venture on a proper footing, discussing what they considered to be fundamental changes for the colony. At that moment, an immense fleet was being prepared to sail for America. The outcome of the venture would determine the fate of the English colony in Virginia.

Chapter Eight

FOR GOD, GLORY, AND GOLD

Thomas Smythe stared out one of the windows of his luxurious mansion on Philpot Lane trying to decide on a course of action to take regarding the Jamestown colony. The bleak winter weather that blanketed London did little to revive his mood. The normally busy streets were sparsely populated with bundled people trying to escape the cold. The poor were in desperate circumstances, hunting down spare pieces of wood to stay warm against the elements. The plague had come to London, further dampening the desires of many to go outdoors in the miserable cold. The wharves along the Thames were generally empty, and the traffic along the river had also slowed to a trickle as winter voyages were among the most perilous of all.

In January 1609 one ship that had braved the elements was captained by the indefatigable mariner Christopher Newport, who was returning from the New World. Newport met with Smythe and other members of the council within days of his arrival in London. Unfortunately, he confirmed their growing suspicions about the dismal state of Virginia and added to the bad news coming out of the colony. He related to them the difficulties that he had had with President John Smith and delivered Smith's letter, which was highly critical of Newport and the Virginia Council itself. The leaders of the anti-Smith faction, Gabriel Archer and John Ratcliffe, returned with Newport and also met with Smythe. They harshly censured Smith in no uncertain terms, blaming him for the problems of the colony.

Yet after Smythe listened to the complaints of Smith's enemies, he and the other members of the council did not place the blame entirely on Smith. Removed from Virginia by thousands of miles and receiving only limited reports, they were intelligent men who appreciated that significant problems would not be resolved by the removal of a single overbearing leader. It was terribly unsettling, but they were honest enough to concede that fundamental changes were necessary. And they were flexible enough to see the changes through to protect their investment. Indeed, they were planning a massive restructuring and sharpening of their vision that they hoped would result in an influx of settlers that would finally establish Jamestown as a permanent colony.

By mid-February, King James granted Smythe and his allies a new second charter, completing reorganizing the Virginia Company. The Crown relinquished its authority over the council and invested the company with full powers to appoint the members of the council. Under the terms of the charter, the Virginia Council of London was expanded to fifty members that read like a who's who of the nation's rich and powerful. These included Francis Bacon, Oliver Cromwell (uncle of the future lord protector), Lord De La Warr, Edwin Sandys, the Earl of Pembroke, and William Shakespeare's patron, the Earl of Southampton. Smythe continued to run the operations of the colony as treasurer.

The Virginia Council assumed "full and absolute power and authority, to correct, punish, pardon, govern and rule" the colony.

It was bound to follow the laws of England, but the members of the council were otherwise granted autonomy to use their wisdom and good discretion to do whatever they "shall think to be fittest for the good of the adventurers and inhabitants there." This time they would take no chances that those they appointed to govern in the colony would fail to follow the will of the council in London.[218]

The faith of the Virginia Council in the system of rule conducted by the local council in Jamestown and its removable president was shattered. After all, overwhelming evidence from the experience of the past two years had led to follies, outrages, and mismanagement by the councilors who were continuously divided by "dissention and ambition among themselves." Factional government that split the colony led to "idleness and bestial sloth, of the common sort, who were active in nothing but adhering to factions and parts, even to their own ruin."[219]

Their solution was to invest "one able and absolute governor" with total authority to rule the colony. When the governor reached Jamestown, the government constituted under the first patent would be thereby abolished, and all documents held by the council were to be handed over to the governor. The Virginia Council would still appoint a local council, but now it was to play only an advisory role to the governor. The council did not have, "single or together, any binding or negative voice or power upon your conclusions, but do give you full authority." The council would be able neither to over-rule the governor nor to depose him at their whim, as had happened previously. The governor's authority was absolute, and this included the power to declare martial law if necessary.[220]

The new charter also expanded the territory of Jamestown two hundred miles north and south of Point Comfort, extending across the continent from the Atlantic to the elusive Pacific Ocean. The unhealthful capital at Jamestown would be moved to three other principal settlements, including Point Comfort. More important, colonists would now be granted private ownership of land. Among the laws would be a prescription to work a certain number of hours per day, and food was still allotted from a common storehouse. The military and corporate organization of the colony was still fundamental to its mission, but a reorientation was occurring that slowly chipped away at the edges of this focus.

The charter enforced religious orthodoxy upon the colonists by requiring them to take the oath of supremacy to the Anglican Church. Worship services were to be conducted according to Anglican forms. Anyone suspected of practicing the "superstitions" of Roman Catholicism was banned from migrating. "Popery" was lumped in with atheism as religious offenses against God that were to be punished.

When the new 1609 charter reorganized the company, the joint-stock company was restructured to make investment more accessible to a wider group of shareholders. Whereas the first charter attracted the money of the very wealthy and influential, the shares of the second charter cost a little more than twelve pounds. The company had discovered that the expeditions carrying supplies and additional settlers to the colony were very expensive. The costs, as well as the risks, could be spread out with a greater number of investors. Moreover, popular enthusiasm for the project would be encouraged if more people and organizations had a stake in the outcome of the mission.

The company planned to pool the money of investors to organize a fleet of ships that dwarfed the original settlement in Virginia. The council members envisioned nine ships that would carry several hundred colonists to Virginia under tighter control. A second, larger expedition would follow the year after. The company turned to two gentlemen adventurers—Sir Thomas West (Lord De La Warr) and Sir Thomas Gates—to lead the ambitious expeditions and Jamestown colony.

Lord De La Warr was only about thirty-two years old but had built up an impressive list of credentials to be selected as the governor of Jamestown. He was related to Queen Elizabeth and had served his queen in the Netherlands, battling the forces of Catholic Spain in the Dutch Revolt. He was knighted for his leadership in fighting the colonial war in Ireland. He followed the common path of gentlemen adventurers in Elizabethan England, and his star was on the rise. Then he was implicated in the Essex rebellion in 1601. Elizabeth nearly had him executed, although he was eventually cleared and actually placed on her ruling privy council. James I asked him to stay on as a member of his privy council. De La Warr naturally supported the national English mission to colonize America in order to challenge Spain in the New World, and the company chose him to be the man who would set things right in Virginia. He would not travel with the first planned expedition, but with the larger second fleet.

Thomas Gates would have the responsibility of bringing over the first group of settlers and establishing order in the colony. Gates was also an experienced gentleman adventurer with a long record of service to the English Crown. He was educated at Gray's Inn and served as an ambassador to Vienna. He had fought in the Caribbean and had been currently fighting in the Netherlands, having to request leave to serve in Virginia. He was a charter member of the original April 1606 patent and intimately acquainted with the London merchants and fellow adventurers who had endeavored to make Jamestown successful for the last several years. Few men were as invested in the outcome of the colony as Gates. The company was confident in selecting him to be the interim governor until De La Warr arrived in Virginia. The two gentlemen were bold, daring, and dedicated to establishing a foothold in the New World to challenge England's greatest rival. They staked their personal reputations and the glory of mother England in agreeing to lead the venture.

Armed with the new charter, and sharing an unambiguous vision and a method of organization to achieve it, the company organized a massive public relations campaign to promote investment and settlement in the new venture. London was soon abuzz with excitement about the Jamestown colony, which quickly drowned out any rumors or hard news of difficulties in Virginia. During the spring of 1609, Londoners were bombarded with glowing words that extolled the bounty of Virginia as well as stirring calls to support the patriotic national mission in the drive to colonize. Ministers preached the message from pulpits around the capital, writers composed numerous pamphlets, and recruiters spread the word in countless conversations in taverns and homes around the city. The promotional campaign reached virtually everyone in London several times.

The message was clear and concise and repeated in all of the venues. It was a broad picture of English national greatness. Jamestown was a focal point of the global struggle with Spain. The colony would reap a growing economic empire that would surpass the wealth of the Spanish treasure fleets. The religious impulse would drive the Christian soldiers onward to convert and civilize the native peoples, especially before they could be converted by Spain to Roman Catholicism. All of this, the promoters argued was God's will, England's national destiny, and a mission for imperial greatness.

The message being promoted was scarcely a new one. The search for great wealth, the mission to convert the natives to Protestantism, and the challenge to the rival Spanish Empire were all elements of the 1606 patent and included in the instructions to the original settlers. Indeed, this national vision had been shaped in the 1570s and 1580s, when gentlemen adventurers plunged into overseas ventures to explore, set up trading companies, fight abroad, and establish colonies. It was the same vision of Sir Walter Ralegh, Sir John Hawkins, Sir Francis Drake, and Richard Hakluyt. It remained a martial vision of winning personal and national glory through strict rule instead of individual liberty. But the message to support the Jamestown colony was repackaged and sold to a much broader spectrum of Londoners than any previous publicity campaign.

Robert Johnson, a merchant and Thomas Smythe's deputy treasurer for the company, penned the pamphlet *Nova Britannia* that grandly described the potential wealth of Virginia in glowing terms. The climate was "most sweet and wholesome." The deepwater harbors supported oceangoing vessels, and Jamestown would be an important part of the highway of goods and trade stretching across the Atlantic. Virginia contained vast lands with "hidden treasure, never yet searched." The soils held valuable minerals and supported an array of crops "in great abundance" to sustain a large population.[221]

Moreover, Johnson asked his readers to imagine the limitless possibilities of wealth that could be produced when "art and nature shall join, and strive together, to give best content to man and beast." The English believed that the native peoples had not exploited the great bounty of the land. The company planned to "set many thousands to work, in these such services," producing timber, hemp and flax, silk, pitch, turpentine, and any number of industries. All the colony needed was "people to make the plantation, and money to furnish our present provisions and shipping now in hand." The sooner interested individuals signed up, their "charge will be the shorter, and their gain the greater."[222]

Another broadside, *Concerning the Plantation of Virginia New*

Britain, spotlighted the fact that the company offered economic opportunity to all classes in the New World. While it had the support of nobles, gentlemen, and merchants, it was advertising to "all workmen of whatever craft they may be…men as well as women, who wish to go out in this voyage." Blacksmiths, bakers, carpenters, weavers, shipwrights—all were invited to consider the opportunity to start over in Virginia and establish a thriving trade. To sweeten the pot a bit, readers were reminded that the company would provide "houses to live in, vegetable gardens and orchards, and also food and clothing" at no expense. Not only that, but every settler would "have a share of all the products and the profits that may result from their labor." In Virginia, the Reverend William Symonds promised, English laborers would find "a land more like the garden of Eden, which the Lord planted, than any part else of all the earth." It seemed almost too good to be true, and it was. There was not a word about the difficulties the colonists had encountered since May 1607, the fruitless searches for gold and the Northwest Passage, or the lack of any significant commodities to export home.[223]

The same message was finely crafted for the "better sorts," who held commoners in contempt, assuring them that the colony would be a dumping ground of sorts for the teeming masses. In *Nova Britannia,* Robert Johnson reminded the nobles and gentlemen, although he did not need to, "Our land [is] abounding with swarms of idle persons, which having no means of labor to relieve their misery, do likewise swarm in lewd and naughty practices." He warned his readers of the dangers they posed because of the resentments caused by "oppression, diverse kinds of wrongs, mutinies, sedition, commotion and rebellion, scarcity, dearth, poverty, and sundry sorts of calamities." The answer was evident: send the "idle persons to Virginia where greater opportunities "will make them rich."[224]

Ministers preached widely of the divine mandate that was calling them to support the efforts of the company. The Reverend William Symonds compared the providential mission of the settlers to that of Abraham and the ancient Jews in the book of Genesis. England was a chosen nation called to "go and carry the Gospel to a nation that never heard of Christ." The Reverend Daniel Price spoke from the pulpit at St. Paul's Cross, arguing that the Indians "know no God but the Devil." It was the responsibility of English settlers to go forth and "obtain the saving of their souls." The version of Christian salvation that the English would instruct the natives in was militantly Protestant and steeped in not a little anti-Catholicism. The imperial, economic, and religious objectives all dovetailed perfectly in the English hatred of their mortal enemy: Catholic Spain.[225]

The national mission of England called on Englishmen to rally around the unity of that mission for the glory of England and the Crown. Anyone who doubted the future success of the colony was construed a traitor. Reverend Price declared, "Every opposition against it [Virginia] is an opposition against God, the King, the Church, and the Commonwealth." Dissenting opinions and honest appraisals of life in the colony were not to be tolerated, since they undermined the national glory.[226]

Of course, the Virginia Company did not depend merely upon pamphlets and sermons to get its message to a broad audience. It also relied upon the personal appeal to the friends and connections of its eminent members. For example, Thomas Smythe met with the heads of some of London's guilds. The Virginia Company followed up, asking council member Humphrey Weld, the lord mayor of London, to sell shares to "the best disposed and most able of the companies." Fishmongers, grocers, clothworkers, tailors, and more than fifty other guilds invested in Virginia.[227]

The Earl of Southampton was Shakespeare's patron and had

connections with James's court, the Globe Theatre, and St. Paul's. He attracted a group of nobles that wrote to the English ambassador in the Netherlands to push subscriptions and military recruitment there. The merchants of London appealed to their counterparts in Plymouth who had worked with them in 1606, inviting them to "join your endeavors with ours."[228]

The results of the campaign were a stunning success for the company. Investors flocked to risk their money on the overseas venture that seemed almost to guarantee great returns on every share. Spanish Ambassador Don Pedro de Zúñiga noted, "The people are mad about this affair."[229] More than 650 individuals bought shares in the new Virginia Company, and 56 companies and guilds invested money as well, corporately representing many hundreds more. The number included nobles as well as commoners in this broad effort to support the national mission for the greatness of England.

Most of the investors risked their fortunes, large and small, on the outcome of the colony in Virginia. They were persuaded the settlement would work by the glowing promotions that flooded London as well as the appeal to their national pride.

But the people recruited by the company to settle in America risked more than a few pounds on a share of stock; they bet their lives on the outcome of the colony. They were in a sense investing themselves in the company, and they received a share for agreeing to settle in Virginia. Those with higher social status received an additional share, but their share of the expected bounty of gold and profits from exports was worth exactly the same as that of the poor laborers who only had themselves to invest. With the positive messages driving excitement, some six hundred people decided to seek opportunity in the New World under the English banner.

During the spring, Zúñiga witnessed the colonial promotion

with great alacrity and correctly judged the national sense of mission among the English against Spanish interests. In a series of insistent letters, he informed Philip III of the preparations for the 600-person expedition that attracted widespread investment among the English public. Zúñiga warned his king that the English enemy sought nothing less than "the exaltation of their religion and its extension throughout the world." The English, he was told, were aiming to alter the character of settlement by ending the previous attempts of "sending people little by little, but now we see that what we should do is establish ourselves all at once, because when they open their eyes in Spain they will not be able to do anything about it." They would also establish a base for piracy to raid Spanish trade routes.[230]

Don Pedro de Zúñiga described English goals as "villany" and "insolent." He urgently advised Philip to take rapid action to "put a bridle" on their overseas ambitions while it was still possible. If "they get away with this, it will not be long before they will give themselves airs," while the appeasing Spanish king would appear weak and have "trouble getting them out of there" as they strengthened their position. Zúñiga became desperate and frustrated that his warnings were again ignored by a complacent king. Philip should not combat the English through "abjurations" or prayer, but through firm action. But still his admonitions fell on deaf ears, and the ambassador disconsolately felt that "It seems that I always fall short," when his king failed to act as he wished.[231]

For all of his bluster, Zúñiga essentially captured the character of the Gates expedition, which signified the promise of a new step foreword in the success of the colony. It heralded a massive wave of settlers inspired by national pride who would create a thriving colony through force of will. As a national mission of such grand importance, there was a sense of national destiny that it would succeed. The existing Jamestown colonists did not conceive of the magnitude of the fleet or its sense of mission.

With the infusion of money and interested settlers, the company made preparations to launch a massive expedition to Virginia that matched its grand expectations. The members of the company worked feverishly to organize the fleet. First, nine ships and smaller boats were bought or leased to carry hundreds of settlers and the supplies they would need for their transatlantic journey and when they arrived in the colony.

The flagship was the *Sea Venture,* a three-masted ship measuring 100 feet and rated at 250 tons. She would sail armed with twenty-four cannons, in case privateers found the fleet an attractive catch. She could carry some 150 closely packed passengers in her decks and tug a tiny ketch behind her. The vice admiral, the *Diamond,* was nearly as big, while the smaller rear admiral was the *Falcon.* Four smaller vessels—*Blessing, Lion, Swallow,* and *Unity*—were smaller ships that kept in the middle of the fleet. The *Virginia* was a pinnace that could be used for exploration.

Captains and crews were found to sail the ships. The company selected Sir George Somers as the admiral of the fleet. Somers was nearing sixty years old, but no one could deny his illustrious résumé. He had fought the Spanish with Drake and Hawkins, making a fortune in the process. He was knighted and held a seat in Parliament. The Virginia Company listed him as one of its charter members in 1606. He now invested a small fortune of £300 in the company and was part owner of the *Sea Venture* and two of her companion ships.

Many of Somers's subordinate captains had been to Virginia before and were well known to the colonists. Christopher Newport served Somers as master of the *Sea Venture* and was the most experienced man in the fleet in crossing the Atlantic, which he had accomplished numerous times since the forty-nine-year-old captain had hunted Spanish treasure ships with the sea dogs. Vice Admiral John Ratcliffe commanded the *Diamond.* He had captained the *Discovery* on the original Jamestown voyage and served as the colony's president until he was deposed. His thoughts were not favorable toward John Smith as he prepared for the crossing. John Martin was also returning to Jamestown, this time as the commander of the *Falcon.* His ship's master was the experienced Francis Nelson, who had arrived late on the *Phoenix* while sailing on the first relief expedition with Newport. Nelson understood the importance of this mission, considering the state of the colony the last time he was there.

Mariners were not hard to recruit, especially since peace with Spain had given them less opportunity to work. They read broadsides and spoke with recruiters at seedy taverns about the voyage and negotiated their wages. Even though most were in their twenties, they were weathered and experienced old salts. Some had even been to Jamestown previously and based their decision on that trip. They were hired for their specific skills: carpenters, cooks, coopers, and ordinary sailors.

Tons of beer, biscuits, salt pork and fish, peas, cheese, and butter was purchased. They were loaded into the holds of the ships at wharves along the Thames. The food would turn rancid and spoil during the voyage. Passengers and sailors would have to pick out worms or cut off mold. They also would suffer from scurvy.

Sailors brought aboard pigs, chickens, and some other live animals, making a small racket aboard the *Sea Venture* and some of the larger ships. They would supply fresh meat for the passengers and crew during the voyage and populate the farms in the colony. The unfortunate consequence of ferrying the animals was the variety of smells that emanated from their pens, especially in the heat of the tropics.

Large guns and a supply of shot were also loaded on the *Sea Venture*. Other weapons in the ships' arsenals included matchlock pistols, swords, and daggers, in case the ships were boarded. The sailors laded the ship with the usual rigging, sails, and ropes. Navigational charts and instruments were brought aboard.

This third supply mission was a highly organized venture, as were most overseas voyages. Merchants and captains had lengthy experience in exploration, privateering, fishing in Newfoundland, and establishing companies like the East India Company or the Muscovy Company, and were well acquainted with the needs for a long voyage. The provisions for the voyage and the colony were loaded, the fleet was properly armed against attack, and equipment was ready in case of emergencies, which were always expected at sea. It was a dangerous trip under the best of circumstances, not lightly undertaken, but the crew would use their experience and wits to adapt to any difficulties. The only thing they needed now were their passengers.

In mid-May hundreds of Englishmen and women traveled to the town of Woolwich's docks on the Thames, ten miles downriver from London. Most walked individually or in small groups. Some family members made the trek in the spring weather to see their loved ones off. Others paid to be ferried along with their belongings by a London wherry. Wealthier gentlemen made the bumpy ride in their carriages, accompanied by servants who handled the baggage. They arrived in Woolwich and boarded the ships with a mixture of unspoken dreams and trepidation.

Among their number was only one Anglican minister, the Oxford-trained Reverend Richard Buck. He believed in England's mission to settle the New World and planned to minister to the souls of his congregants in Jamestown as well as the Indians of Virginia.

Yet not everyone on board believed in the tenets of the Anglican Church. Stephen Hopkins and others were religious dissenters who were sympathetic to the growing Puritan movement, which was equated with sedition against king and church.

Another passenger was William Strachey, a poet on the fringes of London's literary and theater circles. His friends included John Donne and Ben Jonson, but he produced little significant literature of his own. Dreaming of literary greatness, the aspiring poet had consumed most of his inheritance and loans. He had recently served as a secretary to the English ambassador in Turkey, but that ended badly, and he was in debt. He stowed his writing materials for the journey, hoping to compose a travel narrative of the exotic New World that would become popular reading throughout Europe.

Two other persons who boarded embodied the exotic in the New World. Namontack, Powhatan's emissary to the English, was returning from his second trip to London. He wore English clothes, as his chaperones dressed him in the garb of civilization, but he stirred the imagination of Londoners as an American native nonetheless. Machumps, another Powhatan, joined Namontack for the voyage, returning to their people with wondrous tales from the world's largest city.

On May 15, seven of the ships slipped their moorings at Woolwich and rode the ebb tide toward the coast. Their English colors flew proudly in the breeze. Investor Stephen Powle came to see the fleet off and watched it sail out of sight. He listened with the passengers of the ships and other well-wishers to the prayers of Reverend Buck. "God bless them and guide them to his glory and our good," he prayed.[232]

The Englishmen and women who were voyaging with the fleet and those that remained at home truly felt blessed by heaven. They were embarking on a mission to fulfill their national destiny and rightfully take their place under heaven as a great empire. They believed they were divinely favored because of their piety and entrepreneurial spirit, that fortune would favor those who served God devoutly and boldly risked everything in pursuit of their righteous cause. But the Atlantic was full of great dangers that might be interpreted as divine anger should they encounter them. Indeed, in the coming months, they would perhaps see just how much the Almighty was displeased with their national mission to colonize Virginia.

Chapter Nine

A FATEFUL DAY FOR THE *SEA VENTURE*

The fleet of seven ships sailed around the southern coast of England to rendezvous with the two other ships, some passengers, and Thomas Gates and George Somers. The ships put in at the seafaring port of Plymouth on the southwestern coast for a few weeks. In Plymouth Harbor, dockworkers laded the ship with dozens more barrels of provisions and coaxed eight horses on to the *Blessing.*

Meanwhile, the passengers grew bored and consumed provisions as they waited for Interim Governor Gates, who had remained in London, attending at Westminster Hall to receive the revised charter from the king. Gates was handed the charter on May 23, and after some final preparations with the company, he immediately made his way to Plymouth to link up with the fleet.

When he arrived, he conferred with Admiral Somers and Vice Admiral Christopher Newport about the voyage. The three gentlemen adventurers squabbled over their positioning in this historic voyage as they jockeyed for fame. Somers was the admiral of the fleet and would not contemplate sailing on any vessel other than his flagship, *Sea Venture*. Governor Gates also wanted to take his rightful place aboard the flagship. Newport, too, was accustomed to command and would not tolerate being consigned to a lesser vessel. John Smith later wrote, "All things being ready, because those three captains could not agree for place, it was concluded they should go all in one ship." Gates stowed the colony's sealed instructions in a locked box in his cabin on the *Sea Venture*. Having the leaders of the fleet and of the colony all in one ship, along with the instructions for the governance of the colony, was imprudently risky and foolish. It would prove to be a fateful decision that would determine the course of the Jamestown colony.[233]

On the pleasant evening of June 2, 1609, the *Sea Venture* and her convoy of ships departed from Plymouth on a southward course around the Devon coast. The passengers were headed for a new life, willingly sailing into the unknown.

The ships were soon "crossed" by gusting "southwest winds," which delayed the fleet just as the original Jamestown fleet had been stalled in the winter of 1607. The fleet put in at Falmouth and remained there until June 8, waiting for more favorable winds. The brief delay had a dramatic impact on the journey.[234]

After conferring with his captains, Somers decided that it was safe to sail and tried again. They set course for the Canary Island as was usual for voyagers to the New World. Somers, Gates, and Newport agreed that the fleet would then continue westward along the new path sailed by Samuel Argall in order to avoid any trouble with the Spanish in the West Indies. The commanders wisely agreed on a meeting place at Barbuda in the Caribbean "should [they] chance to be separated." The only possible place to rendezvous along their chosen course was Bermuda, and superstitious sailors would do anything to avoid the "Isle of Devils," where evil spirits would consume the bodies and souls of the unfortunate who landed there.[235]

"We ran a southerly course for the Tropic of Cancer," reported Gabriel Archer from the deck of the *Blessing,* "where having the sun within six or seven degrees right overhead in July, we bore away west."[236] The fleet mostly enjoyed fair weather, even if it grew terribly hot—especially so for the passengers in the crowded decks below.

The sailors had a rough idea of their bearing as they progressed across the Atlantic. They determined their latitude with a cross-staff, viewing the sun in its relative position and comparing it with their astronomical tables. They attempted to use dead reckoning to discover their longitude, which was no more than guess. Still, they knew their approximate course, and considering that they had encountered few problems, experienced navigators such as Christopher Newport could roughly estimate when they might make landfall.[237]

Fortunately, the fleet was able to "keep in friendly consort together, not a whole watch at any time losing the sight each of other" for almost seven weeks.[238] They rode the gentle breezes to their destination and were on schedule to make landfall in Virginia well ahead of the four months it took the original fleet during the winter of 1607. All seemed well.

That the trip was relatively uneventful so far did not mean that it was a pleasant voyage. Most of the passengers were seasick at least at the beginning of the journey, while their bodies grew accustomed to the swaying of the ship. The food and drink was starting to turn after nearly two months in the hold. A few persons showed some of the initial symptoms of scurvy. The quarters were cramped and uncomfortable, with the fetid, stale air from unwashed bodies, spilled chamber pots, and livestock between decks. A breath of fresh air on the top deck brought a welcome respite. The boredom of staring across the unrelieved expanse of the blue ocean was starting to grate on everyone's nerves. The conditions of the passage resembled most of the other relatively successful ocean crossings—miserable but tolerable.

Then things took a turn for the worse. Gabriel Archer blamed the "fervent heat and easy breezes" for the rapid spread of disease on a few of the ships. He reported that "many of our men fell sick of the Calenture," which was a fever on ships in the tropics. Archer and the other frightened passengers saw that "out of two ships was thrown overboard thirty-two persons."[239]

Rumors started flying throughout the fleet, and Archer heard that the *Diamond* "was said to have the plague in her," which was a possibility because of the plague then raging through London and the presence of shipboard rats. Fortunately, Archer wrote, on "the *Blessing* we had not any sick, albeit we had twenty women and children," whom he apparently believed were especially susceptible to disease because of their supposed weak constitutions.

With each body cast into the sea, the passengers and crew wondered who would be next or whether all would perish in the middle of the ocean with no escape.[240] The seamen whispered such terms that the dozens of dead had "come to port" or been "boarded" by the grim reaper. Everyone aboard wanted to have a Christian burial on land and not simply be flung overboard. But it was not possible to keep dead bodies on board because of the health risk and stench, which according to the prevailing miasmatic theory of disease would have made others sick. Sometimes bodies were tied down with cannonballs to give them the closest thing possible to a marked grave in the ground.[241]

People aboard the ships would have been horrified to witness sea creatures feeding off their dead. One time a sailor noted that "ten or twelve sharks hankered about the ship for another such meal, they having met with the poor greasy cook." Another seaman wrote that anyone who died at sea inevitably became "meat for the fishes of the sea."[242]

Since so many people died from fever and presented such an immediate threat to the health of all, there was little ceremony for the dead. The Reverend Richard Buck from the *Sea Venture* would have said a few words to calm the passengers of that ship, although the captains of the ships would have overseen any burial ceremony. Others joined in silent prayers both for the souls of the dead and for themselves. Family members and friends wept and sought comfort. It was customary to fire off cannons to commemorate the dead, although the fleet preferred to continue in stony silence, especially since it did not lose any of the important gentlemen adventurers.[243]

Meanwhile, the summer sun boiled the cauldron of equatorial Atlantic waters, which absorbed the heat and were heated to over eighty degrees. The heat evaporated massive amounts of unseen water vapor, which rode upward convection currents and cooled as it rose higher and higher. The water vapor encountered lower temperatures and pressures in the updraft and condensed into tiny water droplets. Sailors could see cumulus and cumulonimbus thunderclouds forming overhead.

The sailors noticed the winds picking up and building into a gust. The sails bellied tautly in their lines, and the ships crested over the growing ocean swells. The men of Neptune knew that a storm was blowing in.

Menacing thunderclouds could no longer hold the water and dropped heavy downpours of rain back into the ocean. George Somers and the other captains calmly ordered their crews into action, and men not on watch sprang from their hammocks. Most of the storms were spent quickly and finished with an anticlimactic light tropical rain.

A few survived, however. They were fed by the warm ocean waters. The storms grew and the pressure continued to drop. The planet's rotation and the easterlies caused a slow vortex to form that proceeded on a westward drift around ten miles per hour, paralleling the equator.

The hurricane began its slow, steady crawl across the Atlantic. As it grew, the storm developed a more clearly defined shape and center eye. The storm intensified and became a full-fledged hurricane, a deadly monster.

The hurricane was only a few hundred miles across and unlikely to cause a direct hit on any ships crossing the Atlantic. Unfortunately, the trajectory of the hurricane and the English fleet were on a collision course.

As dawn emerged in the early morning light of July 25, the crews aboard the fleet bound for Virginia were roused from their hammocks for their regular four-hour shift and set about their tasks. The early morning was pleasant as the sun peeked over the horizon. The Caribbean heat was mitigated somewhat by brisk winds. It was the Feast of St. James Day.

Saint James was a fisherman called by Jesus to be one of the twelve apostles. He was later martyred by King Herod's grandson in 44 AD. During the Middle Ages, his bones were treated as relics and moved to Spain, where they were visited by pilgrims. The English sailors aboard the fleet had a somewhat ambiguous regard for the saint. They revered him as a patron saint of fishermen who was associated with the symbol of the oyster shell. On the other hand, he was the patron saint of Spain, the hated enemy.

Indeed, the English sailors might not have celebrated the feast day at all. Although Europeans had an annual calendar so filled with holy days that many employers complained that their workers feasted more than worked, at sea it was a different story. "All the days were alike to us, and many times it fell out that we had more work on a Sabbath day than we did on other days," noted one sailor. They simply had neither the time nor inclination to spend their hours in devotion. Moreover, the Protestant Reformation had attacked the veneration of the Catholic saints, and as a result many feast days were eliminated (to the chagrin of many workers).[244]

The captains and crews quietly noted the strengthening winds throughout the day. Taking advantage of the opportunity, they rode the winds whipping their unfurled sails toward their destination at a brisk four to five knots. As the morning progressed, the steadily increasing winds caused whitecaps to appear and choppy swells to shake the ship with a growing intensity.

Gabriel Archer thought that they were "about one hundred and fifty leagues distant from the West Indies, in crossing the Gulf of Bahama." John Hawkins also believed they were very close to the Bahamas, but their exact location is unknown. They were probably a few hundred miles to the east, roughly in the vicinity of longitude 70° west and latitude 26° north.[245]

In the distance, a sailor's worst nightmare—a massive hurricane—appeared across the breadth of the horizon, "the clouds gathering thick upon us and the winds singing and whistling most unusually."[246] The hurricane approached the ships at a steady pace of ten or twelve miles per hour. Lightning flashed and peals of thunder boomed louder with each moment as the fleet inexorably moved closer to the storm.

The captains barked orders and the mariners furled the sails to prevent tearing. The crew of the *Sea Venture* was forced to cut loose the ketch with twenty persons aboard. They "cast off our pinnace, towing the same until then astern"; the people aboard the boat were consigned to the angry seas. They were never heard from again.[247] The passengers on the other ships went below and sought shelter; many of them prayed.

Hurricane-force winds began howling in every corner of the ships. Rain started to deluge the ships. The massive seas underneath the behemoth reached twenty feet high. William Strachey recorded, "A dreadful storm and hideous began to blow from out the northeast, which swelling and roaring as it were by fits, some hours with more violence than others."[248]

The eight ships quickly lost sight of one another as they were tossed about by the dreadful storm. In the driving rain, men could barely make out the entire length of their own ships. As one eyewitness wrote, "This tempest separated all our fleet one from another." They could not do anything to help one another under such conditions anyway—each crew was completely on its own.[249]

Day turned to night in the inky darkness of the swirling storm clouds, frightening the passengers even more. The hurricane "beat all light from heaven, which like a hell of darkness turned black upon us, so much the more fuller the horror, as in such cases horror and fear use to overrun the troubled and overmastered senses of all."[250] Another report stated, "The heavens were obscured and made an Egyptian night of three days perpetual horror."[251]

The hurricane overwhelmed sailors' and the passengers' senses completely as they numbly held on for their lives, expecting death at any second. The screeching winds topped seventy and eighty miles per hour. Soon, however, they blew almost one hundred miles per hour, drowning out all but the loudest screams and shouts. "The ears lay so sensible to the terrible cries and murmurs of the winds."[252]

The passengers huddled closely together and clung to one another. Occasional screams were heard above the din and only served to dampen everyone's spirits and instill greater fear.

"Sometimes shrieks in our ship amongst women and passengers not used to such hurly and discomforts made us look one upon the other with troubled hearts and panting bosoms." However, most of their "clamors drowned in the winds, and the winds in thunder."[253]

Prayers muttered by the passengers were only heard by God. "Prayers might well be in the heart and lips, but drowned in the outcries of the officers," not to mention the fierce winds. Their prayers, however, went unanswered when the fierce screams of the winds increased in intensity hour after hour. "Instantly the winds (as having gotten their mouths now free and at liberty) spoke more loudly and grew tumultuous and malignant."[254]

While the passengers prayed, they were surprised to hear the crew singing songs and hurling curses at the tempest. Besides the fact that sailors usually declared impieties and expletives anyway, the seamen believed that praying during a storm was bad luck.[255]

The pounding rain struck the sailors on deck, painfully stinging them with what felt like millions of tiny darts. Visibility was reduced to zero. "It could not be said to rain," William Strachey noted ironically, "the waters like whole rivers did flood in the air." The imperiled ships rocked violently in the thrashing seas, barely recovering from one wave when another struck. The "seas were as mad as fury and rage could make them." Everyone was soaked from head to foot.[256]

The ships were completely at the mercy of the violent seas. "Our sails wound up lay without their use." The men took turns struggling mightily to control the whipstaff steering the ship, if only a little so that the waves would not crash into the ships broadside. "Sometimes eight men were not enough to hold the whipstaff in the steerage and the tiller below in the gunner room—by which may be imagined the strength of the storm."[257]

The hurricane was "so violent that men could scarce stand upon the decks."[258] Tables and chairs, game boards, and cooking pots rolled back and forth across the decks, threatening to batter and bruise or break an exposed limb. The cannons and their lead cannonballs, weighing almost ten pounds, were secured before they destroyed the *Sea Venture*. People were thrown about, crashing into bulkheads like rag dolls. Some of the immense waves crashed completely over the decks, inundating the ships and threatening to drag them down or roll them over. "There was not a moment in which the sudden splitting or instant oversetting of the ship was not expected."

The passengers were not the only ones who were afraid; the crew was similarly terrified but kept their fear at bay in front of the passengers. "The company, as who was most armed and best prepared was not a little shaken."[259] Another wrote, "The skill of the mariners was confounded."[260]

Finally, the clouds parted and the sun presented a very welcome sight. The sea began to calm as the winds died down. Some passengers began to cry from the stress; others prayed in thanksgiving to God for ending the storm. Some did both. They hugged one another and checked themselves to make sure they were in one piece. They rubbed their bruises and helped those who were more severely injured. "For four and twenty hours the storm in a restless tumult had blown so exceedingly, as we could not apprehend in our imaginations any possibility of greater violence."[261]

Their joy, however, was soon crushed after the brief respite—they had just been in the eye of the hurricane. From their view another hurricane apparently struck the ships; this one more violent yet. They found the second storm, "not only more terrible, but more constant, fury added to fury, and one storm urging a second more outrageous than the former; whether it so wrought upon our fears or indeed met with new forces." Strachey added, "It pleased God to bring a great affliction yet upon us." The fleet was drawn into the deadly right quadrant of the hurricane. With redoubled effort, the hurricane unleashed the worst of its strength against its fatigued victims.[262]

For two days the ships were tossed about by the tempest. The crew was utterly exhausted and moving only by instinct. The passengers regretted ever deciding to come aboard and thought the end was at hand. They were losing all hope that they would survive the hurricane. They said prayers, but "nothing heard that could give comfort, nothing seen that might encourage hope." The ships could not endure such a beating forever. Sooner or later a mighty wave would crush the ships, and they would sink to their watery graves.[263]

The ships struggled individually to remain seaworthy and regroup with each other. Meanwhile, it seemed that God's worst affliction was sent against the flagship and the colony's leaders.

~ Chapter Ten ~

THE SINKING OF THE *SEA VENTURE*

The *Sea Venture* eventually succumbed to the power of the hurricane. The incessant hammering of the waves tore open the caulked seams in the hull, which started taking on water quickly. The ship began to sink. "In the beginning of the storm we had received likewise a mighty leak. And the ship, in every joint almost having spewed out her oakum before we were aware (a casualty more desperate than any other that a voyage by sea draweth with it) was grown five feet suddenly deep with water above her ballast, and we almost drowned within whilst we sat looking when to perish from above. This, imparting no less terror than danger, ran through the whole ship with much fright and amazement, startled and turned the blood."[264]

Even the most experienced and bravest sailor was frightened, perhaps because he knew precisely how much danger they were in because of the leak. "The most hardy mariner of them all, insomuch as he that before happily felt not the sorrow of others, now began to sorrow for himself when he saw such a pond of water so suddenly broken in, and which he knew could not (without present avoiding) but instantly sink him."[265] Their blood ran cold.

The *Sea Venture* was not destroyed, as the crew and passengers feared, but she was badly damaged. Numb from fatigue and cold, they could not believe they had survived the hurricane when gradually the winds stilled, the rain ended, and the sea calmed. They had no time to reflect on their situation, however, because they were not yet out of danger.

The flagship, still carrying Governor Thomas Gates, Admiral George Somers, Vice Admiral Christopher Newport, and Jamestown's instructions and charter, survived the storm but had a gash in its bottom that was taking in copious amounts of seawater. She could still sink at any moment.

Moreover, they were all alone on the wide ocean. The might of the hurricane had scattered the fleet. For all Somers and his men knew, the other ships were lost and their crews and passengers dead. The *Sea Venture* was in no condition to make for Virginia. "Without bearing one inch of sail," she drifted in the currents. The leaders hoped to link up with the rest of the ships along the way by chance and by some miracle save their ship.[266]

The exhausted crew immediately went below to search for the leak so they could seal it and prevent the sinking of the *Sea Venture*. The ship still rocked in the giant swells as they carefully examined the hold by candlelight, silently "creeping along the ribs viewing the sides, searching every corner, and listening in every place, if they could hear the water run." The crew found and plugged many small leaks with chunks of dried beef that expanded when they became waterlogged. But it was "to no purpose," as the men could not find the source of the major leak that was steadily filling the boat with water.[267]

The men worked continuously at the vessel's rudimentary pumps, the muscles of their arms straining with the effort. Others formed a line and hoisted weighty buckets of water to the top deck, where they were dumped and returned below. Despite the Herculean effort by the fatigued men, the water in the hold continued to rise inexorably. The men cursed when the pumps became choked with soggy biscuits, since tons of hardtack floated in the murky water. But they also thought that it might be a clue to discovering the source of the leak. Since they believed that the water was pouring in through a leak in the bread room, the carpenter went down and "ripped up all the room." But still the leak remained hidden from view.[268]

The countermeasures failed to work because the violent seas rocked the ship and tore at her seams. A passenger noted, "So much water as covered two tier of hogsheads above the ballast, that our men stood up to the middles with buckets, barricos, and kettles to bail out the water and continually pumped for three days and three nights together without any intermission, and yet the water seemed rather to increase than to diminish."[269]

Somers tried his best to rouse the spirits of his men. He "most comfortably encouraged the company to follow their pumping, and by no means to cease bailing out of the water." Somers stayed on the poop deck, "where he sat three days and three nights together without meals and little or no sleep, steering the ship to keep her as upright as he could (for otherwise she must needs instantly have foundered)." His example motivated the crew and passengers to exert themselves beyond their normal endurance to save the vessel.[270]

For his part, Thomas Gates was a governor who would rule once they landed but had no formal authority on the wide ocean. The gentleman adventurer sprang into action, helping Somers control the perilous situation and provide much-needed leadership for the terrified people on the ship. Gates divided the 140 men on the *Sea Venture* into three work crews and assigned them to different parts of the ship. Each man had alternated an hour of grueling labor and an hour to recover his strength and sleep. They stripped to their waists and worked day and night, losing track of time in their exhaustion. Soon the fatigued men became confused and had difficulty performing the simplest tasks. "Then men might be seen to labor (I may say well) for life, and the better sort, even our governor and admiral themselves, not refusing their turn…kept their eyes waking and their thoughts and hands working, with tired bodies and wasted spirits, three days and four nights."[271]

The men were suffering from their grueling efforts, working "destitute of outward comfort and desperate of any deliverance." But they continued nevertheless, working together to save their own life and that of everyone else on board. Their actions were "testifying how mutually willing they were yet by labor to keep each other from drowning, albeit each one drowned whilest he labored." No one stopped working, lest he let down the others who continued pumping water from the hold.[272]

During these exertions, a colossal wave broke "upon the poop and quarter [decks and] upon us, as it covered our ship from stern to stem." The seamen coughed up buckets of salt water and desperately tried to scream. "Like a garment or a vast cloud, it filled for a while within, from the hatches up to the spar deck." Tons of water violently swept the men and women off their feet and threw the helmsman so roughly that "it was God's mercy it had not split him." Several more feet of water filled the sinking ship.

A second wave—this one of a wave of terror amongst the people—engulfed the ship just as surely as the ocean had. One man said, "For my part, I thought her already in the bottom of the sea."[273] Governor Gates responded to the despondency that overtook the men. He heartened their spirits with inspiring speeches and by the authority of his person. He waded out of the flooded hold and confidently asserted that if he were going to die, he would do so under the open sky "in the company of his old friends." They recovered their determination and "not a passenger, gentleman or other, after he began to stir and labor but was able to relieve his fellow and make good his course."[274]

Those who struggled to keep the *Sea Venture* afloat worked mostly in darkness while it was still caught in the clutches of the storm; the hurricane blotted out daylight and starlight. "The heavens looked so black upon us that it was not possible the elevation of the Pole might be observed, nor a star by night, not sunbeam by day was to be seen." Then, suddenly, Somers was on watch on the deck when he called to the sailors and passengers and pointed toward the top of the mainmast. They were amazed when they looked up and saw "an apparition of a little round light like a faint star, trembling and streaming along with a sparkling blaze half the height upon the mainmast, and shooting sometimes from shroud to shroud, tempting to settle as it were upon any of the four shrouds." The men stood completely still, mouths gaping open, mesmerized by the phenomenon.[275]

As they drifted along, the blue light of St. Elmo's fire danced on the masts for "three or four hours together, or rather more, half the night it kept with us; running sometimes along the mainyard to the very end, and then returning." To their disappointment, it abruptly vanished: "But upon a sudden, toward the morning watch, they lost the sight of it and knew not what way it made." William Strachey reported that the "superstitious seamen make many constructions of this sea fire, which nevertheless is usual in storms."[276]

Strachey knew that sailors from different regions of Europe had slightly different names for what they had seen. The Italians, for example, "who lie open to the Adriatic and Tyrrhene Sea, call it (a sacred body) *Corpo sancto*." The Spaniards called it St. Elmo's fire "and have an authentic and miraculous legend for it."[277] St. Elmo's fire was a "corposant" or starlike mass that appeared after a storm at sea. Saint Elmo was a diminutive of Saint Erasmus, the patron saint of Mediterranean sailors. He generally appeared "like a Great Ball of fire" or a "small star" affixed to a mast.[278]

Similarly, the Greeks looked back into their mythical past and regarded the lights as Castor and Pollux. This pair of brothers spent half of their time on earth and half in heaven. Their mother was Leda, the wife of a Spartan king, who bore Castor and Clytemnestra (the wife of Agamemnon) by the mortal king and Helen and Pollux by Zeus. Castor and Pollux were regarded as the special protectors of sailors.

Strachey relates the common belief that "if one only appeared without the other, they took it for an evil sign of great tempest."[279] Another seafarer agreed: "The seamen have an observation that when the meteors called Castor and Pollux come not together, that it was a bad omen." If the brothers appeared together as two lights, it portended fair weather and good fortune.[280]

Strachey believed that hard work would determine the fate of the ship, not a superstitious sign. "Be it what it will, we laid other foundations of safety or ruin, then in the rising or falling of it." If the light had actually helped them to reckon their position, it "struck amazement, and a reverence in our devotions, according to the due of a miracle." But as it was, "it did not light us any whit the more to our known way." They continued to drift "now (as do hoodwinked men) at all adventures, sometimes north, and northeast, then north and by west, and sometimes half the compass."[281]

They were lost, wandering aimlessly on the ocean and ready to sink at any moment. They continued their losing battle with the leaks in the ship. Despite bailing several tons of water every day, *Sea Venture* still held ten feet of water in her bottom.

Somers concluded that they would have to lighten their load

and ordered the men to throw tons of materials overboard. They tore down the ship's rigging and jettisoned it. They dumped their trunks and chests, conceding that their lives were more valuable than any of their possessions. They threw over "many a butt of beer, hogsheads of oil, cider, wine, and vinegar," deciding to save themselves from the sinking ship and later worry about provisions. Recognizing that the ocean presented a much more imminent threat than any Spanish privateers, they "heaved away all our ordnance on the starboard side." They were leaving a trail of debris and hope behind the drifting ship.[282]

They considered cutting down the mainmast, a move that would improve the ship's seaworthiness but simultaneously doom her ability to sail. The men hardly cared, "for we were spent, and our men so weary as their strengths together failed them with their hearts, having travailed now from Tuesday till Friday morning, day, and night, without either sleep or food."[283]

The work teams pumped out an estimated hundred tons of water every four hours, and still the *Sea Venture* slowly took on more water. They were expecting their deaths and were ready to consign themselves to the sea. They saw no escape from their immediate predicament. After four fruitless and exhausting days there was a "general determination to have shut up hatches, and commending our sinful souls to God, committed the ship to the mercy of the gale."[284]

Even the typically irreverent sailors commended themselves into "the mercy of their mighty God and redeemer." They lost all hope of rescue and "inevitable danger, which ever man had proposed and digested to himself, of present sinking."[285]

As they faced their deaths, a few opened up the barrels of rum and other spirits and drank themselves into a stupor. "Some of them, having some good and comfortable waters in the ship, fetched them and drunk the one to the other, taking their last leave one of the other, until their more joyful and happy meeting in a more blessed world." Luckily for the nearly 150 people aboard, most of the crew had an instinct for survival, and they had excellent leaders. [286]

Somehow they found the will to press on for just a little bit longer with their final reserves of energy. Sylvester Jourdain believed he saw God working through the efforts of the men to help themselves by bailing out the water: "Through which weak means it pleased God to work so strongly as the water was stayed for that little time (which, as we all much feared, was the last period of our breathing)." [287]

Just when all hope was lost and "no man dreamed of such happiness," Somers cried "Land!" when he spotted a large island chain in the distance. The ship was completely at the mercy of the elements, when Jourdain wrote, "It pleased God out of his most gracious and merciful providence, so to direct and guide our ship (being left to the mercy of the sea) for her most advantage." [288] The spent men, who had been lying down in every corner of the ship, suddenly revived and renewed their efforts to bail out the water. "Every man bustled up and gathered his strength and feeble spirits together to perform as much as their weak force would permit him." [289]

Somers ordered the boatswain to take a sounding to measure their depth. He dropped the knotted line and discovered that they were floating in thirteen fathoms of water as they approached the island with its dangerous reefs. Another sounding recorded the water's depth at seven fathoms and then only four. Since they could not safely drop their anchor and disembark, Somers ordered the crew to "run her ashore as near the land as we could." [290] Although it was a highly dangerous maneuver, the sight of land cheered everyone's souls, and they braced for impact. The island loomed larger in their sight as they came within a mile of the beautiful beaches.

The *Sea Venture* struggled over the last leg of her final, desperate journey. The passengers and crew lurched forward as the ship ground over a reef and then shuddered to a stop between two massive rocks. The ship was lodged firmly and not going any farther.

The *Sea Venture* had massive tears rent into the bottom of the hull from the collision with the coral reef below. Normally, such a position would have been a horrible predicament. But in this case, the ship was fortunately stuck and gave the crew sufficient time to load as many passengers as they could safely aboard the skiffs and rowed them through the crystal-clear waters to the beaches before going back for the rest.

The weary sailors saved every person on the *Sea Venture* and even brought ashore the mastiff and several pigs. But as the mariners soon realized and the passengers would soon discover, they had landed on Bermuda, the "Isle of Devils." They were castaways who had survived the horrific ordeal of the sinking of the *Sea Venture* only to drift to an island that would surely seal their doom. This new discovery frightened them as much as the tempest had.

Chapter Eleven

THE FALL OF JOHN SMITH

The condition of the rest of the fleet bound for Jamestown was only marginally better than its lost flagship *Sea Venture*. The hurricane had nightmarishly held the fleet in its grips for forty-eight hours before finally swirling off, leaving the weather-beaten and scattered fleet on the wide Atlantic.

The first thing each of the captains did was to check on his crew and passengers. Some were lost in the storm, and many were injured with bruises and broken bones. All were waterlogged and seasick.

All hands assessed the damage to the ships; some were in a terrible state. Masts were damaged or blown down, sails were torn and in need of mending, rigging was broken, and leaks had to be patched as best as possible to keep the boats seaworthy.

Meanwhile, the captains sent boys up any safe masts to scan the horizon for any sign of the other ships. Within a few days, four ships sighted one another and managed to sail together.

The sailors were eager to help out their fellow jack-tars. Some boarded the *Unity* to aid her because many of her crew were incapable of doing their jobs. "The *Lion* first, and after the *Falcon* and the *Unity,* got sight of our ship [the *Blessing*]…The *Unity* was sore distressed when she came up with us, for of seventy land men, she had not ten sound, and all her seamen were down, but only the master and his boy with one poor sailor, but we relieved them."[291]

The *Sea Venture* remained separated from the four ships, but that was hardly surprising due to the severity of the hurricane. It was certainly troubling that the governor, admiral, vice admiral, and the instructions for the colony were missing. "Four ships came together again, but they heard nothing of the admiral."[292]

The captains assumed the others were sunk or on their way to Virginia. Either way, in their condition, they decided it was safer to sail directly for the colony rather than rendezvousing in the West Indies. Perhaps the *Sea Venture* and the rest of the fleet would be waiting there when they arrived. It was not unprecedented for a separated fleet to meet at their destination. A favorable wind pushed the injured ships over the waves. "So we lay a way directly for Virginia, finding neither current nor wind opposite."[293]

Capt. John Ratcliffe of the *Diamond* was not heard from either by the larger remnant of the fleet. But the *Diamond* linked up with the *Swallow,* and the captains made the same decision to sail toward Virginia.

The first group of ships limped into Jamestown on August 11, and the second arrived a few days later. Their tumultuous journey was finally over.

The first fleet was likely met with much fanfare. The colonists were hungry and relieved to see the relief fleet arrive. After viewing the distressed condition of the newcomers, however, the colonists ran to help the seafarers disembark and inquired into their well-being. As they unloaded belongings and supplies from the ships, ate a meal, and took a well-deserved rest, the travelers told of their terrifying encounter with the hurricane. The arrival of the second group of boats raised expectations that the flagship might also have survived and would be sailing for Virginia. But these hopes faded and tensions grew with every passing day.

It quickly became apparent that each group—the newcomers and the existing colonists—was profoundly disappointed with the other. The ships brought precious few supplies; most of these had been aboard the *Sea Venture.* All the fleet had really brought were four hundred hungry mouths to feed at a time when there was little food. On the other hand, the newcomers quickly discovered that they had been duped. Virginia was not exactly the land flowing with milk and honey as they expected. What they found instead was shocking and frightening.

The Virginia Company intended for the new settlers in Gates's fleet to swell the population of Jamestown to ensure the colony's survival. It did not foresee that rather than contributing to the colony's success, the new settlers would significantly add to its woes.

Virginia had experienced a terrible drought all summer. The settlers had been able to store very few provisions for the winter, so their larders stood virtually empty. "Those provisions at a small allowance of biscuit, cake, and a small measure of wine or beer to each person for a day" was all they had to eat. The hundreds of new colonists rapidly ravished the supply of corn. "They fell upon that small quantity of corn…and in three days at the most wholly devoured it."[294] The outlook for the coming year was bleak.

With Gates and the instructions for the colony missing, plus the return of President John Smith's greatest enemies, the colony broke into factions and anarchy. John Ratcliffe, Gabriel Archer, George Percy, and other newly arrived gentlemen fiercely contested Smith's right to continue as president of the colony. They asserted their rightful authority to rule the colony, because the fleet had received a patent from the king and had been sent by the Virginia Company. Gates and the instructions may have been lost, but they averred that those were a mere technicality. Archer complained that Smith was an ambitious tyrant who sought to "strengthen his authority…and gave not any due respect to many worthy gentlemen that came in our ships."[295] Ratcliffe agreed, writing that Smith "reigned [as] sole governor without assistants, and would at first admit of no council but himself."[296]

John Smith hotly contested their right to rule the colony. Smith believed that he had single-handedly saved the colony by engaging in tough trade with the Indians for corn, setting the men to work, placing the settlement's pigs on Hog Island, and thwarting Indian attacks. In his mind, only he understood what was needed to survive. He viewed his foes as "factious spirits" who tried to "strengthen themselves with those new companies so railing and exclaiming against him" and conspiring in any number of plots against him. Smith believed they were attempting to "usurp the government" with their rebellious and ambitious nature. In this struggle of wills, the only losers were the colonists. Factionalism divided them and left them without any form of government when it was never more sorely needed.[297]

Amid the chaos, and with so many new colonists and few provisions to feed them, Smith dispersed the colonists in several groups to other locations. He removed them from Jamestown to relieve the demand for food among the 250 settlers who remained. Some of the gentlemen who contended with him for power were sent away as well. He sent Francis West (Lord De La Warr's younger brother) to the falls with 140 colonists, while John Martin and George Percy took 60 settlers to Nansemond near the mouth of the James.

The werowance at Nansemond refused to trade with the English and declined any offer to sell a small island so that they would settle there. Martin sent two messengers to negotiate a price, including copper hatchets and other useful items. They were not heard from for some time, and the Indians informed the English that "they were sacrificed, and that their brains were cut and scraped out of their heads with mussel shells." The Englishmen responded savagely to the violence, driving the Indians from the island, burning their homes, ransacking their sacred areas, and carrying away bracelets, copper, and pearls. They also took the chief's son and another Indian hostage. A boy accidentally shot the chief's son, who escaped wounded and bleeding. Percy wanted to plunder the Indians' supply of corn, but Martin refused because of the hazard to his men. Percy returned to Jamestown to deal with the political struggle.[298]

At the falls, several of West's men were killed or wounded when they straggled from the fort. Smith visited the garrison a few times and argued with West about where best to situate the men. Smith wanted West to settle in the village of Powhatan, recently acquired from Wahunsonacock's son, Parahunt, because it was a more defensible location. After West refused to do so, some Powhatan warriors killed several Englishmen outside of the protection of the fort and then assaulted the fort itself. "They slew many and so frightened the rest as their prisoners escaped, and they retired with the swords and cloaks of those who had been slain."[299]

George Percy and others accused Smith of betraying his countrymen in his lust for power. They charged that he had "incensed and animated" the Indians against the English settlers, even informing the enemy that "our men had no more powder left them than would serve for one volley of shot." Although the accusations were false, Smith returned to the falls a third time while West went to Jamestown. Smith ordered the settlers to relocate to the village of Powhatan, which West bitterly resented when he returned and discovered what Smith had done.

While Smith was sailing back to Jamestown, he had a terrible accident that may have been perpetrated by his enemies: his powder bag exploded. It burned "his flesh from his body and thighs nine or ten inches square in a most pitiful manner." With his clothes aflame and his skin bubbling, Smith screamed and desperately leaped into the river "to quench the tormenting fire frying him in his clothes." The people aboard fished his nearly lifeless body out of the river "nearly bereft of his senses by reason of his torment." Without any medical attention, he traveled the rest of the way to Jamestown in excruciating pain. He was carried from the ship to his bed when they disembarked.[300]

As if that were not enough, Smith reported that the conspirators—Martin, Ratcliffe, Archer, and their confederates—plotted to dispatch him while he was sleeping "in his bed." The would-be assassins apparently lost heart, but they settled for deposing him and seizing the reins of government while he lay dying.[301]

Smith saw that he was defeated and needed a doctor, and he resolved to sail for England. His enemies decided to follow up the attempt on his life by discrediting him before the company. His longtime enemy, John Ratcliffe, informed Lord Salisbury, "This man is sent home to answer some misdemeanors whereof I am persuaded he can scarcely clear himself from great imputation of blame." In October, John Smith left Jamestown in disgrace, despite his best efforts for more than two years to help the colony succeed.[302]

Since they were rid of Smith, the gentlemen of the colony elected a new president. Not surprisingly, Martin, Ratcliffe, and West, along with a few allies, formed the governing council. They selected George Percy, the twenty-nine-year-old son of an earl, to be the new president. He, like many other gentlemen adventurers, had been educated at Oxford and the Middle Temple. Percy may have sought adventure in Virginia, but he was a dandy and was a very weak leader to select in Smith's or Gates's absence.

When Wahunsonacock learned of Smith's departure, he concluded that his most formidable foe among the English no longer presented a challenge to his desire to be rid of the infernal invaders. Moreover, he understood how short of provisions the English were. He launched an all-out war to drive them out of Virginia, using his warriors to besiege the Jamestown settlement and banning trade among the Indians to starve them out.

President Percy sent Ratcliffe to Point Comfort to build a fort and fish for food, the latter to relieve some of the pressure on the dwindling food supply. Meanwhile, when Martin left Nansemond for Jamestown to escape an impending mutiny, seventeen men stole a boat, pretending to be departing on a trade mission. As they attempted to flee from the colony, they were slaughtered by Indians. The president thought that they "were served according to their just deserts, for not any of them were heard of after, and in all likelihood were cut off and slain by the savages."[303]

A few days later, Martin's subordinate, Michael Sicklemore, and his desperately hungry men went to the Indians to "seek for bread and relief among them." They were killed, and their mouths were scornfully "stopped full of bread" as a sign of what would happen to any Englishmen who sought food from the Indians. The remaining men decided that staying at Nansemond was suicidal and sailed back to Jamestown. Unfortunately, their return further strained the settlement's dwindling food supplies, as they "[fed] upon the poor store we had left us." Indian attacks claimed several of West's men and forced him to abandon the falls and return to Jamestown.[304]

The return of the dispersed settlers to Jamestown in early November 1609 was extremely troubling. President Percy could not turn the men away. "In charity we could not deny them to participate with us," he wrote, even if it meant only "a poor allowance of half a can of meal for a man a day." When Percy asked Daniel Tucker to estimate how long their stores would last, Tucker reported that he expected their pitiful rations to last only three months, perhaps four if they somehow tightened their belts even more.[305]

Wahunsonacock continued to pressure to the Jamestown settlement. Young Indian interpreter Henry Spelman had been among the Powhatans for three weeks when Wahunsonacock sent him to Jamestown with a message: "Tell them that if they would bring their ship and some copper, he would fraught her back with corn." The werowance's subsequent actions reveal that he was plotting to murder the Englishmen who came.[306]

Spelman delivered the message to the president and waited for an answer. Although the settlers had lost dozens of men to Indian attacks, a desperate George Percy decided that he had no choice but to send a trade delegation to Wahunsonacock. He ordered John Ratcliffe to take fifty men to "procure victuals and trade by the way of commerce and trade." Ratcliffe was a poor replacement for the tough John Smith, whom he had helped drive out of the colony.[307] He lacked the skill that Smith had demonstrated in trading with the Indians and made numerous mistakes that led to disaster.

Although Ratcliffe had "Powhatan's son and daughter aboard his pinnace," he did not use them properly. Smith would have held on to them as bargaining chips. Even Percy recognized that Ratcliffe should have detained them, since they would have been "a sufficient pledge for his safety." But the "credulous" Ratcliffe made his first mistake when he but allowed them to "depart again on shore."[308]

The "subtle old fox" Wahunsonacock received Ratcliffe warmly and seemed willing to trade, leading the Englishman to a storehouse "above half a mile from the barge." The pair exchanged gifts and then began trading the following day, Ratcliffe offering "pieces of copper and beads and other things according to the proportion of baskets which they brought." Unfortunately, Ratcliffe—like Christopher Newport—offered terms that were far too generous. Powhatan, who already had the upper hand over the English generally and was toying with them, offered few bushels of corn for the copper.[309]

The Powhatans also deceived the English by "pulling or bearing up the bottom of their baskets with their hands, so that the less corn might fill them." Ratcliffe and his men discovered the fraudulent practice and angrily protested, but Wahunsonacock denied the charge and simply left.

Meanwhile, Ratcliffe foolishly allowed his men to be lured into small groups by Powhatan women in different homes. Wahunsonacock, the "sly old king," bid him time until the Englishmen were separated and then "cut them all off." The men were easily slaughtered when warriors surprised and overwhelmed them. Ratcliffe was taken alive, and the chief ordered him "bound unto a tree naked with a fire before." Powhatan women scraped the flesh "from his bones with mussel shells [which were then] thrown into the fire" while he was still alive. Poor Ratcliffe witnessed the grisly scene of his own torture and slow execution until he lost consciousness.[310]

Wahunsonacock dispatched his warriors to assault the few Englishmen remaining in the pinnace. William Phetiplace and a few sailors were anxiously awaiting word from Ratcliffe when they were assaulted. Several were hit by arrows in the assault, and many were killed. The English returned fire with their muskets and pistols. War cries and the screams of the wounded filled the air as the Phetiplace frantically tried to sail away. The Powhatan warriors and English exchanged fire until the pinnace was safely out of range.

The few survivors of the expedition disembarked at Jamestown and quickly dashed the expectations of the settlers at the fort. They had lost three dozen men and returned without any corn. Percy was running out of options to feed the settlers.

Percy understood that the tribes under the dominion of the Powhatans were overtly hostile and would continue to kill Englishmen or refuse to trade with them. He had no choice but to send Francis West to the more distant Patawomecks in the Chesapeake to trade for "maize and grain." The lives of the settlers depended upon his success. West sailed with thirty-six men and emulated Smith's "harsh and cruel" strong-arm tactics in forcing the Patawomecks to part with some of their food supplies and killed two of them in the process. After West cut off "two of the savages' heads and other extremities," the frightened Patawomecks loaded the pinnace with corn.[311]

On their return to Jamestown, West's party passed by Point Comfort. There, James Davis and his small garrison hailed the *Swallow,* calling out and "acquainting them with our great wants, exhorting them to make all the speed they could to relieve us." The starving men expected West to pull in and share some of the bounty to mitigate their condition temporarily.[312] Rather than disembarking and sharing their provisions, the mariners suddenly hoisted the sails and turned with the wind, sailing directly for the Atlantic. A stunned Davis watched the small ship disappear on the horizon.

The company of men on the *Swallow* had mutinied and demanded that they be allowed to sail for England to have a chance at survival. They understood that returning to Jamestown was a death sentence. West was sympathetic to their (and his own) plight and acceded to his men's wishes to make for home. They had enough provisions to cross the Atlantic and make it safely to England.

The settlers at Jamestown waited in vain for the *Swallow* to return with a supply of corn. The famished men continued to hope until it became clear that West's company would not be returning.

They assumed the Patawomecks had slaughtered West's trade party just as they had Ratcliffe's. When they learned from James Davis that West had sailed east for England, they were furious at being betrayed by their countrymen and being left with neither food nor ship for launching additional trade expeditions.

The Jamestown colonists now faced a terrible predicament. They were starving to death on their meager provisions, and unlike the past few years, they could not get supplies from the native peoples. Those tribes had also killed dozens of the settlers over the last couple of months and pinned them down within the fort. There was very little food, no way to get any more, and no expected supply fleet coming from England. The colony teetered on the brink of disaster as the settlers hourly contemplated their own deaths. If only Thomas Gates and the *Sea Venture* had arrived, though, things would have turned out differently.

Chapter Twelve

THE ISLE OF DEVILS

Hundreds of miles to the east, the survivors of the disastrous hurricane and shipwreck of the Sea Venture were stranded in Bermuda. The leaders, however, were determined to keep everyone alive. Admiral George Somers proudly watched over the rescue effort and directed his men. His first priority, after getting everyone ashore, was to salvage their provisions. During the early afternoon, the sailors had time "to save some good part of our goods and provision which the water had not spoiled." The next priority was to anticipate what materials they would need to get off the island. The sailors rowed between the wreck and the shore over and over, eventually going for whatever was "available for the building and furnishing of a new ship and pinnace, which we made there for the transporting and carrying of us to Virginia." The mariners dismantled the rigging that remained aboard the ruined *Sea Venture* as well as any ropes, sails, nails, planks, and tools. They gathered up loose articles of clothing and household items that might contribute to their survival. After they stripped the ship, all that was left looked like the ribs of a large whale. Within a few days, the pounding of the surf destroyed the last remnants.[313]

The settlers thanked God for providentially landing them on an island where all of their basic necessities were bestowed upon them. The Reverend Richard Buck led the colonists in prayers of thanksgiving when they were deposited on shore. The next day was the Sabbath, and Buck preached two sermons during a morning and afternoon Anglican service. Most of his sermons were appropriately focused on "thankfulness and unity," for he supported the social order and exhorted everyone to obey the will of Thomas Gates as an extension of their fidelity to the king, God and His church, the Great Chain of Being, and the traditions of the English rule of law. Moreover, "every morning and evening at the ringing of a bell we repaired all to public prayer." They had much to be thankful for, although any shirkers were "duly punished." Buck held Communion and performed all the offices and rites of the Anglican profession, including marrying a few couples and christening a few babies.[314]

As the sun dipped brilliantly below the horizon on the first night, the crew and passengers feasted on the fresh food that the island provided. They took generous swigs of the alcohol being passed around. Their moods were finally lightened after their harrowing escape from the hurricane. The campfire gave off welcome heat that dried out their clothes after days of bailing out water. "Our delivery was not more strange in falling so opportunely and happily upon the land, as our feeding and preservation was beyond our hopes and all men's expectations most admirable."[315]

Not everything was as it seemed, however. In fact, the people became downright frightened as the leaders of the expedition and a few sailors informed them that they had landed on Bermuda, nicknamed the "Isle of Devils." They discovered with great shock that it was "the dangerous and dreaded island or rather islands of the Bermuda." The island was superstitiously reputed by sailors to be "so terrible to all that ever touched on them, and such tempests, thunders, and other fearful objects are seen and heard about them, that they be called commonly the Devil's Islands, and are feared and avoided of all sea travelers alive above any other place in the world."[316]

Another chronicler of the shipwreck confirmed that "every man knoweth" from rumors that Bermuda was "a most prodigious and enchanted place affording nothing but gusts, storms, and foul weather." Sailors avoided Bermuda as "they would shun the Devil himself; and no man was ever heard to make for the place, but as against their wills, they have by storms and dangerousness of the rocks, lying seven leagues into the sea, suffered shipwreck." Bermuda was certainly a dangerous place to sail near, with its underwater reefs and tempests, but it was also considered to be occupied by evil spirits.[317]

After a few weeks on the island, though, the people discovered that their horrific fears were completely unfounded. The bountiful land was free of disease, had a temperate climate, and provided for their every need. Thus the island was not a place where devils and wicked spirits lived, nor a place of mythical sea monsters. William Strachey personally hoped that the publication of his account would "deliver the world from a foul and general error" that Bermuda was uninhabitable.[318] The survivors now knew through firsthand experience the island was as "habitable and commodious as most countries of the same climate and situation." Strachey for one had learned an important lesson in the ordeal: "Men ought not to deny everything which is not subject to their own sense." In other words, one had to make up one's own mind rather than relying on the opinions of others.[319]

Once the *Sea Venture* crew and settlers bound for Virginia reached land, they came under the authority of the governor of the colony.

Thomas Gates opened the sealed box with the instructions for the colony and asserted his just and near absolute authority under the command of the Virginia Company. He directed the crew and passengers of the shipwrecked *Sea Venture* to attend to their survival needs immediately. "Every man disposed and applied himself to search for and to seek out such relief and sustentation as the country afforded." He organized them into foraging groups and sent them out to find food and water. There were no rivers or freshwater springs, but one group dug a well near the beach that provided enough water for their needs. They also collected armfuls of firewood to cook whatever food they could find. Others searched for saplings and palm leaves to gather to build primitive shelters.

Some of the crew stayed on the beach and rummaged through the piles of recovered supplies for fishing line and hooks and went out into the gentle surf. George Somers led them, personally casting his line and taking in a great haul of fish. The admiral "went and found out sufficient of many kind of fishes, and so plentiful thereof that in half an hour he took so many great fishes with hooks as did suffice the whole company."

Initially, the men caught baskets of fish and could almost scoop them out of the surf. "Fish is there so abundant that if a man step into the water they will come round about him; so that men were fain to get out for fear of biting. These fishes are very fat and sweet and of that proportion and bigness that three of them will conveniently feed two men."[320]

When they caught much of the fish populations near the shore, they made a flatboat that enabled them to go a little farther out, hooking "angelfish, salmon, bonitos, stingray, horse mackerel, snappers, hogfish, sharks, dogfish, pilchards, mullets, and rockfish." They hunted among the rocky shore for "crayfishes oftentimes greater than any of our best English lobsters." Likewise, they had an abundance of crabs and oysters to feed the company.[321]

The colonists discovered ready sources of meat on the island, much of it from the massive flocks of migratory birds in the area during the autumn and winter. The most abundant birds were nocturnal cahows, which were easily snared when they flew on to the men's arms. They took as many as "three hundred in an hour." One survivor described the scene:

> Our men found a pretty way to take them, which was by standing on the rocks or sands by the seaside and holloing, laughing, and making the strangest outcry that possibly they could. With the noise whereof the birds would come flocking to that place and settle upon the very arms and head of him that so cried, and still creep nearer and nearer, answering the noise themselves; by which our men would weigh them with their hand, and which weighed heaviest they took for the best and let the others alone. And so our men would take twenty dozen in two hours of the chiefest of them; and they were a good and well-relished fowl.[322]

The colonists also easily collected the eggs of the cahows without encountering any aggressive defense by the birds. They were very similar in size and taste to a hen's egg. The eggs were simply plucked out of their nests, even with the birds present.

The islands were also the nesting place of mammoth sea turtles that the company baked and roasted. They were so immense that "one tortoise would go further amongst them than three hogs. One turtle (for so we called them) feasted well a dozen messes, appointing six to every mess." They were easily captured, although it might require three or four men to carry the large creatures.

Most of the company "liked the meat of them very well."[323] The men also consumed their eggs, which were "sweeter than any hen egg; and the tortoise itself is all very good meat and yieldeth great store of oil, which is as sweet as any butter; and one of them will suffice fifty men a meal, at the least."[324]

When there were no fish, birds, or turtles, the men went hunting for wild hogs, which inhabited the islands by the hundreds with no natural predators. The Spanish had deposited them on the island in order to have a ready food supply should sailors be forced to go ashore. The colonists learned of their presence when a wild boar smelled the English swine and came down to investigate. The colonists went out to hunt them with their mastiff and brought home forty or fifty in a single outing, sometimes even alive, because "the dog would fasten on them and hold whilst the huntsmen made in." The colonists "made sties for them," feeding them on berries and slaughtering them for meat when other sources of food were more scarce.[325]

The settlers also ate large palm leaves, which they either roasted to make them taste like fried melons or stewed in order to give them a cabbage flavor, although thankfully "not so offensively... to the stomach." Berries, fruit, and a variety of other natural crops rounded out their diet. The berries also were fermented into an alcoholic drink.

The colonists made salt by boiling seawater and used it to preserve the meat and fish. "Our governor dried and salted and, barreling them up, brought to sea five hundred, for he had procured for salt to be made." Three or four pots were kept constantly boiling to meet the demand.[326]

The provisions on the *Sea Venture* were largely ruined, but the island was endowed with all that they needed to survive and more. Contrary to their expectations when they learned they were on Bermuda, "the air [was] so temperate and the country so abundantly fruitful of all fit necessaries for the sustentation and preservation of man's life that, most in a manner of all our provisions of bread, beer, and victual being quite spoiled in lying long drowned in salt water, notwithstanding we were there for the space of nine months (few days over or under) not only well received, comforted, and with good satiety contented."

They had so much food, Sylvester Jourdain explained, that they even had extra to bring with them to Virginia. "Out of the abundance thereof provided us some reasonable quantity and proportion of provision to carry us for Virginia and to maintain ourselves and that company we found there, to the great relief of them, as it fell out, in their so great extremities."

The people of Virginia were starving and, ironically, were fed by their compatriots who had been shipwrecked on the Isle of Devils. After seeing that their fears were unjustified, the marooned settlers started to believe that God had landed them in Bermuda to gather supplies in order to feed the starving Virginians. "It pleased God that my Lord's coming thither their store was better supplied."

In short, many of the settlers believed Bermuda to be "the richest, healthiest, and pleasing land...and merely natural, as ever man set foot upon."[327] It was a paradise. William Strachey thanked God for bringing the *Sea Venture* to such a beautiful, bountiful island. They never would have sailed for Bermuda—in fact, they would probably have avoided it at all costs had they known what it was. But he thought they were providentially brought there. "It pleased our merciful God to make even this hideous and hated place both the place of our safety and means of our deliverance."[328]

Thomas Gates and the other leaders were eager to get off the island and head for their Virginia destination because that was their national mission. Gates could not abandon that mission and had to pursue every possible means of getting to Virginia. Gates opened the instructions for the colony and discovered the names of the men whom the Virginia Council selected to be members of the local council. They began organizing the men into work teams to fulfill the needs of the settlers and their mission to reach Virginia.

Gates ordered the carpenters and other artisans to refit their longboat to sail to Virginia ahead of the other survivors and make contact with the Jamestown colony. The scouts would then borrow one of Jamestown's boats and sail back to rescue the rest of the survivors. The workers used a combination of the salvage from the *Sea Venture* as well as materials from the island.

The carpenters fit the boat "with a little deck, made of the hatches of our ruined ship...gave her sails and oars." The leaders selected a knowledgeable Plymouth pilot, the master's mate, Henry Ravens, to lead the expedition. Eight hardy sailors volunteered to make the journey in the small boat so soon after their horrific experience during the hurricane and wreck of the *Sea Venture*. Thomas Wittingham, the cape merchant in charge of the storehouse, also agreed to join the venture. Admiral Somers aided their chances for success by making a survey of the treacherous waters around Bermuda.

Governor Gates then had to inform the colony who should govern the settlement in his temporary absence. He imagined the anarchy and struggle for leadership among the ambitious gentlemen when at least a few of the ships had escaped the clutches of the hurricane and arrived without the governor or the instructions for the colony. "For by a long-practiced experience, foreseeing and fearing what innovation and tumult might happily arise amongst the younger and ambitious spirits of the new companies to arrive in Virginia," Gates composed a letter to the colony and gave a commission to the leaders of the colony until he arrived in Jamestown.[329]

Gates chose Peter Winne to serve as temporary governor. The

Virginia Council's instructions listed George Somers as the next ranking official after Gates. John Smith and John Ratcliffe were next, but they had disputes with each other and might polarize the settlement into factions again. John Martin was also named as a council member, but he might have gone down with the *Falcon.* Peter Winne was the next man on the list, outranking two other men at the bottom of council, and Matthew Scrivener was appointed as the council secretary.[330]

Gates also wrote a letter to the Virginia Council, which was to travel indirectly to England. The governor described the predicament of the survivors of the *Sea Venture* wreck, but he informed the council that he was alive and well and preparing to sail to Virginia. Ravens and Wittingham would deliver the letter to the colony, which would dispatch a ship to England with the news. Gates also expressed the hope that the council might charitably dispatch Lord De La Warr's expedition earlier than expected to "redeem us from hence" if it proved necessary.[331]

After stocking the boat with adequate provisions for the trip and working out their position relative to Virginia so that Ravens could plot a course for Jamestown, the eight men boarded the small boat. On Monday, August 28, 1609, they shoved off.

The colonists were not expecting to see them, or any other rescuers, for at least a month. But much to the surprise and dismay of the settlers, Ravens and his crew returned on Wednesday night. The boat could not sail clear of the shoals around the island.

Ravens set sail again in early September. He promised that if he made it to the Jamestown colony, he would return to Bermuda "the next moon with the pinnace belonging to the colony."

Gates appointed "fires prepared as beacons" on high points on the island, and the settlers diligently tended the fires that would signal their position to any ships searching for them. But after a month, they wondered whether any ship would come. After two months, most abandoned hope. "Two moons were wasted upon the promontory...and gave many a long and hopeful look round about the horizon, from the northeast to the southwest, but in vain." The survivors would have to rely upon their own industry and creativity to find a way off the island.[332]

Ravens and his daring crew were never seen again.

Gates faced even more challenges, and a mutiny among his own men on Bermuda nearly doomed his attempt to get to Virginia. He had to establish the rule of law on this island to ensure that the people under his command would survive their predicament. But, he would have to weigh his rule against their rights and liberties, especially when some of them sought to set themselves up as rulers or decided that the island paradise was a good place to settle instead of Virginia.

When Thomas Gates exercised his absolute authority over the colony in the military fashion to which he was accustomed, the individualistic, free men among the colonists bristled. Despite the assertion of what was tantamount to martial law, four major mutinies erupted in the ten months the crew and passengers of the *Sea Venture* resided on Bermuda. Although each plot had its own character, there were a few similarities rooted in the problems of leadership here and at Jamestown. First, free Englishmen refused to be governed according to the martial organization of the colony. Second, the trouble in Jamestown stood in stark contrast to the wonderful experience on Bermuda.

The first mutiny began when Ravens and his crew left on August 28. Gates ordered the men to start building a second pinnace to get them to Jamestown. He commanded Richard Frobisher, a "well-experienced shipwright and skillful workman," to organize the building of the ship. Frobisher had four carpenters and a team of workers at his disposal. They laid the keel for the ship at the water's edge in Building Bay so that the high tides could pull the completed ship into ocean. Frobisher and his carpenters took a careful inventory and used the oak beams, nails, and other materials salvaged from the sunken *Sea Venture* for the forty-foot keel. Every item was used or repaired so that nothing was wasted.

Governor Gates worked just as hard as any man. He felled trees with an axe, hefted them onto his shoulder with some other men, carried them to the work site, and sawed them into planks. He followed the directions of the carpenters without question. Gates spared "no travail of body, nor forbear any care or study of mind" in order to set an example of industry and diligence for the colonists. He used his "own performance [rather] than…authority" to drive them to their best efforts. His leadership style sought to inspire the others with the idea that "example prevails above precepts, and how readier men are to be led by eyes than ears." Yet not everyone was impressed or persuaded.[333]

On September 1, John Want—a religious dissenter who was sympathetic to a radical Puritan view called Brownism, which rejected any civil or ecclesiastical authority in favor of allegiance to the higher authority of God and one's conscience—encouraged six seaman and laborers to stop working on the pinnace. These included carpenter Nicholas Bennett, another religious dissenter against the Anglican Church, and Christopher Carter. The conspirators agreed "not to set their hands to any travail or endeavor which might expedite or forward this pinnace." William Strachey called Bennett a "mutinous and dissembling impostor," because he had made much public "profession of Scripture" in front of the company. Want additionally had made "his own prayers much devout and frequent" but was "both seditious and a sectary in points of religion."[334]

These mutineers told their fellow colonists that Virginia held "nothing but wretchedness and labor must be expected, with many wants, and a churlish entreaty, there being neither that fish, flesh, nor foul." Compared to the difficulties of Virginia, they could remain where they were and plant a successful colony, enjoying a life of "ease and pleasure." The Isle of Devils was actually a beautiful island paradise that provided everything they needed.[335]

The conspirators believed that the shipwreck was a providential sign not only for their temporary survival but for a permanent settlement that resembled a Garden of Eden. Consequently, they proposed to "break from the society of the colony and like outlaws retired into the woods to make a settlement and a habitation there on their party, with whom they proposed to leave our quarter and possess another island by themselves." They could incidentally seize the reins of power of their small island kingdom and govern themselves according to their own consent. Their religious dissent was closely tied to their opposition of Gates's civil authority.[336]

The plot was discovered, and the rebels were hauled before the governor for trial. Gates punished them by granting their wish, sending them to live apart from the colony and fend for themselves on a nearby barren island. It was not long before "they missed comfort, who were far removed from our store." The small island did not have the water, fish, and fowl of the main island, and the mutineers nearly starved to death. They humbly petitioned the governor "fraught full of their seeming sorrow and repentance and earnest vows to redeem the former trespass" if they were allowed to return. Gates pardoned them and readmitted them to the colony of the shipwrecked.[337]

During the fall, George Somers surveyed the waters around the island and mapped the area. Meanwhile, his mariners fished the waters around the island and hunted for game ashore. In late November, it was obvious that Henry Ravens had not succeeded in securing a rescue voyage. Moreover, the castaways had split into two rival camps under Gates and Somers that viewed each other suspiciously. Some in the admiral's camp complained that they recognized "how the pinnace which Richard Frobisher was building would not be of burthen sufficient to transport all our men from thence into Virginia." They suspected that Gates intended to sail off and leave them to their fate.[338]

Somers therefore conferred with Gates and asked him for two skilled carpenters and twenty men to build a second pinnace. The penurious governor claimed that he could spare few men, tools, and materials for the admiral. He gave twenty of "the ablest and stoutest of the company," but only such "tools and instruments as our own use required not." Somers received only a single iron bolt for the entire ship. His men had to adapt and shape dowels to hold the planks together. They also had to innovate with the caulking of the ship. Whereas a supply of oakum and a barrel each of pitch and tar helped seal the *Deliverance* (Somers's ship), the *Patience* (Gates's ship) was caulked with a creative mixture of "lime made of whelk shells, and a hard white stone which we burned in a kiln, slaked with fresh water, and tempered with tortoise's oil."[339]

That winter brought terrible storms that helped feed the frightening reputation of Bermuda. "The islands are often afflicted and rent with tempests—great strokes of thunder, lightning, and rain in the extremity of violence," Strachey reported. During the winter months, "the winds kept in those cold corners, and indeed then it was heavy and melancholy being there." A storm on January 2, 1610, depressed their spirits and nearly destroyed the *Deliverance*. The cradle that held the unfinished ship "being almost carried from her" was set right only with "much difficulty, diligence, and labor" amid the hollowing winds and heavy surf. Gates ordered the men to carry huge stones into the surf and make a breakwater "round about her ribs from stem to stem." More storms—in the form of further mutinies—were gathering over the colony.[340]

In the weeks that followed, Stephen Hopkins began to question the governor's authority. Hopkins was respected because he "had much knowledge in the Scriptures and could reason well therein" and served as the Reverend Buck's assistant in reading the Psalms and biblical verse at Sunday services. Hopkins made complex political arguments about the nature of government on Bermuda. Admiral Somers justly ruled them on the ocean, and General Gates would rightly govern them according to the company's instructions in Virginia, but Hopkins argued that the castaways governed themselves on Bermuda. He argued that "it was no breach...to decline from the obedience of the governor, or refuse to go any further led by his authority, except it so pleased themselves, since the authority ceased when the wreck was committed, and, with it, they were all then freed from the government of any man, and for a matter of conscience it was not unknown to the meanest how much we were therein bound each one to provide for himself and his own family." In other words: the shipwreck disaster broke apart their social compact and placed them in a state of nature, freeing them "from the obedience to the governor." It was every man for himself according to the higher law of one's conscience and obedience to God. Hopkins's dissenting views denied the authority of king and church over an individual's conscience.[341]

Hopkins wanted to remain on the island and enjoy its "abundance by God's providence of all manner of good food." When they "grow weary" of the island paradise, they could always have carpenter Nicholas Bennett "build a small bark" and eventually "get clear from hence [to Virginia] at their own pleasures."

Samuel Sharp and Humphrey Reed had heard enough of this talk and feared being convicted of joining Hopkins's conspiracy if they did not inform the authorities. Sharp and Reed went to Governor Gates and informed him of Hopkins's radical views. The governor immediately ordered Hopkins to be arrested for his "fractious offence" of mutiny and rebellion and clapped him in manacles. Gates presided over a court-martial, which found Hopkins guilty and sentenced him to death. Hopkins penitently and remorsefully pled for his life, crying that his execution would lead to "the ruin of his wife and children." With the entreaty of several gentlemen, Gates was persuaded to pardon the condemned man from the noose.[342]

By March 1610 a great deal of progress had been made on the two pinnaces. But there was a rising tide of resentment among the men in Somers's camp that broke into a "deadly and bloody" conspiracy "in which the life of our governor with many others were threatened." They stole swords, axes, hatchets, saws, and hatchets to execute their nefarious scheme. When some of the conspirators lost their nerve, they went to Gates and informed him of the scheme. The governor could not uncover the names of the ringleaders and told his men to "wear his weapon" and doubled the "sentinels and nightwarders" of the camp. Everyone was advised to "stand upon his guard, his own life not being in safety whilest his next neighbor was not to be trusted."[343]

On the night of March 13, Henry Paine, a gentleman, was deviously collecting weapons when his commander called Paine out for his turn on watch. Paine and the senior officer exchanged heated words, and then Paine "struck at him" and "doubled his blows." He walked away from his duty, scoffing at the governor for appointing the extra watch because of the threat of violence.[344]

The guards warned Paine to close his mouth because "if the governor should understand of this his insolence, it might turn him to much blame." Paine sneered irreverently, with so much cursing that it would, in the words of the chronicler, "offend the modest ear too much to express it in his own phrase." He said that the "governor had no authority...whatsoever in the colony." Paine mocked that the governor could "kiss [off]."[345]

The guards told Gates about Paine's disrespectful words and violent actions. Gates believed the "transgression so much the more...odious as being in a dangerous time." Such impudence would not be tolerated, and the governor summoned Paine. In front of the whole company, many witnesses testified that Paine had slandered the governor. Gates, with the "eyes of the whole colony fixed upon him," instantly "condemned him to be hanged."[346]

Since the gallows was already erected and the "ladder being ready," the hangman prepared to put the noose around Paine's neck. Paine proudly stated that he was a gentleman and preferred that he "might be shot to death." Toward the evening, a firing squad carried out the sentence. The shots echoed in silence, and Paine "had his desire, the sun and his life setting together."[347]

Fortunately, the pinnace that Gates's men was soon finished, and the one Somers's men were building was "ready to launch in short time from that place...to meet ours at a pond of fresh water where they were both to be moored until such time as, being fully tackled, the wind should serve fair for our putting to sea together." But Gates had more trouble before they departed. Some who sympathized with Henry Paine saw his fate and "like outlaws betook them to the wild wood" to hide out. They wanted to remain on the island forever and sent an "audacious and formal" petition to the governor demanding "two suits of apparel and [provisions] for one whole year" for each of them. Gates answered simply that duty bound him to transport them to Virginia rather than leave them there "like savages." Somers agreed and rounded up almost all of the rebellious men in his camp, except Christopher Carter and Robert Waters.[348]

Carter had joined John Want's group, which had refused to work on Gates's pinnace back in September and probably feared a harsh punishment in Virginia. Waters also was anxious about justice in Virginia, even though he had barely escaped the noose for a brutal crime on Bermuda. Soon after the wreck of the *Sea Venture,* Waters had argued with another sailor, and Waters grabbed a shovel and dealt the man a deathblow.

Gates tried and convicted Waters, sentencing him to die the following day since it was already twilight. Waters was tied "fast to a tree" all night, with five or six guards watching him. When the sentinels fell asleep, some sailors freed Waters and "conveyed him into the woods, where they fed him nightly."

Somers intervened and asked Gates to pardon the convicted man. The governor assented to the admiral's wishes. Now, inclined to stay on Bermuda, Waters and Carter decided to take their chances on the island, lest Gates have a change of heart in Jamestown.[349]

The two small ships were now ready to sail. They were products of the creative use of salvaged and local materials. It had taken nearly ten months, but when no help came, the castaways took the initiative and built oceangoing vessels that would bear them to their destination. Still, many wanted to remain on Bermuda, but their governor was intent on fulfilling his mission.

The appropriately named *Deliverance* was the bigger boat, with a forty-foot keel and nineteen feet broad. The *Patience* had a twenty-nine-foot keel and a width of fifteen feet. The castaways loaded the ships with salted pork and fish, fresh water, and tortoise oil for frying.

Thomas Gates then ordered the erection of a memorial to commemorate their remarkable experience. He selected the tallest cedar tree in Admiral Somers's garden, and some men lopped off the top branches to prevent its blowing over in a tempest, so it might endure as a symbol of English imperial ambition. In the middle of the arm of the cross, which was appropriately fashioned from a piece of wood from the *Sea Venture,* Governor Gates nailed a silver coin bearing the image of King James as well as a piece of copper with a Latin and English engraving. It read: "In memory of our great deliverance, both from a mighty storm and leak, we have set up this to the honor of God. It is the spoil of an English ship of three hundred tons called the Sea Venture, bound with seven ships more (from which the storm divided us) to Virginia or Nova Britannia in America. In it were two knights, Sir Thomas Gates, Knight Governor of the English forces and colony there, and Sir George Sommers, Knight, Admiral of the Seas. Her captain was Christopher Newport." The named gentlemen adventurers had survived a shipwreck, discovered and claimed an island for England, and fulfilled their destiny to settle in North America.[350]

More than 150 castaways then boarded the salvaged ships. They were leaving their home of nearly a year, one that had served as their deliverance from their terrible ordeal. They carried with them an important lesson: the martial organization of the colony was incompatible with the individualistic, entrepreneurial spirit of free Englishmen.

In May 1610, the *Deliverance* and *Patience* caught a westerly wind for the two-week voyage to Virginia. They could only guess at what God had in store for them when they arrived in Jamestown. If they had known, even more people might have pressured the governor to remain on Bermuda.

Chapter Thirteen

THE STARVING TIME

The castaways in Bermuda weathered the strange environment relatively well during the winter, especially since the island provided most of their needs. The story was very different in Virginia. Winter came on as usual there, and temperatures dropped. The hungry, emaciated colonists felt the cold even more than usual. The storehouses were virtually empty—by February 1610 there was no food to eat. The colonists felt the "sharp prick of hunger." President George Percy thought that no man could truly describe the awful experience except "he which hath tasted the bitterness thereof." He recorded the events, portraying the winter as a "world of miseries."[351]

Entrepreneurship involved calculated risks, and losses sometimes occurred. These settlers though had not merely gambled their fortunes but also risked their lives on migrating to the New World. They were now about to lose everything.

The people were barely subsisting on meager rations that did not provide them with the nutrition or calories needed to sustain life. They were malnourished and slowly starving to death. The "eight ounces of meal and half a pint of peas for a day, the one and the other moldy, [was] rotten, full of cobwebs and maggots, loathsome to man, and not fit for beasts." Yet that was their only food, and they eagerly consumed it, although it did little to relieve their hunger.[352]

Some forlorn individuals ignored the consequences and desperately broke into the storehouse to "satisfy their hunger" by stealing the last precious morsels. They were caught, however, and Percy had no choice but to execute them. He was forced to make an example of them, chaining one man to a tree with a "bodkin thrust through his tongue" until he starved to death. Others believed their only option was to "flee for relief to the savage enemy"; they were all slain by the Indians.[353]

With their hunger growing more acute, the surviving colonists searched the village for food. They slaughtered horses and roasted them. They fed on the tough meat, eating it greedily and not conserving enough for another day. "Having fed upon horses and other beasts as long as they lasted," Percy explained, they continued to think about what they could kill for their next meal.

Although the dogs and cats in the village were thin themselves, they were also killed for food. By catching mice and rats, the pets were actually competing with the settlers for food. Tempers flared as the wretched villagers fought over who would get to eat one of the animals. The cats and dogs were roasted, but there were too few of them to feed over two hundred people. Everyone thought only of themselves.

With the cats and dogs out of the way, the colonists hunted for rats and mice. Without large stores of corn in the storehouse, the vermin did not exist in large numbers. The settlers caught a few and cooked them, and then carefully picked the meat off every bone, leaving nothing that was even partially edible. Although it seemed like a feast to the famished diners, they still suffered hunger pangs.

The villagers would have caught fish except there were none to be caught. Sturgeon were absent now from the James River. Fish would have supplied some necessary protein but not enough calories to make a difference. The winter cold also made it impossible to "endure to wade in the water as formerly to gather oysters to satisfy our hungry stomachs." Moreover, the settlers could not venture out of Jamestown.[354]

Hundreds of Wahunsonacock's warriors surrounded the fort and killed anyone who ventured outside it. They killed dozens of colonists over the winter. Despite the great danger, several Englishmen risked leaving the safety of the fort's palisade. Those who were strong enough to stand skulked through the woods with as much stealth as possible. The hunters overturned rocks or looked in holes in the frozen ground for any creatures, including "serpents and snakes." Anything creeping or crawling was fair game.

The Englishmen also tried to "dig the earth for wild and unknown roots" and were "constrained to dig in the ground for unwholesome roots, whereof we were not able to get so many as would suffice us." They crammed just about anything into their mouths. While they frantically searched for food on their hands and knees, they were picked off by Indian arrows or beaten to death. "Many of our men were cut off and slain by the savages," Percy reported.[355]

Back in the village, the colonists found a few other items to "satisfy their cruel hunger." When friends began to die around them daily, the colonists starting chewing on "boots, shoes, or any other leather some could come by." As they tried to work the leather in their mouths, they did not look into each other's eyes. They knew that eating their shoes would not delay the inevitable. They even resorted to choking down the "excrement of man," but they retched it back up. There was nothing else in their bellies to regurgitate. They continued to die of starvation.[356]

In such critical circumstances, civilization broke down. The colonists were "beginning to look ghastly and pale in every face that nothing was spared to maintain life and to do those things which seem incredible." They "were driven through unsufferable hunger unnaturally to eat those things which nature most abhorred, the flesh of man." And they ate not only the "flesh of man" but woman as well.[357]

The stronger preyed upon the suffering of the dying as they "licked up the blood which had fallen from their weak fellows." Many died where they were standing or in their beds at night and were rapidly set upon by the living. The cannibals did not bother to cook the flesh but instead ate it raw.[358]

Even the bodies in the graveyard were consumed. Using shovels and hands, a corpse was "dug by some out of his grave after he had lain buried three days. They "wholly devoured him." The graveyard became the cannibals' storehouse.[359]

When the dead failed to satisfy their hunger, the living were driven mad by hunger to murder and eat the warm, meager flesh of their victims. One man murdered his pregnant wife "as she slept on his bosom." He "ripped the child out of the womb and threw it into the river and after chopped the mother in pieces and salted her for his food." The man's evil deeds were soon discovered, and Percy had the culprit hanged by his thumbs and attached weights to his feet until he confessed his crime. He was executed and welcomed death as a release from his suffering. No one fed on his roasted flesh—although they may have wanted to.

The Jamestown colonists knew that they would perish even as the inevitable spring brought new life to the land with budding plants and singing birds. The Christians made peace with their Savior and prayed for death. The Jamestown experiment was over.

In May 1610, two small ships appeared off Chesapeake Bay as the sun peeked over the horizon. Checking their depth, the sailors discovered they were in only nineteen and a half fathoms of water. It was not long before someone saw land. Their first impression of Virginia was magnificent. "We had a marvelous sweet smell from the shore...strong and pleasant, which did not a little glad us."[360]

A few days later they entered the bay and sailed to the mouth of the James River. Within two miles of Point Comfort, they encountered a hostile welcome from the fearful settlers at the fort who thought they might be a pair of Spanish warships. They were approaching the fort "when the captain of the fort discharged a warning piece at us." Considering what the survivors of the *Sea Venture* had been through for the last year, they did not appreciate the greeting. Nevertheless, they understood that it was a reasonable precaution considering the belligerent intent of their European enemies.[361]

Moreover, Thomas Gates, George Somers, and Christopher Newport aboard the *Deliverance* and *Patience* understood that the Virginia colonists presumed them dead. They dropped anchor and put a skiff into the water to make contact with the fort. After establishing their identity, the governor went ashore and exchanged news. The colonists were amazed to see Gates and the other survivors and enthusiastically listened to the tale. However, the news the captain of the fort shared was less welcome. Gates learned of "new, unexpected, uncomfortable, and heavy news of a worse condition of our people above at Jamestown."[362]

Gates received the news with wonder. After all, the garrison at Point Comfort did not seem to lack provisions. President Percy had visited them and found that they had plenty of crabs and hogs to eat. In fact, they had such a bounty of crabs that they fed the surplus to their hogs. Percy commented that any share of the food "would have been a great relief unto us and saved many of our lives" upriver at the settlement. The garrison "concealed their plenty from us above at Jamestown," and Percy suspected that "their intent was for to have kept some of the better sort alive and with their two pinnaces to have returned to England, not regarding our miseries and wants at all." The president was planning to bring the surviving colonists down to the fort "to save our lives" just before the two ships from Bermuda appeared. Gates probably wondered why the people at Jamestown were not already at the fort.[363]

As the small fleet set off on the quick thirty-mile journey up to Jamestown, a storm darkened the sky and their moods. "A mighty storm of thunder, lightning, and rain gave us a shrewd and fearful welcome." The weather seemed to represent the gloomy news of the state of the colony.[364]

Although Gates and his men had been warned about Jamestown's condition, they were shocked at what they found. They had expected to find a thriving colony with several hundred people and well stocked with provisions. They were the ones who had survived a harrowing Atlantic crossing and hoped for a grand welcome and reprieve. But ironically they were in much better condition than the colonists.

When they came within sight of the shore, a few curious, pathetic people came to the dock to see who had arrived. Most were too weak to climb out of their beds and walk to the river. The eyes of the new arrivals widened and registered shock at what they saw. The people of Jamestown "were lamentable to behold." They "looked like skeletons, crying out, 'We are starved! We are starved!'"[365] The governor looked at Somers and Newport as he vigorously went ashore to find out exactly what was going on. The sailors and passengers followed behind.

John Smith had left five hundred settlers at Jamestown the previous fall. Thomas Gates expected to find that number or something close to it, allowing for some deaths or expeditions that were away in the wilderness. Moreover, he knew when he sent instructions that some anarchy might result from his absence, but he never expected the colony to be in complete disarray. As he marched toward the fort, he was both shocked and angered by what he saw. "Viewing the fort," he found "the palisades torn down, the ports open, the gates from off the hinges." Several of the houses were empty or "rent up and burnt" for firewood during the winter. It looked like the scene of a major battle.[366]

Gates strode over to the Anglican church to summon the Jamestown residents together. He wanted to see who was in charge in his absence and why the colony was in such a decrepit condition. The church itself was in ruins. "Our much grieved governor, first visiting the church, caused the bell to be rung, at which all such as were able to come forth of their houses repaired to church." Even so, many could not stir from their houses.

Minister Richard Buck opened the assembly with a prayer. He mostly prayed for God to relieve the pitiable condition of the colonists who sat unmoving in the pews. Buck "made a zealous and sorrowful prayer, finding all things so contrary to our expectations, so full of misery and misgovernment." Some may have started weeping that someone actually came with food—their ordeal seemed to be over.[367]

Although exactly what the minister or governor said to the small congregation is lost to history, William Strachey and other gentlemen blamed the settlers themselves and defended Virginia as an abundant land for anyone who would work hard. He averred that "sloth, riot, and vanity" were responsible for "all these disasters and afflictions descended upon our people." He warned his readers not to blame their "wants and wretchedness…on the poverty and vileness of the country." He affirmed that the new arrivals tested the soil and found that it supported English crops. Some might be absolved of guilt, but the fault clearly lay in the "ignoble and irreligious" practices of the inhabitants. The "debauched" people only had themselves to blame.[368]

After the impromptu religious service, the governor held another ceremony in which his commission was read and President Percy surrendered his authority. Gates learned the story of what had happened as he surveyed the rest of the settlement. The new governor walked around the shattered colony and noted its fallen buildings. He only "found some three-score persons living."[369]

The irony of the scene played out in the minds of the newly arrived settlers. They had crossed the Atlantic, barely survived a hurricane at sea, spent almost a year on the Isle of Devils, rebuilt their ships, and finally reached their destination by a pure act of perseverance. They had come to get wealthy and have a better life. Instead, they found all their troubles were for naught and their dreams dashed in an instant.

A disconsolate Thomas Gates had to admit that he did not know the solutions to what seemed insurmountable difficulties. He did not expect these problems and was having trouble discerning the same innovative ideas that had helped the castaways survive in Bermuda *and* get off the island. "In this desolation and misery our governor found the condition and state of the colony and which added more to his grief," Gates had "no hope how to amend it or save his own company."[370]

Gates crushed the hopes of the starving people who thought he had enough food for their immediate needs and long-term survival. He shared a gloomy truth with the starving colonists. With a heavy heart and a great deal of reticence, he informed them that the ships "had brought from the Bermudas no greater store of provision (fearing no such accidents possible to befall the colony here) than might well serve one hundred and fifty for a sea voyage."[371]

A hasty count of the provisions revealed that they only had about sixteen days of food for everyone. Nor was there any real possibility of securing an adequate supply of provisions. "It was not possible at this time of the year to…have little more than from hand to mouth, it was now likewise but their seedtime and all their corn scarce put into the ground." The hostile Indians who had surrounded the fort during the starving time and killed scores of colonists could not be counted on for trade or gifts. "The Indians were themselves poor [and] were forbidden likewise by their subtle King Powhatan at all to trade with us." There was also no "means to take fish, neither sufficient seine nor other convenient net, and yet if there had, there was not one eye of sturgeon yet come into the river." They were about to suffer the same horror again, this time in the unhealthiest part of the year.[372]

Upon hearing such dreadful news, a man broke into a hysterical fit, understandably blaming God for their suffering. Hugh Price, "in a furious, distracted mood did come openly into the market place blaspheming, exclaiming, and crying out that there was no god." He alleged, "If there were a God he would not suffer his creatures whom he had made and framed to endure those miseries." In his despair, Price was driven madly into the woods, where he met his death by the Indians just as surely as famine and pestilence would have claimed him within the settlement.[373]

Gates promised the settlers in Jamestown that "what provision he had they should equally share with him, and if he should find it not possible and easy to supply them with something from the country by the endeavors of his able men, he would make ready and transport them all into their native country, England, (accommodating them the best that he could)." His words assuaged the hungry, scared colonists who gave "a general acclamation and shout of joy on both sides."[374]

Afterward, Gates drew up and posted some laws to provide the colony with at least a temporary sense of order. "Our governor published certain orders and instructions which he enjoined them strictly to observe, the time that he should stay amongst them, which, being written out fair, were set up upon a post in the church for everyone to take notice of." Meanwhile, there was work to be done to see if maintaining the permanent settlement would be even remotely possible.[375]

After two weeks, the situation had not changed. They had no stores of food and little likelihood of adding any. The Indians refused to trade their food and were still a threat to any who sojourned outside the palisade. In fact, a small boat that was sent out for food had many settlers killed. Raising enough crops in time was impossible, and fishing the river was still not fruitful.

Gates consulted with Somers, Newport, Percy, and several other members of the governing council. They came to an inescapable conclusion and sobering consensus. "After much debating it could not appear how possibly they might preserve themselves ten days from starving." Considering the state of the colony and the dismal prospects for their survival, Gates decided to abandon Jamestown. "In this desolation and misery our governor found…no hope how to amend it or save his own company and those yet remaining alive from falling into the like necessities." He would not risk the lives of two hundred people in his charge with a vain delusion of his own leadership.[376]

Even if they set sail, they could never make it to England with their meager food supply, which would last at most a month under favorable conditions (and Gates knew firsthand that disasters could happen). Their only choice was to sail for Newfoundland, where they could provision themselves through trade and fishing as well as "meet with many English ships into which happily they might disperse most of the company."[377]

The English had only recently begun to fish for cod around Newfoundland. Henry VII had sponsored John Cabot's voyage to the New World, and he reported that the cod in Newfoundland were so plentiful that they practically jumped into the boats. "The sea there is swarming with fish which can be taken not only with the net but in baskets let down with a stone, so that it sinks in the water."[378]

Word from another discoverer in New England confirmed Cabot's account that the Newfoundland coasts were teeming with cod. "In the months of March, April, and May, there is upon this coast better fishing, and in as great plenty as in Newfoundland." The rocky shores of that northern island seemed to be the Virginia colonists' salvation.[379]

On June 7, 1610, the company collected all of the remaining flour and prepared sea biscuits as well as any remaining foodstuffs, which would be evenly distributed to everyone and closely guarded. Even then they only had "not above…sixteen days, after two cakes a day." They loaded all arms and remaining supplies on their four pinnaces, including the *Deliverance* and *Patience.* Gates had the cannon buried, hopefully for use at some future date by other settlers. He also protected the town, even in its ramshackle state, from arson by the frustrated survivors of the famine. "Because he would preserve the town (albeit now to be quitted) unburned, which some intemperate and malicious people threatened, his own company he caused to be last ashore and was himself the last of them when about noon, giving a farewell with a peal of small shot, we set sail." None wanted to look back at the source of their misery.[380]

The Jamestown colony had failed, and the hardy adventurers who had settled the colony were defeated and sailing back to England.

Chapter Fourteen

MARTIAL LAW

The colonists who were leaving Jamestown for good did not get far. They had sailed down the James and anchored the next morning off Mulberry Island when, to their surprise, they encountered a longboat coming up from Point Comfort.

Aboard the flagship of a three-boat expedition, Lord De La Warr floated from Point Comfort to speak with Thomas Gates. The governor was relieved to see Gates alive, but the wretched condition of the colonists filled him with compassion. De La Warr was "met with much cold comfort as, if it had not been accompanied with the most happy news of Sir Thomas Gates his arrival, it had been sufficient to have broke my heart and to have made me altogether unable to have done my king and country any service."[381]

Nevertheless, De La Warr performed his duty and promptly ordered Gates and his forlorn passengers to return to the place of death. Gates obediently sailed his men back to Jamestown and waited.

The colony was not allowed to fail. Lord De La Warr would put the colony back on a proper footing, but he did not offer the Jamestown colonists any new and innovative leadership ideas. He would rule strictly, as if the authoritarian regimes of John Smith or Thomas Gates were the antidote to the problems that continued to plague the colony since its inception. Discipline and martial rule would supposedly inspire success and work for the collective good.

Two days later, on Sunday, June 10, De La Warr entered the Jamestown palisade with great ceremony. Governor Gates "caused his company in arms to stand in order and make a guard." An honor guard bore flags flapping in the breeze. De La Warr solemnly "fell upon his knees and before us all made a long and silent prayer to himself." He marched through the formations into town, wrote William Strachey, "where at the gate I bowed with the colors and let them fall at his lordship's feet."[382]

De La Warr strode into the half-razed church, and Minister Richard Buck delivered a sermon for the Sabbath and the occasion. A gentleman then read the lord's commission granting him the governorship of the colony. Gates handed over his commission and the council seal with a great deal of relief.

Lord De La Warr stood before he assembled worshipers and dressed them down. He blamed their troubled upon their "many vanities and their idleness, earnestly wishing that he might no more find it so lest he should be compelled to draw the sword of justice to cut off such delinquents, which he had much rather, he protested, draw in their defense to protect them from injuries."[383]

After establishing his authority and laying down the tenor of his domineering rule, De La Warr offered them some comforting thoughts. He informed the hungry colonists that he had a "store of provisions he had brought for them, sufficient to serve four hundred men for one whole year." The members of the congregation smiled, and some cried in relief.

De La Warr then got down to the work of rebuilding Jamestown.

The new governor instituted his regimented government and initiated a series of reforms that he thought would reestablish order. First, on Tuesday, June 12, he chose certain gentlemen to hold office to help him govern, and they elected a council who took an oath of office. Unsurprisingly, Thomas Gates, George Somers, George Percy, Christopher Newport, and William Strachey (as secretary and recorder) comprised the council, with a few others. The governor and council had draconian laws at their disposal to compel obedience and submission to their authority. Crimes such as insubordination, mutiny, trading weapons to the Indians, or murder would receive the death penalty, whereas a host of lesser crimes would earn the whip.

The next thing Governor De La Warr did was to assess the food supply. Even though he had brought enough provisions to last through the winter, he put the men to work to add to the stores to ensure the long-term sustainability of the colony. These men spent their time fishing, although still mostly without success, because they found "in our own river no store of fish." The governor dispatched a pinnace to fish in the Chesapeake, but this, too, was without a great deal of luck. Nevertheless, they did raise various crops and even planted a vineyard.[384]

It did not appear that there was "any kind of flesh, deer, or whatever other kind" that could be hunted and killed. Moreover, the Indians "had the last winter destroyed and killed up all the hogs, insomuch as of five or six hundred, there was not one left alive." Nor was there a "hen or chick in the fort; and our horses and mares they had eaten with the first." In addition, the expedition had not brought any significant amounts of meat.[385]

On Wednesday, June 13, the council debated various solutions to the food problem. Somers proposed to sail to Bermuda to "fetch six months' provision of flesh and fish and some live hogs to store our colony again." De La Warr quickly consented to the plan. On June 19, Somers and Samuel Argall set sail in the Bermuda-built *Patience* and *Discovery*.[386]

Next, Governor De La Warr broke the men into groups of fifty, forming them into militia units for discipline and martial deportment. The groups were further split into labor gangs to start rebuilding the colony and followed strict work routines. Their discipline and unity were reinforced by taking their meals together. Their work and meal schedules were organized by ringing bells throughout the day.

The labor gangs first began "to raise a fortress with the ablest and speediest means they could." It was enclosed by "a palisade of planks and strong posts, four feet deep in the ground." They built several bulwarks, unburied the cannon, and set up the ordnance for safety and security. The settlers rebuilt their houses and made them more durable.[387]

Since the church was both "ruined and unfrequented," the governor ordered it repaired for the spiritual well-being of the colonists. A nicely finished black walnut Communion table and cedar pews and pulpit were crafted. Strict rules of church attendance and prayer were enforced. "Every Sunday we have sermons twice a day, and every Thursday a sermon…and every morning, at the ringing of a bell at ten o'clock, each man prays, and so at four o'clock before supper." The house of worship was now beautified and well used.[388]

The governor himself made a public show of attending church services to encourage others to follow his example. "Every Sunday, when the lord governor and captain general goes to church, he is accompanied with all the councilors, captains, other officers, and all the gentlemen, and with a guard of halberdiers in his lordship's livery, fair red cloaks, to the number of fifty, both on each side and behind him." De La Warr worshiped grandly on a green velvet cushion.[389]

De La Warr believed that he had given the colony a proper foundation for its future. He reestablished the rule of law, gave the men stern work rules for discipline, and attended to their spiritual needs. The reigning authoritarian view of administering the colony had failed for several years but still predominated at Jamestown.

One final priority of the governor was the elimination of the Indian threat. As instructed by the Virginia Company, the governor sought to draw "better terms" as well as peacefully convert the native peoples. The company argued that it was lawful to "possess part of their land" as well as "defend ourselves from them," but it wanted the governor to treat them well.[390] As a result, De La Warr sent an embassy of two gentlemen to reestablish relations with Wahunsonacock. The governor acknowledged the strained relations between the two peoples but hoped to set them aright by blaming the violence over the past year on "his worst and unruly people."[391]

Wahunsonacock perceived that he had the upper hand and proudly stood his ground. In response to the embassy, he warned the Englishmen that they either "depart the country or confine ourselves to Jamestown only, without searching further up into his land or rivers." If they refused to heed his warning, "he would give in command to his people to kill us and do unto us all the mischief which they had at their pleasure." Moreover, he demanded future diplomats greet him in a carriage with three horses, because he understood that European ambassadors were received thus when they went to "visit other great men." Daily he sent several spies to keep an eye on the settlement as a signal of his hostile intentions.[392]

Lord De La Warr was not going to allow Wahunsonacock to maintain the advantage he had gained after Smith's departure and during the starving time. He would not suffer an Indian chief as his equal, nor did he intend to permit the Indians to keep the English bound to the immediate environs of their fort under the threat of violence. The national vision of the English included colonies that were expansionary, dynamic forces with a burgeoning population and bold attempts to explore an area in order to discover sources of wealth. The attempt by Wahunsonacock to keep them static and restrained to a small geographical area was antithetical to the gentlemen adventurers and the company. It would be not tolerated but met with force. This was now a struggle for supremacy by both peoples, and the impact would be felt for years and would determine the outcome of the colony.

Savagery escalated on both sides as the English took the offensive. After the Kecoughtans killed a colonist attempting to recover a lost boat, Gates led an expedition against them. A drummer played some music to "lure the Indians to come unto him." When the Kecoughtans emerged, Gates attacked, killing five and wounded many (some of whom later died from bleeding in the woods). The Kecoughtans fled in terror while the English occupied their "town and the fertile ground thereunto adjacent."[393]

When the governor demanded missing arms and men from Wahunsonacock, the Indian leader responded with "proud and disdainful answers." De La Warr ordered Percy to lead seventy men against the Paspaheghs and Chickahominies. On August 9, 1610, Percy's men sailed in two boats and marched upon the tribes in battle formation. They surrounded the village and attacked when a pistol was fired. The English soldiers killed fifteen or sixteen Indians and put the rest to flight.[394]

After the bloody battle, Percy reprimanded a soldier for sparing an Indian man, the queen, and her children. He ordered the male Indian beheaded while other Englishmen torched the village and stole their corn. The invaders boarded their ships, and Percy hastily convened a war council to decide the fate of the remaining prisoners. They decided to toss the children overboard and shoot them. The grisly task was carried out while their mother watched in horror. Their bodies lay floating as the ships pulled away to "perform all the spoil they could."[395]

Percy's force went ashore two miles downriver and were met with a hail of arrows by some warriors who melted into the woods. The Englishmen marched fourteen miles to the Chickahominies' village and unleashed further savagery. As they rampaged through the countryside, they "cut down their corn, burned their houses, temples, and idols, and amongst the rest a spacious temple."[396]

When they returned to Jamestown and disembarked with their lone prisoner, Lord De La Warr was pleased with their safe return, but he reproached Percy for not slaying the queen when she was captured. The governor ordered her execution and thought that Percy should "burn her." A fatigued Percy pled that he had already seen "so much bloodshed that day, now in my cold blood I desired to see no more." If it must be done, he preferred to get the grisly deed over with quickly, "by shot or sword." She was led into the woods where no one would witness her execution.[397]

The English gained additional firepower when Samuel Argall returned from a failed attempt to reach Bermuda for hogs and fished off the coast of New England. He contributed to the raids, attacking the Warraskoyacks, who were warned by neighboring tribes that the Englishmen's ships were coming. They fled and escaped the attack, but Argall cut down their corn and burned their houses, leaving a wake of destruction behind him.

With the Indians seemingly subdued, De La Warr felt confident enough to send a company of men up to the falls to continue the "search for minerals and to make further proof of the iron mines." When they reached the Appomattocs, the English went ashore to fill their barrels with fresh water and were lured to a feast. "Forgetting the subtleties" of the Indians, the "greedy fools" accepted the invitation and went into the homes. Choosing a time in which the English least suspected an attack, the Appomattocs "did fall upon them, slew many, and wounded all the rest, who within two days after also died." Only Thomas Dowse, a drummer boy, survived the ambush. He fled to the ship and hid behind the rudder as he managed to sail off.[398]

Undaunted by the Indian retaliation, Lord De La Warr's military commander, Capt. Edward Brewster, led a force to the falls to "proceed in the search for minerals" and "attend there for my lord's coming," because De La Warr intended to inhabit the fort his brother, Francis West, had built. Throughout the autumn and early winter the garrison had several encounters with the Indians, and "some of his men being slain, among the rest his [nephew] Captain William West." The Indians shouted cries of victory through the woods that the men in the fort could hear. Nevertheless, De La Warr went to live at this fort for a few months, but eventually he would have to abandon the fort as well as the search for wealth.[399]

George Percy was left in charge of the government at Jamestown in the governor's absence. The Paspaheghs appeared at the settlement to test the defenses, thinking they might surprise the garrison. Percy responded by capturing their chief, Wowinchopunck. The colonists surrounded him, and then several Paspahegh warriors appeared out of the woods and fired a hail of arrows. The "stout Indian lived and was carried away" after suffering several sword wounds.[400]

The violence on both sides persisted, although the English settlers were gaining the upper hand. They suffered some deadly attacks and were driven from the falls, but the situation was a far cry from the days of the starving time when the colonists were surrounded in Jamestown. Moreover, new leaders were coming who would continue the expansionary policies of the colonists and overcome the remaining Indian resistance.

Interim governor Thomas Gates left Jamestown in July 1610, soon after surrendering his commission to Lord De La Warr. Gates returned to England with a letter to the Virginia Company. In the letter, the council in Jamestown summarized recent events for the company and detailed the misery of the settlers during the starving time and the unexpected arrival of Gates and Somers. The council explained and defended their unavoidable decision to abandon Jamestown and the reversal of this decision by Lord De La Warr.

The council rendered its collective judgment that the blame for the difficulties of the colony should be placed squarely on the shoulders of the colonists themselves. The land, they stated unequivocally, was bountiful, and "no country yieldeth goodlier corn or more manifold increase." It abounded with grapes, and English seeds easily grew there, "no sooner put into the ground than to prosper as speedily and after the same quality as in England." Any contrary news claiming the poverty of the land was only rumor and scandalous lies.[401] The lesson that the gentlemen adventurers took away from their challenges over the past few months was that their absolute authority was responsible for saving the colony. "I beseech ye, further to make inference that since it hath been well thought on by ye to provide for the government by changing the authority into an absolute command...of a noble and well-instructed lieutenant, of an industrious admiral, and other knights and gentlemen, and officers, each in their several place of quality and employment, if the other two, as I have said, be taken into due account valued as the sinews of this action, without which it cannot possible have any fair subsisting." Rather than giving the individual colonists greater incentive and initiative to work harder for their success, the gentlemen believed that the settlers were lazy commoners who must be herded like swine and commanded by their lordly masters to work for the common good.[402]

The Virginia Company used Gates's celebrated return to London in the late summer of 1610 in its public relations campaign to promote the national mission of the Jamestown colony. The company published promotional literature that interpreted the disaster of the wreck of the *Sea Venture* and the successes of Lord De La Warr's leadership as the core of the narrative of the providential protection of England's national mission to settle America. Downplaying the struggles to survive, particularly the starving time, the company instead publicized the notion that "God will not let us fall. Let England know our willingness, for that our work is good. We hope to plant a nation where none before hath stood." Attacking any "scandal, false reports, or any opposition," the company again advertised Virginia as the land of milk and honey, promising that the rapidly growing colony would reward every investor with great profits.[403]

George Yeardley, a future governor, had to admit that the fleet of ships that carried Gates back to England imported nothing valuable from Virginia. "At this present I am little or nothing better furnished with any matter of value, either for discovery of mines or ought else worth your knowledge." Yeardley still hoped that the fertile land would reap a bounty of commodities of "pitch and tar, soap-ashes, wood, iron, etc." After several years of futile searching, the company would instruct the governor to continue the search for silver and gold for which it now had "probable intelligence" about its location. Finally, the march to the west to hunt for precious metals would include another voyage of discovery for "finding out the South Sea."[404]

Yet even as the company publicized its efforts to keep its current investors and attract new ones, the settlers faced not only a war with the Indians but summer diseases. During the summer of 1610, as many as one-third of the colonists perished from salt poisoning, dysentery, and typhoid. Many of those who died were the unseasoned new settlers who had been castaways from the *Sea Venture* or with Lord De La Warr's relief expedition. The governor himself was suffering from a chronic health problem, although no one blamed it on his "idleness" as they would for the common settlers.

Back in London in November 1610, the company followed up its attempt at damage control to reassure investors that the bad news from Virginia was nothing but rumors. It published *A True and Sincere Declaration* to "wash away those spots which foul mouths, to justify their own disloyalty, have cast upon so fruitful, so fertile, and so excellent a country." Throughout all of the colony's problems, "Never had any people more just cause to cast themselves at the footstool of God, and to reverence his mercy than our distressed colony!" Besides divine providence, the colony was well governed by trusted gentlemen like Gates and De La Warr. Finally, the land was bountiful and essential to England's national security, because American forests would supply masts and planks for the ships of the navy.[405]

Lord De La Warr wintered upriver at the fort at the falls, but his illness did not abate but worsened. In late March 1611, the governor and fifty of his men sailed for Nevis in the West Indies for the "recovery of his health" at the baths there. He delegated his authority to George Percy, the former president, to rule in his absence. Lord De La Warr's ship, however, met with contrary winds and was forced to return to England.[406]

Because of his premature and unanticipated return, he felt honor bound to defend himself against those who "spare not to censure me in point of duty." He recovered from his infirmity and claimed as a gentleman adventurer that "far from shrinking or giving over this honorable enterprise as that I am willing and ready to lay all I am worth upon the adventure of the action, rather than so honorable a work should fail, and to return with all the convenient expedition I may."[407]

De La Warr defended his leadership in departing by informing the company that he had left two hundred colonists generally in good health and well provisioned with ten months' of food. The settlers had built three forts while he had been in Virginia. The country "is wonderful fertile and very rich, and makes good whatsoever heretofore hath been reported of it." No mention was made of the Indian war or of the unremitting difficulties encountered by the colonists.[408]

~ *Chapter Fifteen* ~

WAR

As the sickly Lord De La Warr arrived in England to the conster-nation of the Virginia Company, the company was preparing yet another supply expedition to Jamestown with hundreds of additional settlers. Sir Thomas Dale was appointed to serve as the marshal of Virginia and commanded three hundred settlers, brought provisions for a year, and transported cattle for livestock to feed the colonists.

The national mission of the expedition remained unchanged. Indeed, the Virginia Company reiterated their grand vision for the colony to keep its investors and maintain public support: "The eyes of all Europe are looking upon our endeavors to spread the Gospel among the heathen people of Virginia, to plant our English nation there, and to settle at in those parts which may be peculiar to our nation, so that we may thereby be secured from being eaten out of all profits of trade, by our more industrious neighbors." The search for profits, imperial competition, national glory, and Christian evangelization were all there. The instructions could as well have been written for the first voyage in 1606.[409]

Nor did Thomas Dale differ from the other gentlemen adventurers who first settled the colony, such as John Smith. Dale served in the Netherlands against the Spanish and was made a captain. He subsequently commanded troops in the colonization of Ireland in the 1590s and then returned to the Netherlands. In 1606, King James knighted Dale. He was a well-heeled and connected gentleman who was acquainted with the likes of Sir Robert Cecil and the Earl of Southampton. The Virginia Company appointed Dale marshal of the colony in order to institute a rigorous system of martial discipline.

The chosen model of harsh punishments, a regular work routine, and tight organization based upon the belief that law and order would save the lives of the slothful commoners remained unaltered, despite the string of failures since 1607. The members of the company dogmatically resisted any fundamental changes in how the colony was organized. They would settle Virginia through sheer force of will, but the sinkhole would continue to drain thousands of pounds of provisions as well as the lives of hundreds of settlers.

In mid-March 1611, Dale's fleet, commanded by the inestimable Christopher Newport, sailed from England and endured the shipboard fevers of the passage across the Atlantic. By May 12, four years after the first settlers had espied land, Dale entered the Chesapeake and was greeted by the garrison at Point Comfort. His first task was to repossess Forts Henry, Charles, and Algernon. He sailed up the James to repair the palisades and buildings and plant corn, because of his instructions to "search further up[river] for a convenient new seat to raise a principal town" away from unhealthy Jamestown. He planned to take two hundred men and build a new town near the falls and then relegate Jamestown to be one of many forts with a garrison of "some fifty men with a sufficient commander" around Virginia.[410]

On Sunday, May 19, with the work progressing at the forts, Dale disembarked at Jamestown and attended Anglican services with the rest of the colony. George Percy formally surrendered his commission, and Thomas Dale had his read aloud. He informed the colonists that Thomas Gates would be following him in a few months with hundreds of new settlers.

When Dale made his inspection of the capital, he was disgusted by what he saw. He found "no corn set, some few seeds put into a private garden or two." The church and the storehouses were falling down. The men had to repair the storehouse for powder and munitions as well as dig a new well.[411]

Dale was appalled by the new settlers, judging them "such disordered persons, so profane, so riotous, so full of mutiny and treasonable intendments—as I am well to witness in a parcel of 300 which I brought with me, of which well may I say not many give testimony beside their names that they are Christians." He wrote that their "diseased and crazed bodies…render them so desperate of recovery as of 300 not threescore may be called forth or employed upon any labor or service." They were of course laid low by the usual summer diseases that wracked their bodies and claimed many lives. But Dale believed the source of their illness was in their disobedient and slothful natures.[412]

Dale instituted the draconian "laws divine, moral, and martial" to regulate almost every aspect of the lives of the colonists and provided harsh punishments for those who violated them. Punishments for those who did not attend church services twice a day were to have their food allowance taken away, be whipped, or, for repeat offenders, be put in chains in the galley for six months. Fornicators would be whipped three times a week for a month and were required to ask for public forgiveness from the congregation. Anyone who criticized the government three times would be put to death, as would those who robbed the common "store of any commodities therein."[413]

Dale put the men and women to work under a strict regime, since they seemed more inclined to spend their days "bowling in the streets" rather than repairing their homes, which were "ready to fall upon their heads." They prepared the planks and other materials for the new capital. His "strict and severe" laws were instituted because "it was no mean trouble to him to reduce his people so timely to good order, being of so ill a condition…for more deserved death in those days."[414] Dale and other gentlemen adventurers uncovered plots to run away to the Indians or the Spanish and meted out severe punishments. "Some he appointed to be hanged, some burned, some to be broken upon wheels, others to be staked, and some to be shot to death." Others who attempted to steal from the common storehouse he ordered "bound fast unto trees and so starved them to death."[415] If the deaths were "more severe than usual in England," the leaders opined, "there was just cause for it." The lowly commoners were "sensible only of the body's torment, the fear of a cruel, painful, and unusual death more restrains them than death itself."[416] Dale extended and systematized the authoritarian regime of his predecessors, enforcing very strict laws to govern the colony.

After setting the colonists right in working for the common good and planning the geographical organization of the settlements around Virginia, Dale had to advance the security of the colony against its enemies. The forts along the Chesapeake would defend against Spanish incursions into the rivers, and Dale now sought to eliminate the Indian threat once and for all. His plan was to subdue the great werowance, Wahunsonacock, and his peoples, so that the English would be the true masters of their colonial territory and the native peoples their subjects.

Dale said, "By the several plantations and seats which I would make I should so overmaster the subtle, mischievous great Powhatan [Wahunsonacock] that I should leave him either no room in his country to harbor in or draw him to a firm association with ourselves." The Powhatans and their subjects had a choice: submit to the English or be driven from their traditional lands.[417]

To these ends, the marshal employed several strategies. First, he forbade "all manner of trading with the Indians lest our commodities should grow every day with them more vile and cheap by their plenty."[418] He also ordered that many of the Indians "who used to come to our fort at Jamestown bringing victuals with them [be] apprehended and executed as a terror for the rest," because they were suspected of spying on the fort and relating intelligence about its weaknesses.[419]

Dale then planned an expedition against the Nansemonds at the mouth of the James to ensure control of the river by eliminating the final threat there. They had many encounters "by land and water."[420]

Dale, Francis West, and John Martin outfitted their men with a complement of arms and armor. The technological superiority of the English and the European way of war were evident as Dale's men sailed toward their enemy and unleashed a terrifying onslaught.[421]

Although the Indians managed to wound a couple of men with arrows, including West in the thigh and Martin in the arm, they were clearly outmatched. The English killed and wounded many Indians who "not being acquainted nor accustomed to encounter with men in armor, much wondered thereat, especially that they did not see any of our men fall as they had done in other conflicts."[422]

In the view of the English, the perplexed Indians relied upon their traditional "exorcisms, conjurations, and charms…necromantic spells and incantations" to call upon their gods to douse their enemy's gunpowder with rain. It did not avail them, as the Englishmen, with relative impunity, "cut down their corn, burned their houses, and, besides those which they had slain, brought some of them prisoners to our fort." Dale conducted additional "invasions and excursions upon the savages, [and] had many conflicts with them."[423]

An increasingly beleaguered Wahunsonacock sent Dale a warning that he would kill the English in "a strange manner" if he persisted in his expansionist policies toward the falls. Dale knew he had the advantage and would not be intimidated by an enemy he considered a pagan savage with inferior weapons. He was reportedly "very merry at this message" and sneered at his enemy's inability to resist the English attacks. It seemed to him as if Wahunsonacock was choosing annihilation.[424] Dale sought to eliminate other threats to Jamestown when a Spanish ship appeared off the coast of Virginia.

In late June, a Spanish caravel entered the Chesapeake Bay and anchored within sight of Fort Algernon at Point Comfort, though the captain wisely kept it out of range of English guns. Dozens of English soldiers armed themselves for battle against the hated enemy that they believed had finally decided to attack the Jamestown colony. They waited tensely for the Spanish to act.

The Spanish commander, Don Diego de Molina, had been dispatched on this reconnaissance mission from Lisbon to provide King Philip III with an assessment of the state of the colony and clues to English intentions. Molina ordered a sloop be lowered and boarded it with his second in command, Marco Antonio Perez, an English pilot employed by the Spanish, Francisco Lembry, and ten armed men. As they neared the land, the Spanish spied sixty or seventy armed English soldiers waiting near the fort. Molina recognized that he was outmatched, should a violent confrontation erupt, and chose a diplomatic approach. He ordered the master to remain behind in the sloop with the men and went ashore with just Perez and Lembry.

Things did not turn out as well as Molina had wished as the English "took the three, deprived them of their arms, [and] carried them to the fort." An hour later, some twenty Englishmen attempted to lure the Spanish ashore to take them prisoner as well, but the master refused to take the bait and demanded the return of his commander. A Spaniard went ashore to discover the fate of Molina and the others but was surrounded by armored men leveling their arquebusses at him.[425]

Soon a smaller group of English soldiers went to speak with the Spanish, and a pilot, John Clark, asked to speak with the master onboard the sloop. The Spanish seized him and took him prisoner. The two sides began negotiating the release of their respective hostages. Tensions escalated as the Spanish approached the shore again, facing twenty English musketeers. The Spanish master threatened that unless the English decided "to surrender Don Diego and his companions, that he would fight [them]." The English retorted "with great anger that they might go to the devil."[426]

The Spanish caravel headed out to sea with Clark while the English retained Molina (both were held for years). Dale feared that the consequences of the encounter could prove disastrous for the colony. The Spanish had gathered a great deal of intelligence about the English position, he feared. "What may be the danger of this unto us who are here so few, so weak, and unfortified, since they have by this means sufficiently instructed themselves concerning our just height and seat; and know the ready way unto us both by this discoverer and by the help likewise of our own pilot," he could only guess. It did not bode well for the future. He suspected that the caravel may have been a point ship for a massive Spanish fleet to attack the colony. The English would soon find out. [427]

After the Spanish prisoners were taken, the colony was on high alert throughout the summer. In early August, Dale received word from the forts at the mouth of the James that six more ships had been spotted. He knew that Gates was expected at any moment with a relief expedition, but he also feared that the Spanish might reappear to attack the colony and liberate the prisoners. The marshal sent two officers and forty men to the bay to discover the identity of the strangers. When they did not return in a timely manner, Dale feared "they were either surprised or defeated" by a Spanish fleet. Therefore he "drew all his forces into form and order ready for encounter" and called a war council to "resolve whether it were best to meet them aboard our ships or to maintain the fort."[428]

As the men were scrambling to prepare the ships and the defenses in the fort, word arrived that Thomas Gates was leading the incoming fleet. The colonists were relieved to see their countrymen and stood down. Gates's fleet landed at Jamestown that evening, and the ships were unloaded while more than three hundred new settlers came ashore to bolster the growing colony. Gates resumed his position as governor, and Dale brought him up to speed on the state of the forts, the crops that were planted, the Spanish prisoners, and relations with the Indians. Roughly 750 colonists now inhabited the colony. The situation was decidedly more favorable than the last time Gates set foot on Virginia and a few dozen starving, desperate colonists greeted him.

Dale and Gates decided to send the first group of settlers to reside permanently at the falls. In early September, Edward Brewster marched about two hundred settlers overland, with a contingent of soldiers to protect them. Dale then sailed up the James accompanied by a small company of men. Wahunsonacock learned of the march, and his warriors ineffectively attacked the column of settlers several times. Although the fierce Nemattanew—whom the English named "Jack of the Feathers" because he went to war "covered over with feathers and swan's wings fastened unto his shoulders as though he meant to fly"—led the Powhatan warriors, they could not stop the procession of well-armed and armored Englishmen.[429]

The settlers arrived at the area where they wanted to build a fort and town named Henrico, in honor of Prince Henry of Wales, a supporter of the company and Dale's patron. They had "diverse encounters and skirmishes with the savages," but the work proceeded nonetheless. The Powhatans continued to apply pressure on the English to prevent the settlement from being erected, "shooting arrows into the fort" and wounding several men. The Indian warriors also killed those who were sent on errands outside the fort. Yet they were simply no match for the English and did not have the firepower to assault the fort directly. They were powerless to stop the English from finishing the fort except to harass them and pick off a few settlers. De La Warr's and Dale's use of overwhelming force with superior technology had sufficiently turned the tide against the tribes, and the English could expand their colony almost at will.[430]

The settlers built "at each corner of the town very strong and high commanders, or watchtowers, a fair and handsome church, and storehouses." When these were completed, they constructed "three streets of well-framed houses, a handsome church, and the foundation of a more stately one laid—of brick, in length a hundred feet, and fifty feet wide." They planted a "great quantity of corn" and erected an Anglican church. Proceeding with their relentless expansion, they planned other settlements. Dale wrote letters to England, imploring the Earl of Salisbury and Thomas Smythe to send two or three thousand settlers to Virginia and promised that "in the space of two years render this whole country unto His Majesty, settle a colony here secure for themselves, and ready to answer all her ends and expectations." Dale wanted credit for subduing the native peoples and putting the colony on a firm footing for imperial greatness and significant financial returns.[431]

From Henrico, Dale was able to launch attacks against any neighboring Indian peoples to secure control of the James River. He invaded the Appomattoc village to "revenge the treacherous injury of those people done unto us." The English destroyed the village and took the corn. Dale surveyed the now empty land and "considering how commodious a habitation and seat it might be for us," decided to occupy it and rename it New Bermuda. Relations with the Indians would soon take an unexpected turn when Pocahontas again affected the course of the Jamestown colony.[432]

In 1612, the company made Samuel Argall an admiral and sent him to Virginia. When he arrived, he explored the Chesapeake Bay to the Potomac River and established trade relations with the Patawomecks for corn. In the spring of 1613, he chanced upon a very surprising opportunity when he stumbled across Pocahontas, who was staying with the Patawomecks on her own trade mission to "exchange some of her father's commodities for theirs."[433]

She was "desirous to renew her familiarity with the English, and delighting to see them would gladly visit" with Argall and his companions. The Englishman, however, had more sinister motives in mind. He met with "an old friend and adopted brother of his, Iapazeus, how and by what means he might procure her capture." Argall hoped to use her as a prisoner to "redeem some of our Englishmen and arms now in the possession of her father." Argall assured Iapazeus that he would treat Pocahontas well. The Patawomeck agreed to help Argall to kidnap the young woman, and the pair worked out their stratagem.[434]

Iapazeus and his wife would bring Pocahontas to Argall's ship, and his wife would feign a "great and longing desire to go aboard and see the ship." Iapazeus would pretend to be angry with his wife for wanting to go without the company of another woman. His wife would shed crocodile tears, and he would accede to her request, provided that Pocahontas accompany her.[435]

When the Indians were aboard Argall's ship, they had supper with the captain. After their meal was complete, Pocahontas was "lodged in the gunner's room" while Iapazeus and his wife departed in secret and were rewarded "with a small copper kettle and some other less valuable toys." Argall came into the room and informed Pocahontas that he would not free her because "her father had then eight of our Englishmen, many swords, pieces, and other tools, which he at several times by treacherous murdering our men taken from them, which though of no use to him, he would not redeliver." She became disconsolate because of her captivity and was brought back to Jamestown as a prisoner.[436]

The governor was very pleased with Argall and immediately sent a messenger to Wahunsonacock with the "unwelcome and trouble-some" news that his beloved daughter was being held hostage by his enemy. The messenger also presented the werowance with the terms of her redemption, including the English prisoners and captured weapons and tools.[437]

Wahunsonacock carefully weighed the diplomatic ramifications of negotiating the release of his daughter. Clearly, the English had the advantage and would further dominate the relationship if he surrendered his prisoners and cache of English weapons. He deliber-ated for as many as three months while his daughter was a captive at Jamestown, and the English suspected that he sought the "long advice" of his council.[438]

Finally, Wahunsonacock agreed to the Englishmen's conditions, although he tried to gain some wiggle room and not abjectly submit to their demands. He "returned us seven of our men, with each of them a musket," although each of the weapons was broken and "unserviceable." Moreover, Wahunsonacock stipulated that when his daughter was released, he would offer the English five hundred bushels of corn in payment for the "rest of our pieces" which he would keep and were supposedly "broken" anyway.[439]

Gates, Dale, and the other Jamestown leaders saw through their adversary's ruse and retorted that they knew "that the rest of our arms were either lost or stolen from him." They informed Wahunsonacock that "till he returned them all we would not by any means deliver his daughter." The English also delivered a warning that "it should be at his choice whether he would establish peace or continue enemies with us."[440]

The English did not receive an answer to their counterdemands from Wahunsonacock for almost a year. He recognized that the English were in control of the relationship and that surrendering his trophies was akin to admitting defeat and appearing weak in front of his own people and subjects around Virginia. Nevertheless, silence was hardly the best means of recovering the control he had over the colony during the starving time. Essentially, he admitted defeat and acquiesced to their rule.

While she lived among the English as their prisoner, Pocahontas was sent to Henrico, where she received instruction in the Christian religion from the Reverend Alexander Whitaker. There she also met with John Rolfe on several occasions, and the pair became close and fell in love. The Englishman agonized over his feelings for the native woman and wrote to Dale, "Nor was I ignorant of the heavy displeasure which Almighty God conceived against the sons of Levi and Israel for marrying strange wives." He rigorously examined his feelings that would provoke a love for a woman "whose education hath been rude, her manners barbarous, and her generation accursed." He felt a Christian duty to convert her to his religion, especially since she had a "desire to be taught and instructed in the knowledge of God." Rolfe asked Dale for permission to marry Pocahontas, and it was granted.[441]

But in March 1613, the English tired of waiting for Wahunsonacock's response and forced the issue. The bellicose Thomas Dale armed 150 men for war, their weapons and armor glinting in the sun as they embarked in Argall's ship and some other vessels. The fleet sailed to the York River. Pocahontas was on board the flagship, frightened for the fate of her father and people. Dale wanted to force the issue, "either to move them to fight for her, if such were their courage and boldness...or to restore the residue of our demands, which were our pieces, swords, and tools."[442]

The Indians who delivered the corn that Wahunsonacock had promised to Jamestown traveled with the English company and evidently showed "great bravado all the way as we went up the river." They bragged that they had always bested the English soldiers "in that river" and reminded them of the brutal death of John Ratcliffe and his men. The Englishmen tired of hearing such bluster and replied that if their werowance did not do as the colonists demanded, they intended to "fight with them, burn their houses, take away their canoes, break down their fishing weirs, and do them what other damages we could." They were armed with cannons, muskets, pistols, and pikes and protected by metal armor.[443]

The Powhatans drew first blood when they shot arrows at the ships from the cover of the woods, according to their way of war. The English responded with overwhelming force. They "went ashore, and burned in that very place some forty houses; and of the things we found therein made freeboot and pillage." They killed five or six Indians for "their presumption in shooting at us."[444]

Dale's men continued on their brief journey upriver and the next day made contact with Powhatans who demanded to know why the English had attacked them. The Englishmen agreed to a temporary truce of twenty-four hours to send messengers to Powhatan to get a response to their demands. The next day the colonists received a message from Wahunsonacock that the prisoners he held had come of their own free will to escape the brutal laws of Jamestown. He also promised to send the weapons and tools the following day. They never arrived, however, and the soldiers went directly to one of the Powhatans' main towns. The Indians put on a show of force, greeting the Englishmen with four hundred warriors armed with bows and arrows.

The soldiers of the rival armies stood nose to nose, each proclaiming that they were ready to go to war. If just one soldier on either side fired their weapon, a terrible bloodbath would follow. In this tense atmosphere, Dale had Pocahontas brought forward as proof for two of Wahunsonacock's sons that she was unhurt. Her brothers rejoiced that she was well and went to relate this good news to their father.

Dale sent two Englishmen, including John Rolfe, to negotiate peace with Wahunsonacock. Although the werowance did not grant them an audience, they were able to conclude a pact with his brother, Opechancanough. It was a sign that the aging Wahunsonacock, whose authority was successfully challenged by the English, would be replaced by Opechancanough. The English saw that he was "one who hath already the command of all the people."[445]

Opechancanough and Rolfe consented to the terms and concluded their peace. The Powhatans would return the weapons and tools as well as any colonists who had run away to the Indian villages. There was an additional provision that Pocahontas would be allowed to live among the English. Rolfe pledged that the colonists would not attack if the terms were observed. Opechancanough made an honorable peace that apparently met with the approval of his people. Meanwhile, the English had won a great deal of territory and established a half dozen settlements and forts away from Jamestown through war and aggressive expansion. With a better survival rate (which was by no means guaranteed even away from Jamestown Island) and additional settlers, the English colony would continue to grow. What the rising Powhatan leader's response would be was anyone's guess.

On April 5, in the wake of the peace pact, John Rolfe married Pocahontas at the church in Jamestown. Dale had given his consent to the union, as did Wahunsonacock. One of Pocahontas's uncles came to Jamestown to give her away, and two of her brothers attended the wedding as witnesses. The marriage was a union of two people in love that touched the core of the English mission in Virginia.[446]

The Chickahominies responded to the peace by aligning themselves closer with the English. "These people, hearing of our concluded peace with Powhatan...sent two of their men unto us, and two fat bucks for [a] present for our king." Dale and Argall then sailed to their town and discussed the terms of an alliance. The Chickahominies, who would be henceforth known as Tassantasses, or Englishmen, submitted to the authority of King James and his governors. The eight chief men who ruled the Chickahominies assented to receive a "red coat, or livery" from the king annually and a picture of King James "engraven in copper, with a chain of copper to hang it about his neck." They also agreed not to launch offensive operations against the colonists and to furnish warriors in case of a Spanish invasion. Dale demanded a tribute of a thousand bushels of corn as a symbol of "their obedience to His Majesty and to his deputy there."[447]

In return, the Indians would receive iron tomahawks and would continue to enjoy "their own liberties, freedoms, and laws, and to be governed as formerly by eight of their chiefest men." The English promised to "defend and keep them from the fury and danger of Powhatan, which thing they most feared, but even from all other enemies domestic or foreign." The two peoples concluded their pact with an exchange of gifts.[448]

With the peace established with the Powhatans and the submission of the Chickahominies, Dale attempted to press his advantage with Wahunsonacock and sent Indian interpreter Thomas Savage and Ralph Hamor to meet with the chief. Hamor left an extensive record of the colony under the leadership of Dale and soon after returned to England, where he could speak intelligently about Wahunsonacock and the Powhatans after being among them. Savage and Hamor delivered a message from Dale asking for another of the werowance's daughters in marriage.

Hamor informed Wahunsonacock that Dale (and the other colonists) had resolved to "dwell in your country so long as he liveth." Therefore, Dale sought to unite the two peoples in a "natural union...of perpetual friendship" by binding them through marriage. The chief declined the offer, telling the ambassadors that his other daughter was already pledged to a husband and "I hold it not a brotherly part of your king [Dale] to desire to bereave me of two of my children at once." Still, he told them that Dale need not fear "any injury from me or any under my subjection." Too many had been killed on both sides, and he hoped that "by my occasion there shall never be more." He added, "I am now old and would gladly end my days in peace." Conceding that the English were too powerful to drive from the land, he stated, "If the English offer me injury, my country is large enough; I will remove myself farther from you." Earlier, when the English were weak, Wahunsonacock dominated the relationship by denying them food to starve them out and surrounding their forts, killing scores of them with impunity. Now, the aggressive expansion of the English forced the aging werowance to withdraw.[449]

On June 12, 1616, Thomas Dale landed at Plymouth aboard Samuel Argall's *Treasurer*. He had "settled to his thinking all things in good order" and chose George Yeardley to serve as deputy governor in his absence.[450] Other passengers on the ship included John Rolfe and Pocahontas, along with their son, Thomas. Pocahontas was accompanied by other Powhatans, including ten female attendants and Uttamatomakkin (or Tomocomo), a priest whom Wahunsonacock sent to "observe and bring news of our king and country to his nation."[451] The prisoners who had been seized from the Spanish vessel, Don Diego de Molina and pilot Francis Lembry, were also carried to England.

Pocahontas and the other Powhatans traveled to London and resided at an inn near St. Paul's Cathedral to finalize their conversion to Christianity. Moreover, they were conspicuous in the city and immediately attracted attention as exotic natives from the Americas. The Virginia Company used the Powhatans as a marketing tool to promote excitement about the Virginia colony and its native peoples, as voyagers had done since the time of Martin Frobisher and other gentlemen adventurers.

As the daughter of Wahunsonacock, the wife of Englishman Rolfe, and an example of the possibility of Indian conversion, Pocahontas was a great sensation among the fashionable elite in the capital. She attended "plays, balls, and other public entertainments" dressed in English clothing as a symbol of her celebrated conversion to England's civilized ways, which trumped interest in the exotic. She was even a guest of the king and queen at a masque presented by playwright Ben Jonson and architect Inigo Jones.[452]

That fall, Pocahontas was reunited with her friend John Smith when she and Rolfe moved to Brentford, west of London. Smith was "preparing to set sail for New England" for the second time that year. In the spring, he had organized two fishing trips to New England for cod. While he was sailing the unexplored regions of the New World, he charted the New England coastline and rivers, which provided invaluable information for another English colonization project less than a decade later. The restless gentleman adventurer continued to search for profit in the New World to advance his personal interest and the imperial interest of the nation.[453]

Smith and Pocahontas had an uncomfortable meeting initially, after a seven-year separation in which she feared that he had died. After seeing him, she "turned about" without a word and went off for a few hours. They finally spoke to each other in an awkward exchange. Pocahontas insisted on calling him "father," just as Smith had used the term with her father when he was a stranger in Virginia. But he would not permit her to do so "because she was a king's daughter."[454] The two parted after their uncomfortable reunion. Pocahontas died of tuberculosis only a few months later, in March 1617.

Whatever the value of Pocahontas and the other Powhatans to the company for the promotion of the colony, there was something of much greater profit to the long-term financial success of the colony aboard the ship that landed at Plymouth. Hundreds of ambitious gentlemen adventurers and common artisans had spent a challenging and often deadly decade fruitlessly seeking gold, the Northwest Passage, and local commodities of even marginal value to send home to frustrated investors. Perhaps the surprising thing was how much risk, bad news, and poor outcomes they had endured.

More importantly, the Virginia Company was finally altering the model of colonization. The decades-old military model, which stretched back to the time of the Elizabethan sea dogs, was giving way to a capitalist and entrepreneurial model that was in close harmony with the longings of English character and human nature. Imperial greatness would be achieved not by harsh discipline and tight organization, but rather by unleashing the energies of private individuals who were seeking wealth.

Chapter Sixteen

AN ENTERPRISING COLONY

The Jamestown colony began to thrive in the late 1610s. It was not merely the discovery of a viable cash crop that could be sold in England that caused this change. Rather, the colony was fundamentally reoriented so that an entrepreneurial ethos provided the foundation for a valuable export crop such as tobacco. Investors had finally found a source of profit and a model on which to build a successful colony.

The *Treasurer* docked in England with cargoes in addition to John Rolfe and his wife, Pocahontas (also known as Lady Rebecca), and her attendants. The vessel also carried a commodity that would contribute more to the long-term success of the Jamestown colony than the exotic people who dazzled London's social circles. Most of the crops delivered by the ship hardly stirred the imaginations of investors, and some of the goods, like hemp and flax, had brought only a pitiful return in England. But Rolfe had also brought a shipment of tobacco, which Thomas Dale believed was "exceeding good."[455]

From 1616 to 1619, the Virginia Company introduced a number of fundamental changes that set the Jamestown colony on the path to success. The company had so far invested more than £50,000 with almost no return. Investors were pulling out or not making scheduled payments, and some were hauled into court to answer a growing number of lawsuits. The problem was that the colonists had not only failed to find great riches in the supposed land of gold, but they had failed to export almost anything of value.

The answer to the problem was to introduce an entrepreneurial element. The colonists had found a cash crop in tobacco. This would sate the nicotine cravings of Londoners who had become addicted to smoking ever since the Spanish discovered the weed in the New World. Even the king had attacked the habit in the pamphlet *Counter-Blast to Tobacco.* He derided tobacco as a "noxious, stinking weed" and smoking "so vile and stinking a custom." Still, the demand was great, and the colonists were eager to supply tobacco to Londoners and profit from the vice. The potential profit for colonists from exporting tobacco trumped any objections raised by moralists, even the king.

Back in Jamestown, in 1612, Rolfe had "first took the pains to make trial" of some West Indian tobacco, which was much milder than the harsh Virginia plant. The result was astounding. "No country under the sun may, or doth, afford more pleasant, sweet, and strong tobacco than I have tasted there." Unfortunately, they did not have "the knowledge to cure and make up." There was little doubt that the crop would "return such tobacco…that even England shall acknowledge the goodness thereof."[456]

In 1614, the colony exported a small shipment after several colonists made close observations of the previous year's crop and successfully experimented with properly drying and curing the weed.

In 1616, although some denounced it as a mere "esteemed weed," Rolfe promoted his high expectations for tobacco and wrote that it was "very commodious, which there thriveth so well that no doubt but after a little more trial and experience in the curing thereof it will compare with the best in the West Indies."[457]

Rolfe wanted to regulate the planting of tobacco "lest the people, who generally are bent to covet after gain, especially having tasted of the sweets of their labors, should spend too much of their time and labor in planting tobacco." Human nature coveted gain, and the Christian Englishmen sought to earn their daily bread by the sweat of their brow. People began working diligently on their crops, because now they were allowed to keep the fruits of their labor. After all, tobacco was "known to them to be very vendible in England."[458]

But they also needed to contribute to the food supplies of the colony, according to the military model of colonial governance. Therefore, Thomas Dale, who had agreed to stay in the colony and serve as governor after acting as marshal, required the colonists to "manure, set, and maintain for himself and every manservant two acres of ground with corn." In addition, the farmers were required to contribute part of their annual food crop to the common store-house "by which means the magazine shall yearly be sure to receive their rent of corn...and many others if need be." If the farmers followed the regulations, they could "plant as much tobacco as they will." If they did not, their tobacco would be "forfeit" and seized by the governor.[459]

Already, tobacco established itself as the "principal commodity the colony for the present yieldeth." The company sent a supply ship with "clothing, household stuff, and such necessaries" that the settlers could purchase with their tobacco as a form of exchange.[460]

Meanwhile, changes were afoot in the colony to allow the settlers to keep other commodities resulting from their hard work. Thomas Dale noted that a number of farmers were "freed from all public works to set corn for themselves." Moreover, every man was provided a sow and allowed to "keep her as his own for five years… so that he is to have all the male pigs every year to kill for his own provision." The encouragement of private initiative yielded many benefits for the colony. The farmers "live most at ease, yet by their good endeavors bring yearly much plenty to the plantation." Blacksmiths, carpenters, shoemakers, tailors, and tanners could "work in their professions for the colony, and maintain themselves with food and apparel, having time limited them to till and manure their ground."[461]

Dale was exaggerating the prosperity of the colonists and the ease of their lifestyle; food shortages still occurred, although they were generally alleviated by the introduction of private property. In 1614, when the seven-year terms of work expired for the original settlers who were servants, Dale allotted them small tracts of land. The enforcer of martial law in Virginia had taken the first halting steps towards private enterprise. In 1616, the year Dale left the colony, the dividend on the investments made in Gates' expedition fell due, and the nearly bankrupt company decided to offer land in Virginia to pay investors and attract new colonists.

When Samuel Argall arrived back in Jamestown as governor in 1617, he and his supporters received land grants to distribute among settlers who took advantage of the company's and attracted the first significant group of immigrants in several years. Those who paid for the passage of servants would receive an additional "headright" of fifty acres. Observers noted that the settlers who owned their own property worked harder in a day than they previously did in a week when they contributed to the common store of food.

The most dramatic changes came with yet another revised charter that formalized the land policies of the company introduced over the previous few years. The "Great Charter" was part of the instructions given to the new governor, George Yeardley, in November 1618. The leaders of the company, particularly Thomas Smythe and Edwin Sandys, sought to establish a set of policies that would achieve the elusive profitability consistent with those originally envisioned as part of the entrepreneurial mission of the colony. If this was to be accomplished, real changes would have to be made. The ensuing reforms fundamentally shifted the colony away from a military form of organization to a model of free enterprise.

The greatest challenge to the failing company was how to attract settlers and investors to a colony with a disastrous reputation in England because of the deathly conditions, draconian set of laws, and pitiful economic returns. The company decided to offer the traditional guarantees of the common law—liberty and self-government—and greater opportunity for those seeking a new life.

Of greatest significance to drawing migrants to Jamestown was the opportunity of owning private property. The new charter stated that any settlers who helped colonize Jamestown before April 1616 would be granted one hundred acres of land "for their personal adventure" and another hundred acres for every share they held in the company. Any who came at the expense of the company would receive the same parcel of land. Colonists who adventured to Jamestown after that date received fifty acres of land. The company stated that the reason later settlers would receive a smaller grant was because the "former difficulties and dangers were in greatest part overcome, to the great ease and security of such as have been since that time transported thither."[462]

The individual ownership of land gave the landless poor in England a great incentive to seek opportunity in the New World. The charter established the headright system, in which individuals would receive an additional fifty acres by paying the cost of emigration for the poor, who would in turn be granted the same amount of land "for their personal adventure" when their term of servitude expired. Rather than struggling to make ends meet in England, settlers could achieve the dream of owning a plot of land to feed themselves and their families while growing a cash crop for export to England. It was a very attractive inducement to risk venturing to the American colony.[463]

The company recognized that the authoritarian character of the colony was highly objectionable and discouraged many potential settlers from going to Virginia. The company sought to quell this source of discontent and revised the martial law that had governed the colony for a set of laws that were consistent with English common law. "The rigor of martial law, wherewith before they were governed, is reduced within the limits prescribed by His Majesty, and the laudable form of justice and government used in this realm, established, and followed as near as may be."[464]

The company instructed Yeardley to set up "a laudable form of government," intended to attract settlers and create a better form of government with the first representative legislature in America. The company directed it to make "just laws for the happy guiding and governing of the people." It was more in accord with the traditional rights and liberties of Englishmen stretching back to the protections of the Magna Carta in 1215 as well as the perennial longings of human nature. In the late 1610s political liberty dovetailed nicely with economic liberty and was a necessary component to it in Jamestown.[465]

The company created a bicameral legislature to govern the colony with just laws. It was the first representative legislature in America and would protect the liberties of the people by separating the branches of government. The people no longer had to submit to strict laws made by an executive and in which they had no voice in creating. One of the legislative houses was a council of state that would advise the governor in discharging his duties. The company would select its members. On the other hand, the free inhabitants of eleven towns, hundreds (subdivisions of an English county with land supporting one hundred families), and plantation settlements would choose two representatives in a body to be known as the House of Burgesses. The "liberty of a General Assembly being granted to them," the free men would be able to "execute those things, as might best tend to their good."[466]

The House of Burgesses was established to make laws for the "public weal" and good order of the colony's affairs. It would convene once a year, unless extraordinary circumstances necessitated its being called into session more frequently. The governor had the authority to veto laws passed by the assembly, and the Virginia Company in London was still the governing authority of the colony and could approve laws made in distant Jamestown. The laws of the colonial government had to be in harmony with English common law.

The company believed that political stability would generate additional investment and settlers willing to move to Virginia for economic opportunities. But the company had a larger purpose in mind. It sought to protect the traditional principle upon which consensual government in England was founded: "Every man will more willingly obey laws to which he hath yielded his consent."[467]

On July 30, 1619, the twenty-two burgesses assembled in the Anglican church at Jamestown and convened the first meeting of the general assembly. The members participated in a solemn prayer service and then took an oath of loyalty to the king of England. The first order of business the assembly took up was to agree to certain parliamentary procedures and accept its members.

It heard petitions for redress and various complaints. The assembly considered Indian relations and rededicated itself to the mandate to convert them to Christianity.

The colonists were required to observe the Sabbath and attend services of the official Anglican religion. Shirkers would be fined and punished. This common impingement on liberty was seen as necessary for the morality and virtue of the individual colonists and the good order of the colony. To this end, the assembly also laid down rules regulating personal behavior, such as excessive drinking, idleness, and gambling.

The assembly regulated the price and quality of tobacco, interfering with the operation of the private market. The members were concerned about the consistency of the quality of tobacco it shipped to England as well as the reputation of that tobacco, since the price would depend on it. But English and European consumers would have given the growers the incentive to uphold the quality of the tobacco they sent or suffer a drop in demand. The assembly also followed the will of the company by encouraging the development of diverse crops and commodities. The company's elusive search for economic diversification was thwarted by a simple fact: individuals could make a lot of money raising tobacco and almost nothing in other endeavors. It was the simple and pure logic of economic self-interest.

From these humble origins, self-government was born in America. It was a special inheritance of Englishmen with their traditional liberties to bequeath to America. Ordered liberty under law and self-government provided the foundation for the protection of private property. The distribution of land grants to settlers allowed them to pursue their own happiness as they determined their own destinies. They were working for themselves rather than for the government under martial discipline.

In August, shortly after the first representative legislature met, a Dutch man-of-war, *The White Lion*, and another privateer, *Treasurer*, arrived at Jamestown with a supply of Africans that they had plundered from the *São João Bautista*. John Rolfe reported that they "sold us twenty-odd Negroes." The Africans' status was vague, but they were probably treated as indentured servants because of the demand for labor. When their terms expired, they held the same property and voting rights as the English, and the successful among them could afford to purchase other indentured Africans and eventually slaves. In the ensuing decades that status would tragically shift from freedom to slavery, and Africans would be denied the most basic liberties and right to the fruits of their labor that were guaranteed to the Europeans.[468]

The results of the land grants and self-governing assembly were startlingly successful. Finally enlarging the Jamestown colony after a decade of failure and frustration. In 1618, the first significant shipment of tobacco—twenty thousand pounds—reached England and fetched £5,250. Investors finally realized some return on their hefty investments. While this sum of money did not put the colony in the black or turn around the company's fortunes overnight, it was a propitious watershed that boded well for future shipments by colonists and future investments by Londoners.

The land grants, expansion of personal liberties, and cultivation of tobacco spurred the kind of migration that Thomas Dale had demanded from the company by force of will. The promise of land and profit led almost four thousand settlers to sail for Jamestown between 1618 and 1621 on an increasing number of ships: six in 1618, fourteen in 1619, thirteen in 1620, and almost two dozen in 1621. Common husbandmen, middling tradesmen and artisans, and some religious dissenters went to Virginia for liberty and opportunity.

Still, the company complained that the colony lacked economic diversification. The leadership of the colony worried that a tobacco craze had seized the people, and as a result the plant was cultivated in "the marketplace, the streets, and all other spare places." John Pory lamented, "All our riches for the present do consist in tobacco." The sudden wealth contributed to a rise of an unlikely conspicuous consumption in a colony that suffered such inhumane conditions only a few years before. Commoners who in England barely eked out a living now walked around Jamestown dressed in "flaming silks" and "fair pearl hatbands and a silken suit." Tobacco was returning a princely profit to many colonists who never would have had such opportunity or riches in England.[469]

Sir Edwin Sandys summed up the effect on the work ethic and financial success of the colonists at Jamestown: "All of them followed their particular labors with singular alacrity and industry, so that through the blessing of God...within the space of three years, our country flourished with many new erected plantations from the head of the river to Kecoughtan." The colonists enjoyed greater prosperity because of tobacco.[470]

The industry shown by the colonists' raising and shipping the profitable commodity was rewarded with great financial returns. In 1620, their harvest reaped some £40,000 to £50,000. Two years later, the amount increased to £60,000 and kept growing rapidly. Moreover, the value of their land increased as additional settlers acquired land and participated in the tobacco bonanza.

Despite their newfound prosperity and plenty, the Jamestown colony was still not the utopia dreamed about for a decade in the company's promotional literature. The settlers did not, of course, participate equally in the riches of land grants and the tobacco trade. The governors and wealthy gentlemen received hundreds and even thousands of acres while others struggled to feed themselves. Disease also continued to plague the colony, and hundreds died annually.

Richard Frethorne, a servant at Martin's Hundred, complained to his parents in England, "I am in a most miserable and pitiful case, for want of meat and want of clothes since I came out of the ship. I never ate anything but peas, and water gruel." He begged his parents to "release me from this bondage, and save my life."[471]

Still, no one could deny the remarkable success the colony had experienced over the past few years. The settlers were free Englishmen who enjoyed liberties and self-government rather than martial law. The colony no longer suffered from the political discord and chaos of the early council during the first days of the settlement. It had discovered an unexpected source of wealth in tobacco, and it used the abundant land to attract settlers and allow them to earn their livelihoods.

But, the Virginia Company was in severe straits in London. Although the leaders of the company had found the solutions to the problems of the colony, they fared much worse in governing the company. Factionalism was tearing apart the company at its core. In 1619, Sandys was able to replace Smythe through a series of machinations, including demands for an audit of company finances. Sandys had his work cut out for him, since the company was in the red to the tune of some £9,000 and almost twice that in uncollected subscriptions.

Sandys instituted a series of reforms including large expenditures on ironworks, which was related to a diversification program to offer alternative forms of investment and profit away from tobacco. He also expected lotteries and subscriptions to raise money for the company's, plans even though they had failed in the past. Sandys's financial administration was an abysmal failure as his lotteries were implicated in charges of corruption and embezzlement, resulting in their termination and leaving the company without a source of income. Meanwhile, the free colonists in Virginia thwarted all attempts to regulate their planting of tobacco. Worst of all, it was painfully evident that company was for all intents and purposes bankrupt in 1621.

The colony itself was thriving, but it was hardly free of difficulties. Challenges persisted that tested the settlers' perseverance. In fact, within only a few years of the beneficent reversal of fortunes, an old danger would threaten to undermine the colony, even as they had found a better model for success.

Chapter Seventeen

A ROYAL COLONY

The tobacco revolution in Virginia led to the expansion of English settlers throughout the fertile farmland along the James River from Elizabeth City up to the falls. And the colonists had recommitted themselves to converting the Indians to Christianity and English civilization. Consequently, they established schools for the Indians with funds from England. Moreover, some Indians were allowed to live among the colonists in order to learn and adopt their ways. In January 1622 the governor happily reported to the company that Virginia was "in very great amity and confidence with the natives."[472]

Wahunsonacock had lost his authority. He eventually died in 1618. His brother Opitchapam replaced the great werowance, although their brother Opechancanough was the real leader of the Powhatans. Opechancanough openly made professions of peace to the English. The new leader visited Jamestown and indicated that he was interested in converting to Christianity. When his greatest warrior, Nemattanew, was shot to death by a settler in March

1622, Opechancanough promised that he would not seek revenge for the slaying. He stated that the death "should be no occasion of the breach of the peace, and…the sky should sooner fall than peace be broken." But his public pronouncements were all subterfuge; Opechancanough was tricking the English into believing he had only peaceful intentions.[473]

In line with their customs, Opechancanough changed his name to Mangopeesomon, and his brother Opitchapam assumed the name Sasawpen, which signaled they were preparing to go to war. The English did not understand the foreboding danger of the name changes. Opechancanough was angry that the English had driven off the Powhatans and their subjects and now occupied the fertile traditional Indian lands along the James River. The war chief knew that he lacked the power to confront the English in a set-piece battle, but unbeknownst to the English, Opechancanough had formed an alliance of tribes who hated the English and wanted to destroy the colony and drive them out of America.

On the morning of March 22, 1622, more than five hundred Powhatan and Pamunkey warriors, along with Appomattocs and other tribes, visited several English settlements as they frequently did to trade deer, turkeys, fish, and other foodstuffs. The Indians had thereby won the confidence and trust of the English. The colonists did not suspect anything out of the ordinary. In fact, they knew many of the traders. The Indians casually spoke and traded with the English in their homes, gardens, streets, and fields. In some places they even "sat down at breakfast with our people at their tables."[474]

Suddenly, the Indians seized farming implements, knives, axes, clubs, and other makeshift weapons. The unsuspecting Englishmen, women, and children were bludgeoned and hacked to death. As the massacre began, screams filled the air. Some wounded individuals fought back and grappled with their attackers. Melees broke out throughout the settlements. Those who were not immediately under attack were frightened, but some women and children managed to grab "spades, axes, and brickbats" and put up a hasty defense and eventually drive off their attackers. The Indians mutilated some of the English and carried off some as prisoners. The captives were never heard from again and were presumably executed. Scores of English colonists and a few Indians were left dead or dying in the afternoon sun.[475]

Some English settlements received an advance warning shortly before the attack and were able to defend themselves. A young Indian boy who had converted to Christianity was instructed to kill his plantation owner and informed that "in the morning a number [of warriors] would come from many places to finish the execution." Instead the boy warned the plantation owner, who informed the governor at Jamestown of the impending attack. Soldiers fired muskets and drove off boatloads of warriors attempting to sneak into the capital. The warning saved their lives, but they were not able to issue a general warning to all the neighboring settlements. The Indians murdered 347 colonists—almost a third of the English colonists in Virginia—that day at more than two dozen sites.[476]

The Indian warriors melted back into the woods after their grisly task was finished, leaving a wake of devastation behind them. In many settlements, only a handful of dazed and confused inhabitants were left alive, reeling from what they had just experienced. In successive days, the Indians came back to finish off the English, forcing the shocked colonists to withdraw to fortified areas. The warriors settled for razing the English homes, burning their towns, destroying their crops, and killing their animals to deprive them of food.

Opechancanough intended the attack to escalate into a war of extermination to kill and drive out the English forever. A few months after the attack, he stated, "Before the end of two moons there should not be an Englishman in all their countries."[477] He very nearly succeeded after killing almost one-third of the colonists. The fear around Virginia among the English was palpable. "The land is ruined and spoiled," one colonist cried. "We live in fear of the enemy every hour…for our plantation is very weak, by reason of the dearth, and sickness."[478]

The English had suffered a major blow but resolved to endure. Indeed, after nearly a decade of relative peace between the two peoples, Opechancanough had loosed the dogs of war and would learn about the English way of doing battle. The colonists would strike a blow much worse than the offensive that Thomas Dale had led in 1611. The English had science and technology at their disposal, far beyond what the Indians could produce.

The Indians had scored a decisive victory based upon their unique fighting style. The psychological effect on the colonists and their supporters in England was profound. The Virginia Company received the news of the sneak attack with a mixture of sadness and anger. The leaders of company expressed their "extreme grief understood of the great massacre executed on our people in Virginia, and that in a manner as is more miserable than the death itself." Still, it was irate with the settlers for not being better prepared for the attack. They were "deaf to so plain a warning…nor to perceive anything in so open and general conspiracy…and almost guilty of the destruction by blindfold and stupid entertaining it." Moreover, their collective sin had brought down the punishing "hand of Almighty God."[479]

The military victory of the natives proved to be temporary. The English prepared a counterattack according to their own devastating methods of warfare. The Virginia Company instructed the governor and council "to root out from being any longer a people, so cursed a nation, ungrateful to all benefit, and incapable of all goodness…let them have a perpetual war without peace or truce."[480] The colony was going to remain firmly planted in Virginia, because moving was tantamount to a "sin against the dead to abandon the enterprise, till we have fully settled the possession, for which so many of our brethren have lost their lives." The company secured the use of thousands of old weapons and armor, which the king released from the Tower of London, and sent them to the colony. [481]

The company reversed its policy of treating the native peoples better than the Spanish and peacefully converting them to Christianity and English civilization. The company did not want the deaths of so many colonists to be in vain. It now instructed the governor to wage a war of annihilation against the Indians, "surprising them in their habitations, intercepting them in their hunting, burning their towns, demolishing their temples, destroying their canoes, plucking up their [fishing] weirs, carrying away their corn, and depriving them of what-soever may yield them succor or relief." In the wake of the massacre, the English view of the Indians as rude, barbarous, brutish, unmanly, and inhumane had hardened. Therefore, the company ordered the colonists to hunt down what they perceived as an uncivilized enemy with bloodhounds and mastiffs to kill or enslave them.[482]

The English would prove themselves to be just as ruthless as the Indians. During the summer and fall of 1622, Governor Francis Wyatt stated, "Our first work is expulsion of the savages to gain free range of the country for it is infinitely better to have no heathen among us." Subsequently, he dispatched raiding parties against the Indians to "revenge their cruel deeds" by unleashing great destruction of their own. The English utilized the mobility provided by their pinnaces and shallops to swoop down on several Indian peoples and destroy their villages, cut down their corn, and torch their fields.[483]

The following spring, with some advanced European weaponry in their hands, the Pamunkey warriors managed to attack some Englishmen in small ships, kill several, and seize their armor and weapons. In another incident, Patawomecks on the Potomac River attacked a group of twenty-six Englishmen who were trading for corn. Even though the Englishmen were protected by armor, they were cut off, surrounded, and killed in revenge for an unprovoked attack the previous year. Only five men escaped in a pinnace, fending off their attackers as they sailed back down the Chesapeake Bay. Frighteningly for the English, the Patawomecks seized the victims' weapons and armor for possible future attacks.

In the spring of 1623 the English succeeded in a deadly ruse to kill off their enemy. Opechancanough's brother, the elderly nominal werowance Opitchapam, offered peace and friendship because "blood enough had already been shed on both sides." He asked to return to his burned lands and village along the Pamunkey River to plant food because his people were starving. In turn, he would return some English prisoners who had supposedly survived after being taken in the massacre of the previous year. Opitchapam also promised that if the English sent a dozen warriors, he would deliver Opechancanough, "who was the author of the massacre into the hands of the English dead or alive."

If Opitchapam was trying to draw some settlers in to slaughter them, the English were prepared with a plan of their own. They feigned friendship with Opitchapam and responded positively to his proffered terms. The governor sent Capt. William Tucker and a dozen soldiers according to Opitchapam's proposal. Tucker offered to seal the deal with a drink of sack wine and made a show of tasting the wine first. But he then passed a bottle of poisoned wine to Opitchapam and his counselors and warriors. While they were feeling the ill effects of the poison, the English fired several muskets volleys and killed scores of Powhatans.[484] Yet they failed to kill Opitchapam, and Opechancanough eluded capture.

The colonists launched another summer campaign against the various Indian tribes, repeating the destruction they had leveled against their villages and stealing their corn. In response, the desperate peoples under Opitchapam decided to fight the well-armed and armored English in a rare set-piece battle. It was bound to favor the English, regardless of Indian numbers.

In July 1624, roughly a thousand warriors defended their village and crops by attacking "not above sixty fighting [English] men" in open battle. As the respective sides confronted each other in the "open field," the Pamunkeys bragged loudly about "what they would do" to the English. Over two days of vicious combat, the Indians fought bravely, but English muskets loosed a withering fire against them. The Indians suffered staggering losses compared to the light English casualties. The victorious colonists took the Indians' corn, and the surviving Indians "dismayedly, stood most ruefully looking on while their corn was cut down."[485]

The war that lasted from 1622 to 1624 had dramatic consequences for both the English and the natives in Virginia. The English victory was complete, and they now dominated the area around the colony. They had mastered the Indians in Virginia and could pursue their profitable tobacco planting. Yet after recovering its strength following the Indian massacre two years before, the colony was never in greater peril. The irony was that the threat came from London rather than Virginia, because the bad news hurt the company, which had already suffered internal divisions tearing it apart.

When the news of the Indian massacre and the starvation among the colonists reached London in the spring of 1623, the state of the colony shocked members of the company and the government. The glowing accounts of Virginia in the company's promotional literature were again contradicted by observers who reported on the continuing struggles. News of the attack was compounded by continuing internal struggles within the company and its relationship with the Crown.

Since 1619, when a seven-year exemption from import duties on the colony expired, the Crown had taxed the attractive burgeoning tobacco trade as a source of revenue. Although it was less than the tariff on Spanish tobacco, the tax significantly cut into the settlers' income and caused resentment. They turned to smuggling the tobacco to Holland, incurring the wrath of the king's ministers. Negotiations between Sandys and the Crown for a tobacco monopoly and tax only divided the company further, as Smythe and his allies attacked Sandys, resulting in bitter factional strife that was brought before the Privy Council.

In May 1623, the Crown established a commission to investigate the colony by examining company records, letters, and questioning former settlers and travelers who had been to Virginia. That autumn a four-man commission traveled to Virginia to inspect the colony.

The failures of the colony were obvious as damning evidence was accumulated. The Indian massacre was evidence that this threat had not dissipated. The colony may have generated profits with the export of tobacco, but these profits were not enough to prevent the company from falling into bankruptcy, nor had the colony established the diversified economy that the company and Crown had wished. On top of that, because of the disease climate, thousands had died since 1607.

The first commission declared that the colony was in a "weak and miserable" condition and argued that the Crown should revoke the company's charter and seize control of the colony. King James ordered Attorney General Sir Thomas Coventry to sue the company in the Court of the King's Bench. On May 24, 1624, almost exactly after seventeen years of struggle and death, the court sided with the Crown and ordered the Virginia Company's charter revoked. The following year, the new king, Charles I, made Jamestown a royal colony dependent upon the Crown rather than a commercial enterprise. The colony's trade and commerce was an attractive target for the king. Yet, it did not take long for the colony to recover from the Indian attack of 1622, and the tobacco trade rapidly grew. Exports of tobacco to England increased dramatically from three hundred thousand pounds in 1630 to one million pounds in 1640 and almost thirty million pounds at the end of the century. The price of tobacco, however, followed the law of supply and demand and gradually fell, causing many farmers to suffer difficult times. Still, tens of thousands of Englishmen and women migrated to Virginia in search of opportunity. The settlers earned money from raising the cash crop, but their success was more fundamentally rooted in the expansion of liberty and opportunity.

The rule of liberty and self-government drew many more settlers than the false promises of the martial regime that predominated during the first decade of settlement. The principles were laid down after a decade of struggling under a failed authoritarian regime. The Virginia Company had introduced and fostered a more capitalist framework of free enterprise that built the American character at the dawn of the colonial era of American history.

Epilogue

During the course of the seventeenth century, Virginia continued to grow and thrive. The Jamestown colony instituted free representative government, governed according to the rule of law, and introduced a system of free enterprise that rewarded industry and individual initiative. These entrepreneurial principles were inherited from England, held by the Elizabethan and Jacobean gentlemen adventurers who first settled North America, and gradually enshrined in the American character. Although the American colonies were part of the mercantilist system of England that limited free trade and heavily regulated American trade, the principles of free enterprise predominated among the colonists.

The development of a capitalist ethic in America was advanced by the American Revolution, as the Declaration of Independence stated that it was an unalienable right that all people could pursue their own happiness unfettered by government. Moreover, the U.S. Constitution was framed to protect liberty and private property and laid the foundation for the rule of law that was necessary for private enterprise to thrive.

The American Dream, which originated along the banks of the James, was perhaps represented most symbolically by the quintessential rags-to-riches story of Benjamin Franklin. In his *Autobiography,* Franklin stated the reason for writing his story: "Having emerged from the poverty and obscurity in which I was born and bred, to a state of affluence and some degree of reputation in the world...my posterity may like to know, as they may find some of them suitable to their own situations, and therefore fit to be imitated."[486]

Franklin's dream was not achieved by all who tried to flee poverty and obscurity, nor was it truly within reach of certain groups who did not enjoy the promise of liberty to pursue their own happiness. Nevertheless, it remained the ideal and part of the American identity. It was attained by many Americans over the centuries, as individuals were free to pursue their own destinies and reach for their dreams with industry, creativity, a bit of pluck, and a great passion to get wealthy.

In the 1830s Alexis de Tocqueville, a French observer of American character, noted the relentless pursuit of wealth among Americans that drove them incessantly forward. In his classic *Democracy in America,* Tocqueville wrote, "In America, therefore, each finds easy ways, unknown elsewhere, to make his fortune or to increase it. Cupidity is always breathless there, and the human mind... gets carried away only in the pursuit of wealth. Not only does one see industrial and commercial classes in the United States, as in all other countries; but what has never been encountered—all men simultaneously occupied with industry and commerce." This ribald individualism made America the most prosperous and dominant global power over the last two centuries.[487]

Despite all the changes in the American economy throughout American history—industrial, transportation, commercial, technological and communication revolutions, globalization, and the growth of government regulation of the private economy—the enterprising American character has proved remarkably resilient, and has endured. Americans are still free individuals doggedly pursuing their wealth in ever-changing ways, taking great risks and sometimes reaping great rewards. The same enterprising spirit that drove the Elizabethan gentlemen adventurers to Virginia, that led to the rise of men like Benjamin Franklin, that characterized the American identity that Tocqueville observed, and that has been responsible for the success stories of countless famous individuals and ordinary persons is alive and well.

And it all started at Jamestown in 1607. The adventurers such as John Smith, Christopher Newport, and Sir Thomas Gates who loomed large in the early history of the colony were free and enterprising English gentlemen, but they could not establish a lasting colony because they built it on the wrong principles. In time, the colony thrived under the leadership of men such as the lesser-known George Yeardley, because it was rooted upon entrepreneurial principles rather than the vain personalities of the first gentlemen. By giving opportunity to all, the colony built the American Dream for all who would work hard to reap the fruits of their labor.

ENDNOTES

1   Samuel Eliot Morison, *The European Discovery of America: The Northern Voyages, A.D. 500–1600* (New York: Oxford University Press, 1971), 157–92 (hereafter cited as *Northern Voyages*).

2   Samuel Eliot Morison, *Admiral of the Ocean Sea: A Life of Christopher Columbus* (Boston: Little Brown, 1942).

3   Henry Kamen, *Empire: How Spain Became a World Power, 1492–1763* (New York: HarperCollins, 2003), 41–42.

4   Kamen, *Empire*, 83–105.

5   Kamen, *Empire*, 125–28.

6   Laurence Bergreen, *Over the Edge of the World: Magellan's Terrifying Circumnavigation of the Globe* (New York: HarperCollins, 2004).

7   Susan Brigden, *New Worlds, Lost Worlds: The Rule of the Tudors, 1485–1603* (New York: Penguin, 2000), 281–82; Arthur Herman, *To Rule the Waves: How the British Navy Shaped the Modern World* (New York: HarperCollins, 2004), 24–29; and Susan Ronald, *The Pirate Queen: Queen Elizabeth I, Her Pirate Adventurers, and the Dawn of Empire* (New York: HarperCollins, 2007), 17–19.

8   Ronald, *Pirate Queen,* 46–52.

9   Herman, *To Rule the Waves,* 1–23; and Harry Kelsey, *Sir John Hawkins: Queen Elizabeth's Slave Trader* (New Haven: Yale University Press, 2003), 13–115.

10 Herman, *To Rule the Waves,* 54.

11 Herman, *To Rule the Waves,* 55–60.

12 Samuel Eliot Morison, *The European Discovery of America: The Southern Voyages, A.D. 1492–1616* (New York: Oxford University Press, 1974), 634–45 (hereafter cited as *Southern Voyages*).

13 Harry Kelsey, *Sir Francis Drake: The Queen's Pirate* (New Haven: Yale University Press, 1998), 93–204.

14 Morison, *Southern Voyages,* 655–85.

15 Morison, *Northern Voyages,* 500–10.

16 Morison, *Northern Voyages,* 561–67.

17 Morison, *Northern Voyages,* 568–78.

18 Peter C. Mancall, *Hakluyt's Promise: An Elizabethan's Obsession for an English America* (New Haven: Yale University Press, 2007), 1–24.

19 Mancall, *Hakluyt's Promise,* 94–101.

20 Mancall, *Hakluyt's Promise,* 138–50.

21 David Beers Quinn, *Raleigh and the British Empire* (London: English Universities Press, 1947), 1–50; and Raleigh Trevelyan, *Sir Walter Raleigh* (New York: Henry Holt, 2002), 1–65.

22 Karen Ordahl Kupperman, *Roanoke: The Abandoned Colony,* 2nd ed. (Lanham, MD: Rowman and Littlefield, 2007), 14–16.

23 David Beers Quinn, *Set Fair for Roanoke: Voyages and Colonies, 1584–1606* (Chapel Hill: University of North Carolina Press, 1985), 55–86.

24 Ronald, *Pirate Queen,* 277–90.

25 Horn, *A Kingdom Strange,* 104–09.

26 Quinn, *Set Fair for Roanoke,* 241–300.

27 James Horn, *A Kingdom Strange: The Brief and Tragic History of the Lost Colony of Roanoke* (New York: Basic Books, 2010), 166–72.

28   Ronald, *Pirate Queen,* 296–302.

29   Colin Martin and Geoffrey Parker, *The Spanish Armada* (New York: Norton, 1988), 125–207; and Garrett Mattingly, *The Armada* (Boston: Houghton Mifflin, 1959), 257–375.

30   Horn, *A Kingdom Strange,* 184–92.

31   Ronald, *Pirate Queen,* 364–65.

32   John Micklethwait and Adrian Wooldridge, *The Company: A Short History of a Revolutionary Idea* (New York: Modern Library, 2003).

33   Kenneth R. Andrews, *Trade, Plunder, and Settlement: Maritime Enterprise and the Genesis of the British Empire, 1480–1630* (Cambridge: Cambridge University Press, 1984), 1–2.

34   John Smith, "The General History," in *Jamestown Narratives: Eyewitness Accounts of the Virginia Colony, the First Decade, 1607–1617,* ed. Edward Wright Halile (Champlain, VA: RoundHouse, 1988), 222 (hereafter cited as *JN*).

35   Smith, "General History," 222.

36   "Letters Patent to Sir Thomas Gates and Others," April 10, 1606, in *The Jamestown Voyages under the First Charter, 1606–1609,* ed. Philip L. Barbour, 2 vols. (Cambridge: Cambridge University Press, 1969), 1:24 (hereafter cited as *JV*).

37   "Letters Patent," *JV,* 1:24.

38   "Letters Patent," *JV,* 1:31.

39   "Letters Patent," *JV,* 1:25.

40   "Letters Patent," *JV,* 1:26.

41   "Letters Patent," *JV,* 1:28.

42   "Orders for the Council for Virginia," December 10, 1606, in *JV,* 1:46.

43   "Instructions for Government," November 20, 1606, *JV,* 1:35–36.

44   "Instructions for Government," *JV,* 1:37–38.

45   "Instructions for Government," *JV,* 1:39–40.

46   George Percy, "Observations Gathered out of a Discourse of the Plantation of the Southern Colony in Virginia by the English, 1606," *JV,* 1:129.

47   Smith, "General History," *JN*, 223.

48   Smith, "General History," *JN*, 223.

49   Percy, "Observations," *JV*, 1:129.

50   Smith, "General History," *JN*, 225.

51   Percy, "Observations," *JV*, 1:129–30.

52   Percy, "Observations," *JV*, 1:130.

53   Percy, "Observations," *JV*, 1:131.

54   Percy, "Observations," *JV*, 1:132.

55   Smith, "General History," *JN*, 223; Percy, "Observations," *JV*, 1:132.

56   Smith, "General History," *JN*, 223.

57   Percy, "Observations," *JV*, 1:133.

58   Percy, "Observations," *JV*, 1:133.

59   Smith, "General History," *JN*, 223.

60   Smith, "General History," *JN*, 223.

61   Percy, "Observations," *JV*, 1:133.

62   Percy, "Observations," *JV*, 1:133–34.

63   Percy, "Observations," *JV*, 1:134–35.

64   Percy, "Observations," *JV*, 1:135.

65   Percy, "Observations," *JV*, 1:135–37.

66   Percy, "Observations," *JV*, 1:137–38.

67   John Smith, "A True Relation," 1608, *JV*, 1:170.

68   Percy, "Observations," *JV*, 1:141.

69   Percy, "Observations," *JV*, 1:141.

70   Smith, "True Relation," *JV*, 1:170.

71   Smith, "General History," *JN*, 224.

72   Smith, "General History," *JN*, 224.

73   Percy, "Observations," *JV*, 1:139.

74   Percy, "Observations," *JV*, 1:140.

75   Gabriel Archer, "A Relation," *JV*, 1:81.

76   Archer, "Relation," *JV*, 1:82–87.

77   Archer, "Relation," *JV*, 1:84–86.

78   Archer, "Relation," *JV*, 1:91.

79   Archer, "Relation," *JV*, 1:93.

80   Archer, "Relation," *JV*, 1:88–89.

81   Archer, "Relation," *JV*, 1:94–95.

82   Archer, "Relation," *JV*, 1:95; Smith, "True Relation," *JV*, 1:172.

83   Archer, "Relation," *JV*, 1:95; Smith, "True Relation," *JV*, 1:172; Smith, "General History," *JN*, 224–25.

84   George Percy, "Discourse," 1608, *JV*, 1:142.

85   Archer, "Relation," *JV*, 1:96.

86   Archer, "Relation," *JV*, 1:96.

87   Archer, "Relation," *JV*, 1:96–97.

88   Archer, "Relation," *JV*, 1:97–98.

89   Archer, "Relation," *JV*, 1:96–98.

90   Smith, "General History," *JN*, 225–26.

91   Archer, "Relation," *JV*, 1:98.

92   Edward Maria Wingfield, "Discourse," 1608, *JV*, 1:214.

93   "Letter from the Council in Virginia," June 22, 1607, *JV*, 1:78–80.

94   Christopher Newport to Lord Salisbury, July 29, 1607, *JV*, 1:76.

95   Sir Walter Cope to Lord Salisbury, August 12, 131607, *JV*, 1:108–11.

96   Sir Thomas Smythe to Lord Salisbury, August 17, 1607, *JV*, 1:112.

97   Pedro de Zúñiga to Philip III, August 22, 1607, *JV*, 1:77.

98   Pedro de Zúñiga to Philip III, September 22, 1607, *JV*, 1:114.

99   Pedro de Zúñiga to Philip III, October 16, 1607, *JV*, 1:120.

100 Philip III to Pedro de Zúñiga, October 28, 1607, *JV*, 1:122–23.

101 George Percy, "Discourse," 1608, *JV*, 1:143–45.

102 Smith, "General History," *JN*, 230.

103 Percy, "Discourse," *JV*, 1:143.

104 Percy, "Discourse," *JV*, 1:144–45.

105 Percy, "Discourse," *JV*, 1:144.

106 Percy, "Discourse," *JV*, 1:144–45.

107 Smith, "General History," *JN*, 230.

108 Percy, "Discourse," *JV*, 1:144–45.

109 Percy, "Discourse," *JV*, 1:145.

110 Wingfield, "Discourse," *JV*, 1:219.

111 Smith, "True Relation," *JV*, 1:173; Smith, "General History," *JN*, 230.

112 Smith, "True Relation," *JV*, 1:173.

113 Wingfield, "Discourse," *JV*, 1:217.

114 Wingfield, "Discourse," *JV*, 1:217–18.

115 Wingfield, "Discourse," *JV*, 1:219–20.

116 Wingfield, "Discourse," *JV*, 1:220.

117 Wingfield, "Discourse," *JV*, 1:221–23.

118 Wingfield, "Discourse," *JV*, 1:218–22.

119 Smith, "General History," *JN*, 230.

120 Wingfield, "Discourse," *JV*, 1:226.

121 Smith, "True Relation," *JV*, 1:174.

122 Smith, "True Relation," *JV*, 1:174.

123 Smith, "General History," *JN*, 232.

124 Smith, "General History," *JN*, 232.

125 Wingfield, "Discourse," *JV*, 1:224.

126 Wingfield, "Discourse," *JV*, 1:225.

127 Smith, "True Relation," *JV*, 1:180.

128 Smith, "True Relation," *JV*, 1:180.

129 Smith, "True Relation," *JV*, 1:180.

130 Smith, "True Relation," *JV*, 1:180–81.

131 Smith, "General History," *JN*, 235.

132 Smith, "General History," *JN*, 235–36; Smith, "True Relation," *JV*, 1:181–82.

133 William White, "Fragments," *JV*, 1:150.

134 White, "Fragments," *JV*, 1:150.

135 Smith, "General History," *JN*, 236.

136 Smith, "True Relation," *JV*, 1:182.

137 Smith, "True Relation," *JV*, 1:182–83.

138 Smith, "True Relation," *JV*, 1:184.

139 Smith, "General History," *JN*, 239; Smith, "True Relation," *JV*, 1:185–86.

140 Smith, "True Relation," *JV*, 1:185–86.

141 Smith, "General History," *JN*, 239.

142 Smith, "General History," *JN*, 240.

143 Smith, "General History," *JN*, 240.

144 Smith, "General History," *JN*, 240–41.

145 Francis Perkins, Letter to England, March 28, 1608, *JV*, 1:159.

146 Smith, "True Relation," *JV*, 1:189.

147 Wingfield, "Discourse," *JV*, 1:227–28.

148 Smith, "General History," *JN*, 236.

149 Smith, "True Relation," *JV*, 1:190.

150 Perkins, "Letter," *JV*, 1:160.

151 Smith, "True Relation," *JV*, 1:191–92.

152 Smith, "True Relation," *JV*, 1:192–93.

153 Smith, "True Relation," *JV*, 1:191.

154 Smith, "General History," *JN*, 245.

155 Smith, "General History," *JN*, 245–46.

156 Smith, "General History," *JN*, 246.

157 Smith, "General History," *JN*, 246.

158 Smith, "True Relation," *JV*, 1:195–99.

159 Smith, "General History," *JN*, 243, 247.

160 Smith, "General History," *JN*, 247.

161 Smith, "General History," *JN*, 247–48.

162 Smith, "True Relation," *JV*, 1:201.

163 Smith, "True Relation," *JV*, 1:201–2; Smith, "General History," *JN*, 242.

164 Smith, "General History," *JN*, 249.

165 Smith, "General History," *JN*, 249.

166 Smith, "General History," *JN*, 251.

167 Smith, "General History," *JN*, 257.

168 Smith, "General History," *JN*, 257–58.

169 Smith, "General History," *JN*, 259–60.

170 Smith, "General History," *JN*, 260–61.

171 Smith, "General History," *JN*, 261–62.

172 Smith, "General History," *JN*, 263–65.

173 Smith, "General History," *JN*, 263–64, 278.

174 Smith, "General History," *JN*, 264.

175 Smith, "General History," *JN*, 264.

176 Smith, "General History," *JN*, 266–68.

177 Smith, "General History," *JN*, 268–77.

178 Smith, "General History," *JN*, 279–80.

179 Smith, "General History," *JN*, 279.

180 Smith, "General History," *JN*, 280–81.

181 Smith, "General History," *JN*, 281.

182 Smith, "General History," *JN*, 281.

183 Smith, "General History," *JN*, 282.

184 Smith, "General History," *JN*, 282.

185 Smith, "General History," *JN*, 283–84.

186 Smith, "General History," *JN*, 286–87.

187 John Smith to the Treasurer and Council of Virginia, *JN*, 287–88.

188 Smith to the Treasurer and Council, *JN*, 287–88.

189 Smith to the Treasurer and Council, *JN*, 289–90.

190 Smith, "General History," *JN*, 293.

191 Smith, "General History," *JN*, 293.

192 Smith, "General History," *JN*, 294.

193 Smith, "General History," *JN*, 296.

194 Smith, "General History," *JN*, 297.

195 Smith, "General History," *JN*, 298.

196 Smith, "General History," *JN*, 298.

197 Smith, "General History," *JN*, 299–300.

198 Smith, "General History," *JN*, 300.

199 Smith, "General History," *JN*, 300.

200 Smith, "General History," *JN*, 301.

201 Smith, "General History," *JN*, 301.

202 Smith, "General History," *JN*, 304–5.

203 Smith, "General History," *JN*, 305–6.

204 Smith, "General History," *JN*, 306.

205 Smith, "General History," *JN*, 306.

206 Smith, "General History," *JN*, 307.

207 Smith, "General History," *JN*, 296–308.

208 Smith, "General History," *JN*, 304.

209 Smith, "General History," *JN*, 304.

210 Smith, "General History," *JN*, 308.

211 Smith, "General History," *JN*, 314.

212 Smith, "General History," *JN*, 314.

213 Smith, "General History," *JN*, 315.

214 Smith, "General History," *JN*, 316–17.

215 Smith, "General History," *JN*, 319–20.

216 Smith, "General History," *JN*, 320.

217 Smith, "General History," *JN*, 320–21.

218 "The Second Charter of the Virginia Company." Alexander Brown, *The Genesis of the United States,* 2 vols. (Boston and New York: Houghton Mifflin, 1891), I: 233.

219 The Council of Virginia, "A True and Sincere Declaration," *JN*, 363.

220 "Instructions to Thomas Gates," Before May 15, 1609," *JV*, 2:262–64.

221 Lorri Glover and Daniel Blake Smith, *The Shipwreck that Saved Jamestown: The* Sea Venture *Castaways and the Fate of America* (New York: Henry Holt, 2008), 57.

222 Glover and Smith, *The Shipwreck that Saved Jamestown,* 57–59.

223 Glover and Smith, *The Shipwreck that Saved Jamestown,* 59, 68–69.

224 Kieran Doherty, Sea Venture: *Shipwreck, Survival, and the Salvation of the First English Colony in the New World* (New York: St. Martin's), 13–14.

225 Glover and Smith, *The Shipwreck that Saved Jamestown*, 62–67.

226 Glover and Smith, *The Shipwreck that Saved Jamestown*, 62–67.

227 Glover and Smith, *The Shipwreck that Saved Jamestown*, 59.

228 Glover and Smith, *The Shipwreck that Saved Jamestown*, 57.

229 Glover and Smith, *The Shipwreck that Saved Jamestown*, 61.

230 Don Pedro de Zúñiga to Philip III, *JV*, 254-61, 269.

231 Don Pedro de Zúñiga to Philip III, *JV*, 254-61, 269.

232 Doherty, Sea Venture, 26.

233 Smith, "General History," *JN*, 327.

234 Gabriel Archer to Unknown Friend, August 31, 1609, *JV*, 1:279.

235 Archer to Unknown Friend, *JV*, 1:279–80.

236 Archer to Unknown Friend, *JV*, 1:280.

237 Dava Sobel, *Longitude: The True Story of a Lone Genius Who Solved the Greatest Scientific Problem of His Time* (New York: Walker, 1995).

238 William Strachey, "A True Repertory of the Wreck," *JN*, 383.

239 Archer to Unknown Friend, *JV*, 1:280.

240 Archer to Unknown Friend, *JV*, 1:280.

241 Marcus Rediker, *Between the Devil and the Deep Blue Sea: Merchant Seamen, Pirates, and the Anglo-American Maritime World, 1700–1750* (Cambridge: Cambridge University Press, 1987), 195–96.

242 Rediker, *Between the Devil and the Deep Blue Sea*, 195–96.

243 Rediker, *Between the Devil and the Deep Blue Sea*, 195–96.

244 Rediker, *Between the Devil and the Deep Blue Sea*, 169–75.

245 Archer to Unknown Friend, *JV*, 1:281.

246 Strachey, "True Repertory of the Wreck," *JN*, 384.

247 Strachey, "True Repertory of the Wreck," *JN*, 384.

248 Strachey, "True Repertory of the Wreck," *JN*, 384.

249 Archer to Unknown Friend, *JV*, 1:281.

250 Strachey, "True Repertory of the Wreck," *JN*, 384,

251 Council of Virginia, "A True Declaration of the Estate of the Colony in Virginia," in *Tracts and Other Papers Relating Principally to the*

Origin, Settlement, and Progress of the Colonies in North America from the Discovery of the Country to the Year 1776, comp. Peter Force, 4 vols. (Washington, DC: W. Q. Force, 1836–46), 1:10 (hereafter cited as *Tracts and Other Papers*).

252 Strachey, "True Repertory of the Wreck," *JN*, 384.

253 Strachey, "True Repertory of the Wreck," *JN*, 385.

254 Strachey, "True Repertory of the Wreck," *JN*, 385.

255 David Cressy, *Coming Over: Migration and Communication between England and New England in the Seventeenth Century* (Cambridge: Cambridge University Press, 1987), 164.

256 Strachey, "True Repertory of the Wreck," *JN*, 385.

257 Strachey, "True Repertory of the Wreck," *JN*, 385.

258 Archer to Unknown Friend, *JV*, 1:281.

259 William Strachey, "A True Repertory of the Wreck," *JN*, 384.

260 Virginia Company, "A True Declaration of the Estate of the Colony in Virginia," *Tracts and Other Papers,* 1:10.

261 Strachey, "True Repertory of the Wreck," *JN*, 385.

262 Strachey, "True Repertory of the Wreck," *JN*, 386.

263 Strachey, "True Repertory of the Wreck," *JN*, 385.

264 Strachey, "True Repertory of the Wreck," *JN*, 386.

265 Strachey, "True Repertory of the Wreck," *JN*, 386.

266 Strachey, "True Repertory of the Wreck," *JN*, 388.

267 Strachey, "True Repertory of the Wreck," *JN*, 386.

268 Strachey, "True Repertory of the Wreck," *JN*, 386–87.

269 Sylvester Jourdain, "A Discovery of the Barmudas, Otherwise Called the Isle of Devils," in *A Voyage to Virginia in 1609: Two Narratives,* ed. Louis B. Wright (Charlottesville: University Press of Virginia, 1964), 105–6.

270 Jourdain, "Discovery of the Barmudas," *Voyage to Virginia in 1609,* 106.

271 Strachey, "True Repertory of the Wreck," *JN*, 387.

272 Strachey, "True Repertory of the Wreck," *JN*, 387.

273 Strachey, "True Repertory of the Wreck," *JN*, 388.

274 Strachey, "True Repertory of the Wreck," *JN*, 388.

275 Strachey, "True Repertory of the Wreck," *JN*, 388–89.

276 Strachey, "True Repertory of the Wreck," *JN*, 389.

277 Strachey, "True Repertory of the Wreck," *JN*, 389.

278 Rediker, *Between the Devil and the Deep Blue Sea,* 181–82.

279 Strachey, "True Repertory of the Wreck," *JN*, 389.

280 Rediker, *Between the Devil and the Deep Blue Sea,* 181–82.

281 Strachey, "True Repertory of the Wreck," *JN*, 390.

282 Strachey, "True Repertory of the Wreck," *JN*, 391.

283 Strachey, "True Repertory of the Wreck," *JN*, 391.

284 Strachey, "True Repertory of the Wreck," *JN*, 390.

285 Jourdain, "Discovery of the Barmudas," *Voyage to Virginia in 1609,* 106.

286 Jourdain, "Discovery of the Barmudas," *Voyage to Virginia in 1609,* 106.

287 Jourdain, "Discovery of the Barmudas," *Voyage to Virginia in 1609,* 107.

288 Jourdain, "Discovery of the Barmudas," *Voyage to Virginia in 1609,* 106.

289 Jourdain, "Discovery of the Barmudas," *Voyage to Virginia in 1609,* 107.

290 Strachey, "True Repertory of the Wreck," *JN*, 390.

291 Archer to Unknown Friend, *JV*, 1:279.

292 Emanuel van Meteren, "Historical Commentaries Relating to the Netherlands, 1610," *JV*, 1:278.

293 Archer to Unknown Friend, *JV*, 1:279.

294 The Ancient Planters of Virginia, "A Brief Declaration of the Plantation of Virginia During the First Twelve Years," *JN*, 895.

295 Archer to Unknown Friend, August 31, 1609, *JN*, 352–53.

296 John Ratcliffe to Salisbury, October 4, 1609, *JN*, 354.

297 Smith, "General History," *JN*, 328–29.

298 Percy, "True Relation," *JN*, 501–2.

299 Smith, "General History," *JN*, 331–32.

300 Smith, "General History," *JN*, 332.

301 Smith, "General History," *JN*, 332.

302 John Ratcliffe to Salisbury, October 4, 1609, *JN*, 354.

303 Percy, "True Relation," *JN*, 503.

304 Percy, "True Relation," *JN*, 503.

305 Percy, "True Relation," *JN*, 503–4.

306 Henry Spelman, "Relation of Virginia, 1609," *JN*, 483.

307 Percy, "True Relation," *JN*, 504.

308 Percy, "True Relation," *JN*, 504.

309 Spelman, "Relation of Virginia," *JN*, 484.

310 Percy, "True Relation," *JN*, 504.

311 Percy, "True Relation," *JN*, 504–5.

312 Percy, "True Relation," *JN*, 505.

313 Jourdain, "Discovery of the Barmudas," *Voyage to Virginia in 1609*, 107.

314 Strachey, "True Repertory of the Wreck," *JN*, 412–13.

315 Jourdain, "Discovery of the Barmudas," *Voyage to Virginia in 1609*, 107–8.

316 Strachey, "True Repertory," Wright, 16.

317 Jourdain, "Discovery of the Barmudas," *Voyage to Virginia in 1609*, 108.

318 Strachey, "True Repertory," Wright, 16.

319 Strachey, "True Repertory," Wright, 16.

320 Jourdain, "Discovery of the Barmudas," *Voyage to Virginia in 1609*, 110.

321 Strachey, "True Repertory of the Wreck," *JN*, 397.

322 Strachey, "True Repertory of the Wreck," *JN*, 399.

323 Strachey, "True Repertory of the Wreck," *JN*, 400.

324 Jourdain, "Discovery of the Barmudas," *Voyage to Virginia*, 111.

325 Strachey, "True Repertory of the Wreck," *JN*, 399–400.

326 Strachey, "True Repertory of the Wreck," *JN*, 397.

327 Jourdain, "Discovery of the Barmudas," *Voyage to Virginia in 1609*, 109.

328 Strachey, "True Repertory of the Wreck," *JN*, 391.

329 Strachey, "True Repertory of the Wreck," *JN*, 402.

330 Virginia Company of London, "Instructions to Sir Thomas Gates," Before May 15, 1609, *JV*, 2:263–64.

331 Strachey, "True Repertory of the Wreck," *JN*, 403.

332 Strachey, "True Repertory of the Wreck," *JN*, 402.

333 Strachey, "True Repertory of the Wreck," *JN*, 403–4.

334 Strachey, "True Repertory of the Wreck," *JN*, 404–5.

335 Strachey, "True Repertory of the Wreck," *JN*, 404.

336 Strachey, "True Repertory of the Wreck," *JN*, 404–5.

337 Strachey, "True Repertory of the Wreck," *JN*, 405.

338 Strachey, "True Repertory of the Wreck," *JN*, 403.

339 Strachey, "True Repertory of the Wreck," *JN*, 403, 414.

340 Strachey, "True Repertory of the Wreck," *JN*, 392–93, 414.

341 Strachey, "True Repertory of the Wreck," *JN*, 406–7.

342 Strachey, "True Repertory of the Wreck," *JN*, 407.

343 Strachey, "True Repertory of the Wreck," *JN*, 408–9.

344 Strachey, "True Repertory of the Wreck," *JN*, 409.

345 Strachey, "True Repertory of the Wreck," *JN*, 409.

346 Strachey, "True Repertory of the Wreck," *JN*, 409.

347 Strachey, "True Repertory of the Wreck," *JN*, 410.

348 Strachey, "True Repertory of the Wreck," *JN*, 410–12.

349 Strachey, "True Repertory of the Wreck," *JN*, 412–13.

350 Strachey, "True Repertory of the Wreck," *JN*, 415.

351 Percy, "True Relation," *JN*, 505.

352 Virginia General Assembly, *JN*, 913.

353 Virginia General Assembly, *JN*, 913.

354 Strachey, "A True Repertory of the Wreck," *JN*, 419.

355 Percy, "True Relation," *JN*, 505.

356 Percy, "True Relation," *JN*, 505.

357 Percy, "True Relation," *JN*, 505.

358 Percy, "True Relation," *JN*, 505.

359 Percy, "True Relation," *JN*, 505.

360 Strachey, "True Repertory of the Wreck," *JN*, 417.

361 Strachey, "True Repertory of the Wreck," *JN*, 417.

362 Strachey, "True Repertory of the Wreck," *JN*, 418.

363 Percy, "True Relation," *JN*, 506.

364 Strachey, "True Repertory of the Wreck," *JN*, 418.

365 Percy, "True Relation," *JN*, 507.

366 Strachey, "True Repertory of the Wreck," *JN*, 419.

367 Strachey, "True Repertory of the Wreck," *JN*, 419.

368 Strachey, "True Repertory of the Wreck," *JN*, 420–22.

369 Jourdain, "Discovery of the Barmudas," *Voyage to Virginia in 1609*, 115.

370 Strachey, "True Repertory of the Wreck," *JN*, 419.

371 Strachey, "True Repertory of the Wreck," *JN*, 419.

372 Strachey, "True Repertory of the Wreck," *JN*, 424.

373 James Horn, *A Land as God Made It: Jamestown and the Birth of America* (New York: Basic Books, 2005), 178.

374 Strachey, "True Repertory of the Wreck," *JN*, 420.

375 Strachey, "True Repertory of the Wreck," *JN*, 420.

376 Strachey, "True Repertory of the Wreck," *JN*, 423.

377 Strachey, "True Repertory of the Wreck," *JN*, 426–27.

378 Peter E. Pope, *Fish into Wine: The Newfoundland Plantation in the Seventeenth Century* (Chapel Hill: University of North Carolina Press, 2004), 11–12.

379 Mark Kurlansky, *Cod: A Biography of the Fish that Changed the World* (New York: Walker and Co., 1997), 65.

380 Strachey, "True Repertory of the Wreck," *JN*, 426–27.

381 Thomas West, Lord Delaware to Lord Salisbury, September 1610, *JN*, 466.

382 Strachey, "True Repertory of the Wreck," *JN*, 432.

383 Strachey, "True Repertory of the Wreck," *JN*, 432.

384 Strachey, "True Repertory of the Wreck," *JN*, 434.

385 Strachey, "True Repertory of the Wreck," *JN*, 433.

386 Strachey, "True Repertory of the Wreck," *JN*, 433–34.

387 Strachey, "True Repertory of the Wreck," *JN*, 429.

388 Strachey, "True Repertory of the Wreck," *JN*, 429.

389 Strachey, "True Repertory of the Wreck," *JN*, 429.

390 Council of Virginia, "A True Declaration," *JN*, 468.

391 Strachey, "True Repertory of the Wreck," *JN*, 436.

392 Strachey, "True Repertory of the Wreck," *JN*, 436–37.

393 Percy, "True Relation," *JN*, 508.

394 Percy, "True Relation," *JN*, 509.

395 Percy, "True Relation," *JN*, 509–10.

396 Percy, "True Relation," *JN*, 510.

397 Percy, "True Relation," *JN*, 510–11.

398 Percy, "True Relation," *JN*, 512.

399 Percy, "True Relation," *JN*, 513–14.

400 Percy, "True Relation," *JN*, 512.

401 The Governor and Council in Virginia to the Virginia Company of London, July 7, 1610, *JN*, 460–61.

402 Governor and Council in Virginia to the Virginia Company, *JN*, 462.

403 Richard Rich, "News from Virginia," *JN*, 372–79.

404 George Yeardley to Sir Henry Peyton, November 18, 1610, *JN*, 478–79.

405 Council of Virginia, "True Declaration," *JN*, 469–77.

406 Percy, "True Relation," *JN*, 513.

407 Lord De La Warr, "A Short Relation," 1611, *JN*, 527, 532.

408 Lord De La Warr, "Short Relation," *JN*, 527–32.

409 Alexander Brown, *The Genesis of the United States,* 2 vols. (Boston and New York: Houghton Mifflin, 1891), 1:463.

410 Sir Thomas Dale to the Council of Virginia, May 25, 1611, *JN*, 522, 524.

411 Dale to the Council of Virginia, *JN*, 522–23.

412 Sir Thomas Dale to the Earl of Salisbury, August 17, 1611, *JN*, 555.

413 "Laws Divine, Moral, and Martial," in Warren M. Billings, ed., *The Old Dominion in the Seventeenth Century: A Documentary History of Virginia, 1606–1689* (Chapel Hill: University of North Carolina Press, 1975), 29–33.

414 Ralph Hamor, "A True Discourse," *JN*, 822.

415 Percy, "True Relation," *JN*, 517–18.

416 Hamor, "True Discourse," *JN*, 822–23.

417 Dale to the Earl of Salisbury, *JN*, 554.

418 Dale to the Council of Virginia, *JN*, 524.

419 Percy, "True Relation," *JN*, 518.

420 Percy, "True Relation," *JN*, 514–15.

421 Percy, "True Relation," *JN*, 514–15.

422 Percy, "True Relation," *JN*, 514–15.

423 Percy, "True Relation," 514–15.

424 Horn, *Land as God Made It*, 199.

425 "Report of the Voyage to the Indies as far as Virginia," *JN*, 535.

426 "Report of the Voyage to the Indies as far as Virginia," *JN*, 536-37.

427 Horn, *A Land As God Made It*, 204.

428 Percy, "True Relation," *JN*, 516–17.

429 Percy, "True Relation," *JN*, 517.

430 Percy, "True Relation," *JN*, 517.

431 Hamor, "True Discourse," *JN*, 824–25.

432 Hamor, "True Discourse," *JN*, 825–26.

433 Hamor, "True Discourse," *JN*, 802.

434 Hamor, "True Discourse," *JN*, 802.

435 Hamor, "True Discourse," *JN*, 803.

436 Hamor, "True Discourse," *JN*, 803–4.

437 Hamor, "True Discourse," *JN*, 804.

438 Hamor, "True Discourse," *JN*, 804.

439 Hamor, "True Discourse," *JN*, 804.

440 Hamor, "True Discourse," *JN*, 806.

441 John Rolfe to Sir Thomas Dale, *JN*, 850–57.

442 Hamor, "True Discourse," *JN*, 806.

443 Hamor, "True Discourse," *JN*, 806.

444 Hamor, "True Discourse," *JN*, 806–7.

445 Hamor, "True Discourse," *JN*, 808.

446 Hamor, "True Discourse," *JN*, 809.

447 Hamor, "True Discourse," *JN*, 809–12.

448 Hamor, "True Discourse," *JN*, 809–12.

449 Hamor, "True Discourse," *JN*, 830–35.

450 Smith, "General History," *JN*, 858.

451 Samuel Purchas, "Pilgrimage," *JN*, 880.

452 Horn, *A Land as God Made It*, 227.

453 Smith, "General History," *JN*, 863.

454 Smith, "General History," *JN*, 864.

455 Sir Thomas Dale to Sir Ralph Winwood, June 3, 1616, *JN*, 878.

456 Hamor, "True Discourse," *JN*, 828.

457 John Rolfe, "A True Relation," *JN*, 869.

458 Rolfe, "True Relation," *JN*, 871.

459 Rolfe, "True Relation," *JN*, 871.

460 Rolfe, "True Relation," *JN*, 871–72.

461 Thomas Dale, "Letter from Henrico," June 10, 1613, *JN*, 778.

462 Virginia Company: Instructions to George Yeardley, November 18, 1618, in Susan M. Kingsbury, *The Records of the Virginia Company of London* (Washington, DC: Government Printing Office, 1906–1935), 3: 98–99.

463 Virginia Company: Instructions to George Yeardley, November 18, 1618, *The Records of the Virginia Company of London*, 3: 98–99.

464 Wesley Frank Craven, *The Southern Colonies in the Seventeenth Century, 1607–1689* (Baton Rouge: Louisiana State University Press, 1970), 133.

465 Virginia Company: Instructions to George Yeardley, November 18, 1618, *The Records of the Virginia Company of London*, 3: 98–99.

466 Horn, *Land as God Made It*, 240.

467 Craven, *Southern Colonies*, 136.

468 John Rolfe, "A Relation," Billings, ed., *The Old Dominion*.

469 Horn, *Land as God Made It*, 246.

470 Horn, *Land as God Made It*, 246.

471 Horn, *Land as God Made It*, 247.

472 Council in Virginia to Virginia Company of London, January, 1621, in Kingsbury, ed., *The Records of the Virginia Company*, 3: 583–84.

473 Council in Virginia to Virginia Company in London, January 20, 1623, in Kingsbury, ed., *The Records of the Virginia Company*, 10–11.

474 Edward Waterhouse, "A Declaration of the State of the Colony and Affairs in Virginia with a Relation of the Barbarous Massacre," in Billings, ed., *The Old Dominion in the Seventeenth Century*, 220–21.

475 Waterhouse, "Declaration," in Billings, ed., *The Old Dominion in the Seventeenth Century*, 221.

476 Waterhouse, "Declaration," in Billings, ed., *The Old Dominion in the Seventeenth Century*, 224.

477 Philip L. Barbour, ed., *The Complete Works of Captain John Smith, 1580–1631* (Chapel Hill: University of North Carolina Press, 1986), 2: 308.

478 Richard Frethorne to his Father and Mother, March 20, April 2 and 3, 1623, *The Records of the Virginia Company*, 4: 58–59.

479 Treasurer and Council for Virginia to Governor and Council in Virginia, August 1, 1622, *The Records of the Virginia Company*, 3: 666–67.

480 Treasurer and Council for Virginia to Governor and Council in Virginia, August 1, 1622, *The Records of the Virginia Company*, 3: 672.

481 Virginia Company to the Governor and Council in Virginia, October 7, 1622, *The Records of the Virginia Company*, 3:683.

482 Treasurer and Council for Virginia to Governor and Council in Virginia, August 1, 1622, *The Records of the Virginia Company*, 3: 672.

483 Governor in Virginia: A Commission to Sir George Yeardley, September 10, 1622, *The Records of the Virginia Company*, 3: 678–79.

484 Robert Bennett to Edward Bennett, June 9, 1623, *The Records of the Virginia Company*, 4: 221–222.

485 Council in Virginia to the Earl of Southampton and the Council and Company of Virginia, December 2, 1624, *The Records of the Virginia Company*, 4: 507–508.

486 Benjamin Franklin, *Benjamin Franklin's Autobiography*, ed. J. A. Leo Lemay and P. M. Zall (New York: Norton, 1986), 1.

487 Alexis de Tocqueville, *Democracy in America*, ed. Harvey C. Mansfield and Delba Winthrop (Chicago: University of Chicago Press, 2000), 429.

BIBLIOGRAPHY

PRIMARY SOURCES

Barbour, Philip L., ed. *The Complete Works of Captain John Smith, 1580–1631.* 3 Vols. Chapel Hill: University of North Carolina Press, 1986.

_____. *The Jamestown Voyages under the First Charter, 1606–1609.* 2 vols. Cambridge: Cambridge University Press, 1969.

Bemiss, Samuel M., ed. *The Three Charters of the Virginia Company of London.* Williamsburg, VA: The Virginia 350th Anniversary Celebration Corporation, 1957.

Billings, Warren M., ed. *The Old Dominion in the Seventeenth Century: A Documentary History of Virgina, 1606–1689.* Chapel Hill: University of North Carolina Press, 1975.

Brooke, Christopher. "A Poem on the Late Massacre in Virginia," *Virginia Magazine of the History and Biography* Vol. 72 No. 3 (July, 1964): 259–292.

Brown, Alexander, ed. *The Genesis of the United States.* 2 vols. Boston and New York: Houghton Mifflin, 1891.

Hakluyt, Richard. *Voyages and Discoveries: The Principal Navigations, Voyages, Traffiques and Discoveries of the English Nation.* Edited by Jack Beeching. New York: Penguin, 1972.

Halile, Edward Wright., ed. *Jamestown Narratives: Eyewitness Accounts of the Virginia Colony, the First Decade, 1607–1617*. Champlain, VA: RoundHouse Press, 1988.

Kingsbury, Susan M., ed. *The Records of the Virginia Company of London*. 4 vols. Washington, DC: Government Printing Office, 1906–1935.

"Letter of Sir Francis Wyatt, Governor of Virginia, 1621–1626." *William and Mary Quarterly*. 2nd Series Vol. 6 No. 2 (April 1926): 114–121.

McIlwaine, H.R., ed. *Journal of the House of Burgesses of Virginia, 1619–1658/9*. Richmond: 1906.

Thompson, John M., ed. *The Journals of Captain John Smith: A Jamestown Biography*. Washington, DC: National Geographic Society, 2007.

Wright, Louis B., ed. *A Voyage to Virginia in 1609: Two Narratives*. Charlottesville: University Press of Virginia, 1964.

SECONDARY SOURCES

Andrews, Kenneth R. "Christopher Newport of Limehouse, Mariner." *William and Mary Quarterly* 3rd Series Vol. XI No. 1 (January, 1954): 28-41.

_____. *Trade, Plunder, and Settlement: Maritime Enterprise and the Genesis of the British Empire, 1480-1630*. Cambridge: Cambridge University Press, 1984.

Barbour, Philip L. "A Possible Clue to Samuel Argall's Pre-Jamestown Activities," *William and Mary Quarterly* 3rd Series Vol. XXIX No. 2 (April, 1972): 301–306.

_____. *The Three Worlds of Captain John Smith*. Boston: Houghton Mifflin, 1964.

Bergreen, Laurence. *Over the Edge of the World: Magellan's Terrifying Circumnavigation of the Globe*. New York: Harper Collins, 2004.

Billings, Warren M. *A Little Parliament: The Virginia General Assembly in the Seventeenth Century*. Richmond: The Library of Virginia, 2004.

Brands, H.W. *Masters of Enterprise: Giants of American Business from John Jacob Astor and J.P. Morgan to Bill Gates and Oprah Winfrey*. New York: Free Press, 1999.

Brigden, Susan. *New Worlds, Lost Worlds: The Rule of the Tudors, 1485–1603*. New York: Penguin, 2000.

Brown, Kathleen M. *Good Wives, Nasty Wenches, and Anxious Patriarchs: Gender, Race, and Power in Colonial Virginia.* Chapel Hill: University of North Carolina Press, 1996.

Bruce, Philip Alexander. *Economic History of Virginia in the Seventeenth Century.* 3 Vols. New York: Macmillan, 1896.

Craven, Wesley Frank. *Dissolution of the Virginia Company: The Failure of a Colonial Experiment.* New York: Oxford University Press, 1932.

_____. *The Southern Colonies in the Seventeenth Century, 1607–1624.* Baton Rouge: Louisiana State University Press, 1970.

_____. *The Virginia Company of London, 1606-1624.* Williamsburg, VA: The Virginia 350th Anniversary Celebration Corporation, 1957.

Deans, Bob. *The River Where America Began: A Journey Along the James.* Lanham, MD: Rowman Littlefield, 2007.

Doherty, Kieran. *Sea Venture: Shipwreck, Survival, and the Salvation of the First English Colony in the New World.* New York: St. Martin's Press, 2007.

Elliot, J.H. *Empires of the Atlantic World: Britain and Spain in America, 1492–1830.* New Haven: Yale University Press, 2006.

Fausz, J. Frederick. "An 'Abundance of Blood Shed on Both Sides': England's First Indian War, 1609–1614." *Virginia Magazine of History and Biography* Vol. 90 No. 1 (January, 1990): 3–54.

_____. "Indians, Colonialism, and the Conquest of Cant: A Review Essay on Anglo-American Relations in the Chesapeake." *Virginia Magazine of History and Biography* Vol. 95 No. 2 (April, 1987): 133–156.

Glover, Lorri, and Daniel Blake Smith. *The Shipwreck That Saved Jamestown: The Sea Venture Castaways and the Fate of America.* New York: Henry Holt, 2008.

Gookin, Warner F. "Who Was Bartholomew Gosnold?" *William and Mary Quarterly* 3rd Series Vol. VI No. 3 (July, 1949): 398–415.

Gordon, John Steele. *An Empire of Wealth: The Epic History of American Economic Power.* New York: Harper Collins, 2004.

Greene, Jack P. *The Intellectual Construction of America: Exceptionalism and Identity from 1492 to 1800.* Chapel Hill: University of North Carolina Press, 1993.

Hashaw, Tim. *The Birth of Black America: The First African Americans and Their Pursuit of Freedom in Jamestown*. New York: Carroll and Graf, 2007.

Hayek, Friedrich A. *The Road to Serfdom*. Chicago: University of Chicago Press, 1944.

Herman, Arthur. *To Rule the Waves: How the British Navy Shaped the Modern World*. New York: HarperCollins, 2004.

Hobbler, Dorothy, and Thomas Hobbler. *Captain John Smith: Jamestown and the Birth of the American Dream*. Hoboken, NJ: Wiley, 2006.

Holifield, E. Brooks. *Era of Persuasion: American Thought and Culture, 1521–1680*. Boston: Twayne, 1989.

Horn, James. *Adapting to a New World: English Society in the Seventeenth-Century Chesapeake*. Chapel Hill: University of North Carolina Press, 1994.

————. *A Kingdom Strange: The Brief and Tragic History of the Lost Colony of Roanoke*. New York: Basic Books, 2010.

————. *A Land as God Made It: Jamestown and the Birth of America*. New York: Basic Books, 2005.

Johnson, Robert C. "The Indian Massacre of 1622: Some Correspondence of the Rev. Joseph Mead." *Virginia Magazine of History and Biography* Vol. 71 No. 4 (October 1963): 408–410.

Kamen, Henry. *How Spain Became a World Power, 1492–1763*. New York: Harper Collins, 2003.

Kelsey, Harry. *Sir Francis Drake: The Queen's Pirate*. New Haven: Yale University Press, 1998.

————. *Sir John Hawkins: Queen Elizabeth's Slave Trader*. New Haven: Yale University Press, 2003.

Kelso, William M. *Jamestown: The Buried Truth*. Charlottesville: University of Virginia Press, 2006.

Kerr, K. Austin, and Mansel G. Blackford. *Business Enterprise in American History*. Boston: Houghton Mifflin, 1986.

Kupperman, Karen Ordahl. *Indians and English: Facing Off in Early America*. Ithaca: Cornell University Press, 2000.

————. *The Jamestown Project*. Cambridge, MA: Harvard University Press, 2007.

_____. *Roanoke: The Abandoned Colony.* 2nd ed. Lanham, MD: Rowman and Littlefield, 2007.

Lemay, J.A. Leo. *The American Dream of Captain John Smith.* Charlottesville: University Press of Virginia, 1991.

Lynch, John. *Spain, 1516–1598: From Nation State to World Empire.* Oxford: Blackwell, 1991.

Mancall, Peter. *Hakluyt's Promise: An Elizabethan's Obsession for an English America.* New Haven, CT: Yale University Press, 2007.

Martin, Colin, and Geoffrey Parker. *The Spanish Armada.* New York: Norton, 1988.

Mattingly, Garrett. *The Armada.* Boston: Houghton Mifflin, 1959.

Micklethwait, John, and Adrian Wooldridge. *The Company: A Short History of a Revolutionary Idea.* New York: Modern Library, 2003.

Miller, Lee. *Roanoke: Solving the Mystery of the Lost Colony.* New York: Penguin, 2000.

Morgan, Edmund S. *American Slavery, American Freedom: The Ordeal of Colonial Virginia.* New York: Norton, 1975.

Morison, Samuel Eliot. *Admiral of the Ocean Sea: A Life of Christopher Columbus.* Boston: Little Brown, 1942.

_____. *The European Discovery of America: The Northern Voyages, A.D. 500–1600.* New York: Oxford University Press, 1971.

_____. *The European Discovery of America: The Southern Voyages, A.D. 1492–1616.* New York: Oxford University Press, 1974.

Morton, Richard L. *Colonial Virginia.* 2 vols. Chapel Hill: University of North Carolina Press, 1960.

O'Brien, Terence H. "The London Livery Companies and the Virginia Company." *Virginia Magazine of History and Biography* Vol. 68 No. 2 (April, 1960): 137–155.

Picard, Liza. *Elizabeth's London: Everyday Life in Elizabethan London.* New York: St. Martin's, 2003.

Price, David A. *Love and Hate in Jamestown: John Smith, Pocahontas, and the Heart of a New Nation.* New York: Knopf, 2003.

Ransome, David R. "Wives for Virginia, 1621." *William and Mary Quarterly* 3rd Series Vol. XLVIII No. 1 (January, 1991): 3–18.

Ronald, Susan. *The Pirate Queen: Queen Elizabeth I, Her Pirate Adventurers, and the Dawn of Empire*. New York: Harper Collins, 2007.

Roundtree, Helen C. *Pocahontas, Powhatan, Opechancanough: Three Indian Lives Changed by Jamestown*. Charlottesville: University of Virginia Press, 2005.

_____. *The Powhatan Indians of Virginia: Their Traditional Culture*. Norman: University of Oklahoma Press, 1989.

Quinn, David Beers. *Raleigh and the British Empire*. London: English University Press, 1947.

_____. *Set Fair for Roanoke: Voyages and Colonies, 1584–1606*. Chapel Hill: University of North Carolina Press, 1985.

Ronald, Susan. *The Pirate Queen: Queen Elizabeth I, Her Pirate Adventurers, and the Dawn of Empire*. New York: Harper, 2007.

Sanders, Charles Richard. "William Strachey, the Virginia Colony, and Shakespeare." *Virginia Magazine of History and Biography* Vol. 57 No. 2 (April, 1949): 115–132.

Sluiter, Engel. "New Light on the '20. and Odd Negroes' Arriving in Virginia, August 1619," *William and Mary Quarterly* 3rd Series Vol. LIV No. 2 (April, 1997): 395–98.

Tate, Thad W. and David L. Ammerman, eds. *The Chesapeake in the Seventeenth Century: Essays on Anglo-American Society*. New York: Norton, 1979.

Thornton, John. "The African Experience of the '20. and Odd Negroes' Arriving in Virginia in 1619." *William and Mary Quarterly* 3rd Series Vol. LV No. 3 (July, 1998): 421.

Tilton, Robert S. *Pocahontas: The Evolution of an American Narrative*. Cambridge: Cambridge University Press, 1994.

Trevelyan, Raleigh. *Sir Walter Raleigh*. New York: Henry Holt, 2002.

Vaughn, Alden T. *American Genesis: Captain John Smith and the Founding of Virginia*. Boston: Little, Brown, 1975.

_____. "Blacks in Virginia: A Note on the First Decade." *William and Mary*

Quarterly 3rd Series Vol. XXIX (July, 1972): 469–78.

————. "Expulsion of the Salvages: English Policy and the Virginia Massacre of 1622." *William and Mary Quarterly* 3rd Series Vol. XXXV No. 4 (January, 1978): 57–84.

————. "The Origins Debate: Slavery and Racism in Seventeenth-Century Virginia," *Virginia Magazine of History and Biography* 97 No. 3 (July 1989): 311–54.

Woodward, Hobson. *A Brave Vessel: The True Tale of the Castaways Who Rescued Jamestown and Inspired Shakespeare's The Tempest.* New York: Viking, 2009.

INDEX

ABOUT
THE AUTHOR

Tony Williams is the author of three previous books on colonial and Revolutionary America, including *The Pox and the Covenant* and *Hurricane of Independence*. He has taught history and literature for more than ten years and is currently teaching U.S. History at Peninsula Catholic High School in Newport News, VA. He lectures widely on the history of the American colonies and the American Revolution.

photo credit: Paul Harrison